Johnny, aged one

Leon, Nita, Tim, Marion and Joe, Portugal 1964

Claire at the Leon Pie Fest, 2010

Petra, Jeremy, Mima and Hattie, 1978

Leon on his ship of the desert, 1959

Jo Jo and Katherine, 1977

Cookbook library at Leon, Old Compton Street

George, 2011

Liza, Sadie, Kate and Joseph, August 1980

Tom Herbert, 1984

Molly, Liza, Emma, Jossy, Kate, Henry and Anna, 1976

LEON.

Baking & Puddings

BY CLAIRE PTAK & HENRY DIMBLEBY

BOOK **3**

FOOD PHOTOGRAPHY BY GEORGIA GLYNN SMITH • DESIGN BY ANITA MANGAN

CONTENTS

INTRODUCTION 6

A guide to ingredients 10

Baking with alternatives 45

Tools, tips & techniques 24

PART ONE: EVERYDAY

RECIPES

Breakfast 48

Cooking with children 174

Power snacks 68

Bread & yeast 194

Tea time 82

Sweets 220

Puds 106

PART TWO: CELEBRATION

Easter 236

Christmas 260

St George's Day 244

Hogmanay 265

Mother's Day 246

Eid 266

Father's Day 248

Valentine's Day 268

Wimbledon 250

Birthdays 270

Halloween 252

Christenings 275

Bonfire Night 254

Wakes 276

Thanksgiving 258

EXTRA HELPINGS 278

Welcome to Leon Baking & Puddings

Leon was founded on the belief that food should taste good and do you good. In this book we hope to show that this can be the case even where it is often thought impossible – when cooking comfort food. The dishes you will find here look indulgent, sound naughty and taste like the sort of treats that normally come with a side-helping of guilt. Yet three quarters of the recipes are wheat, dairy or sugar free, with plenty of vegan and gluten-free options. You will find an index on page 294 that allows you to look up recipes according to their ingredients – e.g. gluten free, dairy free, and so forth.

The book is divided into two sections. The first part, Every Day, contains recipes for things that you might want to eat throughout the year – breakfast breads, energy bars, biscuits and quick puds. The second part, Celebration, is a collection of recipes designed to celebrate the passing of time, both through the year and through our lives. This is where you will find everything from hot cross buns and toffee apples to a Desperate Dan Pie for Father's Day.

We want this book to be accessible to even the most inexperienced cook – hence our 'how-to' sections on basic techniques and tools. Once you have mastered a recipe you can use our suggested variations to put your own stamp on it. We also want to provide inspiration for the more experienced. Some of the recipes are daring (see Baked Alaska page 139), some draw on ancient wisdom (see Sourdough Bread page 196), and some are downright explosive (see Honeycomb page 220). Each recipe is given a confidence rating – from 'beginner' to 'feeling brave' – but even the more adventurous recipes shouldn't prove too tricky for the careful amateur.

We hope this book finds a permanent place in your kitchen and becomes batter-smattered, tacky with toffee and dog-eared through use.

Claire & Henry

A note on the authors

We have written the book in the first person plural – 'we' – because it represents the fruits of a year of close collaboration. We are lucky enough to live two doors down from each other, which means we spend a lot of time messing up each other's kitchens and feasting on the results.

But obviously, we bring different things to the party. Simply put, Claire is the professional baker and Henry the enthusiastic amateur.

Claire used to be the pastry chef at Chez Panisse, Alice Waters' legendary restaurant in California. She fell in love with a dapper English DJ and followed him home to east London, where she now runs her acclaimed bakery, Violet. An ardent believer in seasonal, natural ingredients, she is the best baker we know, and there is a precision and delicate beauty to all of her cooking.

Henry is a co-founder of Leon (with John Vincent and Allegra McEvedy). He started his career as a commis chef, but soon realized he was too messy to be a professional cook. He never lost his passion for food, however, and he still spends every spare moment in the kitchen, where he always has some experiment on the go (with his long-suffering wife, Mima, following behind him with a J-cloth). Some of these experiments turn into dishes worth sharing (see Henry's Spiced Chicken Mystery Pie, page 292 and the Chocolate & Salted Caramel Ice Cream Bombe, page 160); others are still being chipped off the ceiling.

There are a few recipes that have appeared in previous Leon books. They have become so popular with our regulars, that we thought it would be wrong to print a book on baking and puddings without them.

Key to Symbols

Key to recipe icons:

❤   Low saturated fats

✓   Good carbs (low GI) / good sugars

WF   Wheat free

GF   Gluten free

DF   Dairy free

V   Vegetarian

   Indulgence

Level of confidence:

Beginner

Medium

Feeling brave

TIPS   Cooking tips, extra information and alternative ideas.

Lots of lovely people test the recipes to make sure they are spot on. We've given each one a badge of honour.

GUIDE TO BAKING Ingredients

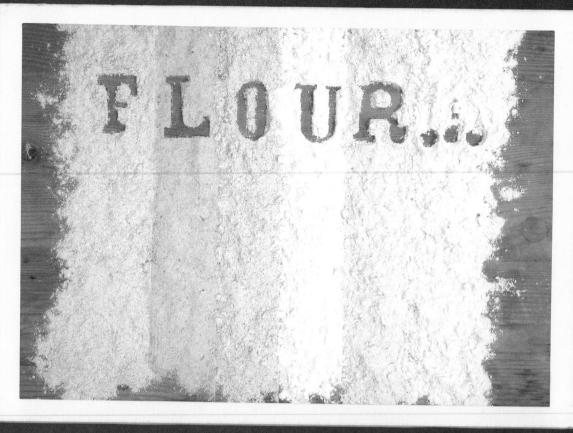

FLOURS FROM LEFT TO RIGHT: WHOLEMEAL SPELT, POLENTA FLOUR, RYE FLOUR, RICE FLOUR, PLAIN SPELT FLOUR & PLAIN FLOUR

The role of flours is to provide structure. The proteins in traditional flours react with water, producing gluten, the strands of which create a lattice in which air bubbles can be trapped, giving your baked goods 'lightness', but some people find flour hard to digest. Recipes using gluten-free flours will be more cake-like, although this effect can often be offset to some degree by adding other structure providers such as eggs or gums.

① TRADITIONAL WHEAT FLOUR
Wholemeal, plain/white strong (or hard) and self-raising

What is it? Ground wheat. Wholemeal is made from the whole grain: the endosperm (proteinous/starchy), the germ (proteinous and full of vitamins), and the bran (fibrous). The other varieties of wheat are made from the starchy endosperm only. Plain flour is used for general baking as it produces less gluten than strong flour which is traditionally used to make bread. Self-raising flour is plain flour with a raising agent (traditionally baking powder) added.
What is it good for? Pretty much anything in traditional baking.
Is it good for me? For a lot of people, no. Wheat has changed beyond recognition in the past 100 years, as farmers have selectively bred it from its naturally occurring forms to the

extremely high-yielding grains that are produced today. These advances have done a lot to help feed a growing global population, but at a cost. Incidences of coeliac disease – a severe allergy to gluten, which causes the immune system to attack the lining of the small intestine – have been doubling every fifteen years since the Seventies. Some people are also allergic to wheat (rather than just to the gluten it contains). In addition wheat intolerance is a growing problem – a less catastrophic but still unpleasant reaction to modern wheat proteins which can leave you feeling heavy, tired, and listless. If you are lucky enough to have a body that can cope with it, wheat is a wonderful thing. If not, there are alternatives.

② SPELT FLOUR
Wholemeal or white

What is it? Spelt is an ancient variety of wheat that has not been transformed by selective breeding.

What is it good for? You can use spelt as a substitute for wheat in many dishes. Although it is higher in protein than many wheat flours, it is lower in gluten. It will not therefore give you the extravagantly risen breads that you can create with wheat flour. It has a delicious nutty flavour. We love spelt.

Is it good for you? People with wheat allergy and intolerance can generally tuck into spelt quite happily. Ceoliacs must avoid spelt because it contains gluten. Our own experience is that it doesn't give you that bloated sensation you get from traditional wheat.

③ RYE FLOUR

What is it? Rye comes from the same family of grasses as wheat. It originated in Eastern Europe, where it grows well in cold climates and in poor soils. It is dense and dark and contains little gluten.

What is it good for? For making traditional rye breads (see page 201). Also strongly flavoured beers, vodka and whisky.

Is it good for you? Many people find it more palatable than wheat, as it has lower gluten levels and has been less intensively bred. It is high in vitamins and soluble fibre, and has a lower glycemic load than many wheat and spelt breads so is less likely to lead to weight gain.

④ BUCKWHEAT FLOUR

What is it? Buckwheat is actually not a wheat at all. It is not even a grass. It is a fruit seed from the rhubarb family and similar to a sunflower seed. It is gluten-free.

What is it good for? We use the flour to make pancakes, the flakes to make granola and porridge, and it can be used as a couscous substitute in its groat form. However, it will not provide sufficient structure to make breads unless you add eggs or xanthan gum. It can also be used alongside other flours for interesting flavour and texture combinations.

Is it good for you? Yes. It is high in nutrients, especially manganese and magnesium, and also provides vitamins, zinc and a whole host of other goodies. It is sometimes called the 'king of the healing grains'.

⑤ GLUTEN-FREE FLOUR

What is it? Any flour that does not contain gluten. You can mix your own or choose shop-bought varieties, which will generally be various blends of rice, potato, buckwheat, and bean and pea flours. They will often have added gluten-substitutes such as xantham gum.

What is it good for? If you want to avoid gluten, you can use it as a flour substitute in instances where the dish you are making does not need the strong structure that gluten provides. In this book, we use it in crumbles, scones, cakes, tarts, and to make a 'cakey' breakfast loaf.

Is it good for you? These flours will not contain gluten, but some are quite refined so they will not necessarily be packed full of nutrients.

⑥ POLENTA

What is it? Coarsely ground dried corn/maize, also known as cornmeal. As opposed to cornflour, which is very finely ground into a starchy white powder.

What is it good for? We use it to give body to cakes while avoiding wheat flour. It has a beautiful yellow colour and a mild, sweet flavour.

Is it good for you? It a relatively complex carbohydrate that also contains protein and some vitamins. A reasonable food – it won't make a superhero of you overnight, but it isn't bad for you either.

⑦ GRAM FLOUR

What is it? Ground-up dried chickpeas.

What is it good for? We use it to add body to some gluten-free cakes. Also good for thickening stews. It can be a little bitter, so we like to use it sparingly.

Is it good for you? Yes. Gluten free, it has a low GL, so it won't set your sugar levels racing. Contains a good bit of protein and iron.

LEAVENERS & THICKENERS

① YEAST

A micro-organism that converts the sugars in flour into carbon dioxide bubbles, thus putting air into the dough. It comes in many forms – fresh, dried and rapid-rise. We specify the type used in each recipe, but if you are substituting one for another, make sure you follow the instructions on the packet.

② BICARBONATE OF SODA

A chemical compound with a slightly alkaline taste, which reacts with acids to form carbon dioxide.

③ BAKING POWDER

A mixture of bicarbonate of soda and an acid compound (typically cream of tartar) that reacts when moistened to produce carbon dioxide. (Some baking powders use wheat as a 'moisture absorption agent'. You can buy gluten-free ones that do not.)

④ ARROWROOT, CORNSTARCH

Starchy powders useful for gluten-free binding and thickening.

⑤ XANTHUM GUM

A thickener/binder that can be used at very low concentrations to thicken sauces. Often used to help give gluten-free breads structure.

⑥ EGG SUBSTITUTE

Also known as whole egg replacer, it is used to replace eggs in sponges and cakes for vegans and people who are allergic. Normally made of soy protein and potato starch. Not something we use often, but nice if you are baking for a vegan.

FATS

Fats play many roles in baking. They add moistness and tenderness. They create barriers between layers of flour, allowing crispy pastries to develop. They help gluten stretch in bread, and are used to stop things sticking to trays. They taste rich and sweet.

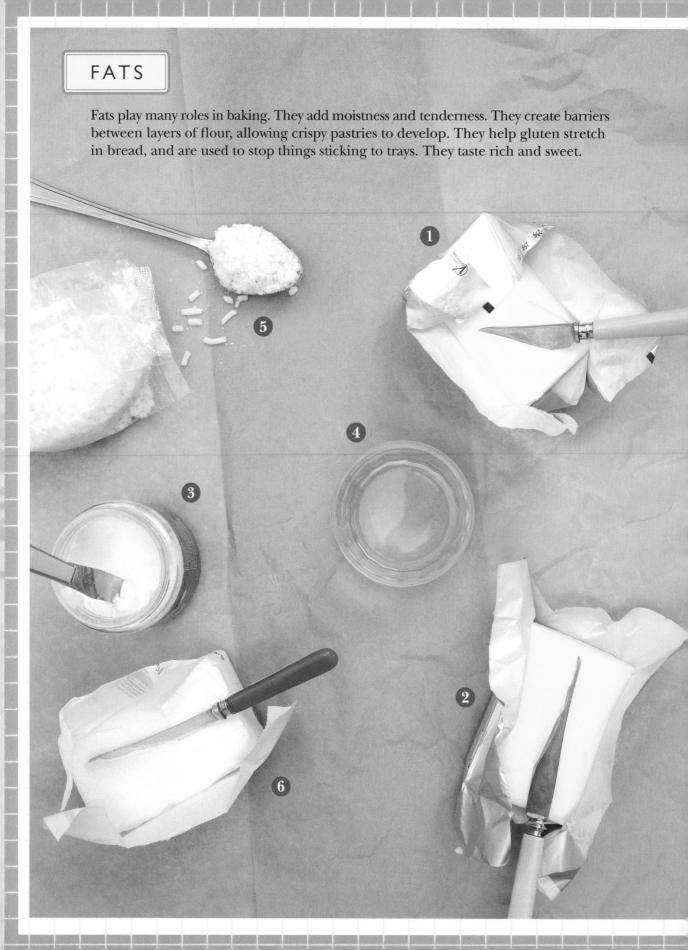

❶ UNSALTED BUTTER

What is it? A golden block of dairy goodness made from churning cream to concentrate the butterfat. It is an emulsion of butterfat (about 80%), water and milk proteins. Unsalted butter is normally used in baking, as it has a sweeter flavour.

What is it good for? The most common baking fat, butter is solid at room temperature and can therefore be used to make all sorts of flaky pastries. It melts at body temperature, so it doesn't taste greasy.

Is it good for me? As with suet (see page 18), butter is mostly saturated fat and is therefore high in calories. These foods used to be considered the devil's work, but they are all natural and recent nutritional research suggests that (within reason) they are likely to do us less harm than processed alternatives. As it is a saturated fat, butter can also be heated without changing its structure and becoming more harmful. Butter contains very little lactose and is therefore rarely a problem for the lactose intolerant.

❷ SALTED BUTTER

What is it? Butter that has had salt added as a preservative and to change the flavour.

What is it good for? Generally we prefer the sweeter flavour of unsalted butter in baking and puddings. But occasionally – e.g. for the Sweet Popcorn with Chocolate Drizzle (see page 79) – the stronger flavour of salted butter gets the nod.

Is it good for me? Much the same as unsalted butter. If you need to watch your salt levels then go for unsalted.

❸ COCONUT OIL

What is it? The oil extracted from coconut flesh.

What is it good for? It is liquid at body temperature, but just about solid at room temperature. This makes it a possible substitute for butter in many applications (although, as you will see from the recipes, you have to handle it differently). Its melting point (about 23°C) is much closer to room temperature than butter (about 32°C) or indeed cocoa butter (about 34°C) – which gives it unique qualities. Coconut oil icing, for example (see page 97), melts in the mouth in a very different way from the richer butter icings. (If you have ever tried Lindt Lindor chocolates – which contain a lot of coconut oil – you will recognize the sensation.)

Is it good for me? There is a great deal of debate over this. When people started trying to cut dairy out of their diet, coconut oil was seen as a perfect substitute. Then nutritionists pointed out that it was also high in calories and saturated fats. More recent evidence has shown that coconut oil actually promotes good cholesterol and that it is easily metabolized into fuel (rather than deposited as fat). Of course this is only useful if you need the fuel. Our feeling is that it is a good fat; some people say it will make you podgy, but many nutritionists disagree. Claire ate loads of it on a recent detox and the weight fell off. (Read labels carefully though, as some coconut oil is still hydrogenated, which is bad news. Always choose organic and unrefined).

4 OLIVE OIL

What is it? Cold-pressed extra virgin olive oil is the oil extracted from olive flesh.
What is it good for? It is liquid at room temperature and therefore less versatile in baking than other fats discussed here. We use it in breads and pizza doughs and to toast granola.
Is it good for you? Yes. It is high in monounsaturated fats that may help protect against heart disease. It also contains a useful source of omega-6 fats, which we must eat because our bodies cannot make them from other foods. (Make sure you get the cold-pressed variety.)

5 SUET

What is it? Raw beef (and sometimes mutton) fat, often taken from around the kidneys. The stuff that you buy in supermarkets has been dehydrated, purified and mixed with flour to stabilize it. If you use real fresh suet, you may need slightly less. (You can also buy vegetarian suet, but choose carefully: most of it is made from hydrogenated trans-fats, which should be avoided.)
What is it good for? Making traditional steamed English puddings. The suet is hard and therefore forms little pockets in the pastry. When the pudding is cooking these melt away, leaving air pockets and giving that wonderful light, spongy and slightly crispy texture. If you substitute butter you will get a much denser, richer pastry.
Is it good for me? It is a high calorie saturated fat. However, the link between saturated fat and heart disease is now under dispute, with recent studies pointing to manufactured trans-fats and sugary foods as the real villains. Therefore: don't eat suet every day, but it's fine as an occasional treat.

6 LARD

What is it? Pig fat – often rendered (melted slowly), purified and then reset.
What is it good for? Generally used to make really flaky pastries (for example, the hot crust pastry used for the pork pie on page 284). It is solid at body temperature and has a distinct soft porky flavour. We don't use it much.
Is it good for you? Very calorific, but probably not as sinful as its reputation would suggest. Eat it about as often as you would suet (see left).

7 MARGARINE

What is it? A butter substitute originally manufactured from beef fat but now more commonly made by thickening vegetable oils and dying them yellow.
What is it good for? Absolutely nothing. Say it again. We don't think that there is any recipe that tastes better when made with margarine.
Is it good for you? Traditional margarines made from hydrogenating vegetable oil were originally marketed as a healthier, cheaper alternative to butter. We now know that the manufacturing process created deadly trans-fats, and these types of marg have all but disappeared from the supermarket shelves. More recent manufacturing methods have produced a slew of margarines with their own advertised 'health benefits'. However, they have only recently entered the food chain and we would council caution. Our general rule of thumb is: avoid using any ingredient in cooking that has been invented in the last 1,000 years.

SUGARS & SWEETENERS

It is one of the tragedies of the human condition that sweet foods were not that commonplace when our palates were evolving. To early man, sugar was a rare and valuable source of energy. As a result, we have evolved to seek it out and wolf it down. Our tastebuds, which usually guide us towards things that are good for us, tell us that sweet things are to be gobbled up with abandon.

Until as recently as 1766, when the Sugar Tax was repealed, it was impossible to get hold of sugar in sufficient quantity to do us harm. But white processed sugar is now cheap and plentiful, and over the last couple of decades has been recognized (alongside processed carbohydrates) as the single greatest threat to our health. In the end, moderation is the answer, but there are some sweet substances out there that enable us to satisfy those evolutionary instincts while offering a little more protection to our bodies.

SUGAR

Sugar is made by distilling a sweet syrup – usually taken from sugar cane or sugar beet – until it crystallizes. It is almost irresistible. We try to use substitutes where possible. Where you do use it, here are a few rules:

Use cane sugar (preferably Fairtrade), not beet sugar. Beet sugar has a funny taste, particularly noticeable in icings.

Use unrefined sugar – it has a slightly nicer taste and at least retains some minerals and nutrients.

Eat as a treat only. Otherwise it will make your blood sugar soar and then slump, leaving you a bit moody and, later, a bit fatter.

Sugar comes in many forms from white caster sugar ✳ to dark brown muscovado. If you are ever holidaying in a sugar-producing country, take an afternoon off the beach to visit a sugar refinery. They are amazing places. The cane is ground by vast grooved metal rollers sprayed with hot water, and the resulting syrup is boiled to varying levels of darkness in bubbling vats. The smell is intoxicating. Unrefined sugars are spun off from the syrups at varying levels of concentration (each darker than the last), using a centrifuge. The final remaining sweet syrup is called molasses, which is dense in nutrients compared to other sugars.

The sugars we use are:

1 UNREFINED CASTER SUGAR

Unrefined means it contains molasses; refined sugar has this source of nutrients and flavour removed. Unrefined cane sugar comes from an early stage of distillation, and the brown of the molasses is hardly visible. The crystals are ground, which makes them easy to mix, melt and dissolve.

2 UNREFINED DEMERARA SUGAR

Darker than caster sugar, with a stronger flavour. Larger crystals give it a satisfyingly crunchy bite.

3 DARK BROWN MUSCOVADO SUGAR

This sugar is not spun in the centrifuge, but is left to dry in the sun. It therefore contains more plant matter, which gives it its rich flavour. It is very different from, and much nicer than, the brown sugar made by adding molasses to white sugar.

4 ICING SUGAR

A very finely ground refined sugar, which generally contains an anti-caking agent.

5 TREACLE

The syrup left over when the sugar crystals have been spun out. Light treacle (or golden syrup) is made from the by-product of the first white sugar production. Black treacle is made from later boilings and contains more plant matter and less sugar (about 55% sugar). It is similar to molasses.

6 FRUCTOSE

The sugar in cane sugar is sucrose, which is made up of glucose and fructose (the latter also occurs naturally in fruit). Sugar can be treated to create fructose, which we use in our brownies because it's less likely to give you a sugar high followed by a sugar low and is therefore good for afternoon concentration. However, there is recent evidence to suggest that it might turn to fat more easily than other sugars. In this book we therefore use a number of other natural sweeteners.

OTHER NATURAL SWEETENERS

Natural sweeteners are generally used because they cause less of a sugar rush than traditional sugar and are less refined – therefore containing more nutrients. However, they still come with some caveats.

7 HONEY

Flower nectar collected by bees.
What is good about it? Completely natural and delicious. Many forms are high in fructose and therefore create less of a sugar rush.
Any problems? Much mass-market honey is made by feeding the bees sugar syrup – and so is nutritionally identical to sugar.

8 MAPLE SYRUP

A syrup from the sap of maple trees.
What is good about it? Like honey, it is natural and delicious.
Any problems? The sweetness in maple syrup comes mostly from sucrose, and therefore it carries the same health warnings as sugar.

9 AGAVE NECTAR

A syrup produced from the Mexican agave plant. It is sweeter than honey, but less viscous.
What is good about it? It tastes good and is much less likely to give you a sugar rush.
Any problems? Due to massive recent demand, much of it is now quite heavily processed. Fructose is its main source of sweetness, and fructose may not be as innocent as once thought. Agave nectar's reputation as a miracle substitute for sugar has suffered as a result.

10 BROWN RICE SYRUP

This is derived by culturing cooked rice with enzymes from dried barley sprouts to break down the starches, which is then strained off and the resulting sweet liquid cooked.
What is good about it? It is a natural product that will not give you a sugar rush and does not contain fructose.
Any problems? It is pretty strongly flavoured. It has not been widely available for long, but so far seems to have a clean bill of health.

11 YACON SYRUP

A dark molasses-like syrup made from a Peruvian root.
What is good about it? Unlike agave syrup, the compounds providing the sweetness in yacon syrup pass through the body without being metabolized at all.
Any problems? It has a pretty strong flavour. As yet, no one has claimed that it is bad for you.

12 STEVIA

A mint-like herb that is very sweet but contains no calories. Recently hailed as the potential solution to the sugar problem.
What is good about it? Sweet without an aftertaste and contains no calories. Will not give you a sugar rush.
Any problems? It is almost impossible to get hold of unless you grow it in your own garden. No detailed research has been carried out on possible side effects so in the UK it still cannot be sold, although it is permitted in many other countries. There is a heated ongoing controversy over whether sweetener companies are exerting political power to prevent it from coming to market.

OTHER BITS & PIECES

SPIRULINA

RICE MILK

BRAZIL NUTS

SHELLED HEMP SEEDS

TAHINI

AGAR FLAKES

OAT BRAN

AGAVE NECTAR

CASHEW NUTS

COCONUT BUTTER

YACAN SYRUP

CHIA SEED

BROWN RICE SYRUP

TOOLS, TIPS & TECHNIQUES

TOOLS

If you are new to baking, the sheer number of available tools and gadgets can be unnerving (and expensive if you find shiny new toys hard to resist). Here are the ones that we use most.

BASIC TOOLS

1 ROLLING PIN
We like a nice long one. Most materials are fine, but wood is nice and light – just make sure the grain is fine or it will leave marks on your dough. You don't need handles – in fact you can get a better feel by rolling your palms over the top of the pin.

2 WHISK
For breaking up eggs, sifting flour (if it does not need to be super-fine), creaming softened butter, and breaking up granita. A silicon whisk is good if you are using it in a non-stick pan (although they are not as long-lasting).

3 SIEVE
Good to have a couple of different sizes – a small one for dusting and a bigger one for sifting. The more sturdy ones with the metal rim will withstand a good bash when you are sifting. (They are beautiful things, sieves, if you look at them closely.)

4 SPATULA (OR LAST LICK)
For making sure that you get everything out of the bowl, even if the last bits are just going straight into your mouth. Great for folding things together (e.g. chocolate and whisked egg whites). The heatproof ones are useful for stirring custard.

5 ELECTRIC WHISK
It's all very well being macho and using a standard whisk when people are about, but when you are on your own an electric one is so much easier. For creaming butter and sugar, making meringues and so forth.

6 GREASEPROOF PARCHMENT
Please don't try to use a thin greaseproof paper in place of proper baking parchment. Parchment makes life much easier – whether you are lining cake tins or pouring hot cracknel on to it, it will not let you down by breaking up into tiny pieces.

7 MICROPLANE ZESTER
For getting the zest off citrus fruits. If you are using a traditional zester you will need to chop it finely. Make sure you aren't so seduced by the microplane's easy action that you absentmindedly shred the white pith into your cake – it is very bitter. These are also great for grating Parmesan.

8 ICE CREAM SCOOP
Use the traditional kind to ensure that your ice cream balls are beautifully proportioned. The quick-release ones are useful for portioning things – e.g. cupcakes – but are often not strong enough for the hardness of ice cream from modern freezers.

⑨ MEASURING SPOONS

Have one set and use them for everything. Whether this is superstition or not, we find that different sets seem to vary slightly. It is safer and your baking will be more consistent if you just get used to one.

⑩ MEASURING JUG

Great as a general receptacle for tidy baking. Use the jug to portion runny batter out into prepared baking tins, for example. Always WEIGH water on the scales (see page 32). You can use a measuring jug to get the rough quantity, but for many recipes the jug is not accurate enough.

⑪ SPEED PEELER

Owning any other kind of peeler is a form of madness – a bit like when Björn Borg tried to make his comeback in professional tennis using a wooden racket. The speed peelers are by far the most effective.

⑫ PARING KNIFE

For all those little jobs: e.g. freeing cakes from tins, trimming fruits, or scoring bread dough.

⑬ JUICER (OR REAMER)

Great for getting all the juice out of a small amount of fruit. Cheap, easy to clean, efficient, durable, beautiful, simple and safe.

⑭ SCALES

Electric scales are brilliant for bakers, because they are so precise (try to get ones that measure in 1g increments, rather than 5g). Otherwise the old weighted scales are fine. The spring-loaded ones tend to be a bit inaccurate.

⑮ BAKING TINS

The basics:
- Two loaf tins (450g/1lb).
- A deep muffin tin (and maybe a mini muffin tin).
- Two 20–23cm sandwich tins (round, with approximately 2.5cm deep edges) – with push-out bases if possible.
- A 20–23cm tart or flan tin with fluted edges (approximately 2.5cm deep) – with a push-out base if possible.
- A deep cake tin for fruit cakes, again with a push-out base (and maybe a springform cake tin for cheesecakes).

(See our pull-out baking tin guide between pages 32–3.)

A BAKER WE LOVE

ELISABETH PTAK

Cakes and sweets were a big part of my mother Elisabeth's childhood. The photograph of her on her fourth birthday (above) tells the story. Her brothers and friends are gathered around the table, where the birthday girl (Mom) has the task of blowing out the candles on *three* birthday cakes.

Usually her mother (my grandmother) or her aunt was in charge of the baking duties, but as soon as she was old enough, Mom happily became the family cake-maker, and passed that love on to me and my brother (who quickly established a reputation for some of the best chocolate chip cookies around).

Mom always lays a beautiful table and has a party whenever she can. She tends to make not one but four or five different desserts, so that there is lots of choice.

Her Lemon Bars (see page 94) are legendary.

CLAIRE

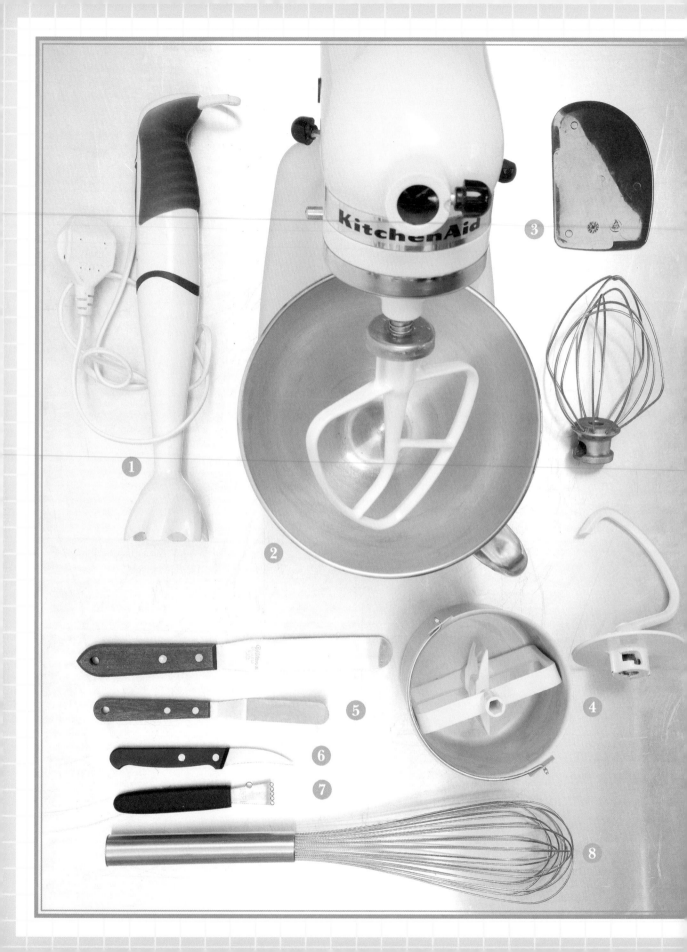

ADVANCED TOOLS

1 STICK BLENDER
For making fruit purées, seed milks, bringing chocolate and butter mixes back if they have split, and mixing flavours, e.g. green peppercorns into the Green Peppercorn Ice Cream recipe on page 250. (Also great for soups and smoothies.)

2 FREE-STANDING MIXER
If you do a lot of baking this will save you a great deal of time and mess.

3 DOUGH SCRAPER
For cutting bread dough, and scraping it (and loose flour) off surfaces. Also useful for folding (e.g. egg white into melted chocolate).

4 ICE CREAM MACHINE
A complete luxury, as you can make great ice cream without one (see pages 150–161). On the other hand, you could have a lot of fun with it and it saves time.

5 PALETTE KNIFES
For icing, levelling cake mixes, and lifting delicate cakes and biscuits on to cooling racks. Good to have a couple of sizes.

6 BIRD'S BEAK
A specialist knife for trimming fruit into particularly pleasing shapes (e.g. for coring the apples in Tarte Tatin on page 116.)

7 ZESTER
For when you need a hit of zesty flavour and you are going to strain out the zest, for example in a poaching liquid or ice cream base. You can also make delicate strands of candied zest by poaching them in a simple syrup.

8 LARGE METAL WHISK
If you are planning to get serious about your baking – either baking in large quantities, or baking for the long term – these professional whisks will offer unflagging support.

TECHNIQUES

Although all the recipes in this book contain enough instructions for you to plunge straight in, what follows is intended as a sort of mini masterclass in baking techniques. The first two sections – Basic Techniques and Advanced Techniques – give a brief run-through for the relatively inexperienced or rusty baker. (Even the more experienced may find they pick up a thing or two along the way.)

The third section – Baking with Alternatives – is a primer on the changes you will need to make to your baking style if you are cooking without that traditional triumvirate of baking ingredients: flour, butter and/or sugar. Many of the recipes in this book are wheat, dairy or sugar free, and this section will get your confidence up before you attempt them. You can also use these guidelines to help you transform your own traditional recipes into healthier ones.

BASIC TECHNIQUES

1 GENERAL TIPS

Make notes
You never know when you will try an experiment that creates something wonderful. Get into the habit of having a pencil and paper to hand to jot down what you have done.

If you are substituting ingredients, be prepared to experiment
For example, if you use spelt flour in place of wholemeal flour, or fructose instead of sugar, you will find that their properties are different. They will produce different textures, absorb different amounts of liquid, and so on. Don't let this put you off experimentation – just be aware of it and observe the results in case you want to tweak the recipes next time.

Measure everything out first
Chefs call this 'mise en place' – literally, 'put in place'. It makes the whole process more ordered and enjoyable. If you are a man, there is a chance that you will forget this advice.

> MAKE SURE YOU HAVE THE RIGHT SIZED PAN/DISH/TIN IN ADVANCE FOR THE RECIPE YOU ARE MAKING.

2 MIXING & MEASURING

Weigh water on your scales
As mentioned previously, measuring jugs can give you a close reading of volume but weighing water leaves less margin for error. Water is the same in weight by grams as its volume in millilitres (1g = 1ml). Milk works like this, too. But some liquids (such as honey) are denser and so weigh a little more than their volume, or are less dense (like cream), so weigh less. For this reason you're better off measuring these.

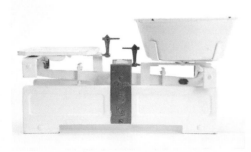

CONVERSION CHART FOR COMMON MEASURES

MEASUREMENTS

5 mm	$^1/_4$ inch
1 cm	$^1/_2$ inch
1.5 cm	$^3/_4$ inch
2.5 cm	1 inch
5 cm	2 inches
7 cm	3 inches
10 cm	4 inches
12 cm	5 inches
15 cm	6 inches
18 cm	7 inches
20 cm	8 inches
23 cm	9 inches
25 cm	10 inches
28 cm	11 inches
30 cm	12 inches
33 cm	13 inches

OVEN TEMPERATURES

110°C	(225°F)	Gas Mark $^1/_4$
120°C	(250°F)	Gas Mark $^1/_2$
140°C	(275°F)	Gas Mark 1
150°C	(300°F)	Gas Mark 2
160°C	(325°F)	Gas Mark 3
180°C	(350°F)	Gas Mark 4
190°C	(375°F)	Gas Mark 5
200°C	(400°F)	Gas Mark 6
220°C	(425°F)	Gas Mark 7
230°C	(450°F)	Gas Mark 8

LIQUIDS

15 ml	$^1/_2$ fl oz
25 ml	1 fl oz
50 ml	2 fl oz
75 ml	3 fl oz
100ml	$3^1/_2$ fl oz
125 ml	4 fl oz
150 ml	$^1/_4$ pint
175 ml	6 fl oz
200 ml	7 fl oz
250 ml	8 fl oz
275 ml	9 fl oz
300 ml	$^1/_2$ pint
325 ml	11 fl oz
350 ml	12 fl oz
375 ml	13 fl oz
400 ml	14 fl oz
450 ml	$^3/_4$ pint
475 ml	16 fl oz
500 ml	17 fl oz
575 ml	18 fl oz
600 ml	1 pint
750 ml	$1^1/_4$ pints
900 ml	$1^1/_2$ pints
1 litre	$1^3/_4$ pints
1.2 litres	2 pints
1.5 litres	$2^1/_2$ pints
1.8 litres	3 pints
2 litres	$3^1/_2$ pints
2.5 litres	4 pints
3.6 litres	6 pints

WEIGHTS

5 g	$^1/_4$ oz
15 g	$^1/_2$ oz
20 g	$^3/_4$ oz
25 g	1 oz
50 g	2 oz
75 g	3 oz
125 g	4 oz
150 g	5 oz
175 g	6 oz
200 g	7 oz
250 g	8 oz
275 g	9 oz
300 g	10 oz
325 g	11 oz
375 g	12 oz
400 g	13 oz
425 g	14 oz
475 g	15 oz
500 g	1 lb
625 g	$1^1/_4$ lb
750 g	$1^1/_2$ lb
875 g	$1^3/_4$ lb
1 kg	2 lb
1.25 kg	$2^1/_2$ lb
1.5 kg	3 lb
1.75 kg	$3^1/_2$ lb
2 kg	4 lb

Working with different types of oven

All the recipes in this book have been tested in an oven without a fan.
If you are using this kind of oven, you should put the cake in the middle of the
middle shelf, because heat rises and the top can be hotter than the bottom.

If you are using a fan-assisted oven, lower the temperature given in the recipe
by 20°C. Modern fan-assisted ovens are very efficient at circulating heat evenly
around the oven, so there's also no need to worry about positioning. Even if
you have a few racks filled, the heat will be pushed by the fan all around the
baking cakes.

Regardless of what type of oven you use you will find that it has its
idiosyncrasies, so don't stick slavishly to any baking recipes. Make sure you
understand how your oven behaves and adjust accordingly.

A GUIDE TO
Baking Dishes

Muffin tin

Spring-form tin

Square cake tin

Deep cake tin

Loaf tin

Baking sheet

Loose-bottomed tin

Small pie dish

Saucepan

Roasting tray

Ramekin

American pie dish

Flan dish /
American tart dish

Griddle pan

Deep baking dish / tray

Sifting

Put the ingredients that you want to sift into a large sieve held over a bowl. Tip the sieve to an angle of 30° and knock the lower edge repeatedly with a metal spoon or the back of a knife until everything has passed through. With icing sugar, you can crush the last few balls through with the back of a spoon.

Combining dry ingredients

Sometimes sifting is not necessary. If you don't mind lumps, and are only trying to evenly distribute raising agents or spices through a large quantity of flour, using a hand-held whisk is a great shortcut.

Creaming

There are two ways to cream your butter and sugar. The recipes in this book will each say which one to use.

Traditional – this method is slightly more painstaking, but gives the lightest cakes. You mix the butter (softened) vigorously with the sugar (ideally with an electric mixer) to trap air. You then mix in the other ingredients gradually in the following order – eggs, then some flour, then some liquid, then the rest of the flour, then the rest of the liquid.

The two-stage mixing method – more common in America – produces soft but slightly heavier cakes. It is quicker. You mix all the dry ingredients in one bowl, then mix the butter into those (as if making pastry) before adding the wet ingredients until incorporated.

Folding

This is how you mix two semi-liquid substances while preserving the air trapped in one of them (for example melted chocolate and whisked egg, or fruit purée and whipped cream). We were taught slightly different ways to fold, but the principle remains the same – do it gently and without any obviously 'crushing' or 'deflating' motions.

Claire's method: Use a rubber spatula to gently but quickly fold together aerated eggs or cream with other ingredients. Swirls will form in the mixture but don't worry about mixing until they are gone, as you run the risk of over-mixing.

Henry's method: Put the mixture with the air in it on top of the other mixture in a large bowl. Take a large metal spoon and cut vertically down into the middle of the bowl. When you hit the bottom, scoop the spoon around towards you, gently lifting the mixture and folding it back on top of the bowl. Rotate the bowl by 45° and repeat until mixed.

EGGS

Buying eggs

Choose a decent-sized, free-range egg. Chickens that have been well fed and cared for produce yolks that are more yellow and lustrous. The yellow or orange yolks are also indicative of the seasons, as the greener the grass that the chickens are eating, the deeper the colour of the yolks.

Storing eggs

If you live in a cold climate or are using your eggs within a matter of days, you can keep them out of the fridge. If you are planning to keep them for a while, or there is a heatwave, put them into the fridge (preferably in an airtight box to keep out smells from other foods, which can permeate the shells).

Bringing eggs to temperature

When baking, eggs should be at room temperature. If you are getting them from the fridge, you can plunge them into warm water for a couple of minutes to speed up the process.

Quick Custard

Makes: 600ml
Preparation time: 5 minutes
Cooking time: 15 minutes
WF GF V

1 **vanilla pod**
500ml **double cream**
100ml **milk**
180g **caster sugar**
5 **free-range egg yolks**, at room temperature
sea salt

1. Halve the vanilla pod lengthwise and put it into a pan with the cream, milk and caster sugar. Bring to the boil, stirring to make sure the sugar dissolves. Take the pan off the heat and allow it to sit for 5 minutes.

2. Meanwhile put your egg yolks into a blender and blend for 2 minutes, or until they go creamy. Add a small pinch of salt.

3. Bring the cream back to the boil, remove the vanilla pod, and pour the mixture slowly into the eggs, blending as you go. Assuming that the cream was good and hot and the eggs not too cold you should be left with great not-too-thick custard. (If you want to make it thicker, heat it gently on the hob, but you shouldn't need to.)

TIPS

❖ By using more cream than in most recipes, and – critically – heating the sugar with the cream, rather than adding it to the egg yolks, you remove the nervous stage of heating the custard over the stove and waiting for it to thicken – or, more often than not, scramble.

Breaking eggs

Break the shells against a flat worktop, rather than against the edge of the bowl or with a knife or spoon. This way, pieces of shell are less likely to get forced into the egg.

Separating eggs

Holding the two halves of the broken egg above a bowl, plop the yolk from one half shell to the other, back and forth, until all the white has fallen into the bowl. Then drop the yolk into another, smaller bowl. (If the yolk starts to break up, move fast and get the yolk into the yolks bowl. It is better to have a little white in the yolks bowl than a little yolk in the whites bowl. Yolk contamination makes it harder to whisk the whites, see below.)

Whisking egg whites

This is one of the few cases where fresher is not better. It is actually slightly easier to whisk the whites of older, runnier eggs. (The whites of a fresh egg will be very coagulated.) MAKE SURE THE BOWL AND THE WHISK ARE VERY CLEAN. A little dirt – particularly fat, which you find in egg yolks – can prevent a good voluminous cloud of whites (although a speck of yolk won't matter). A pinch of salt or cream of tartar helps the whisking. Be careful not to over-whisk egg whites: once they have formed stiff peaks, whisking them further will cause them to granulate and break down.

4 CHOCOLATE – BASIC
(see also page 44)

Buying

Most of the recipes here call for a high cocoa solid chocolate (over 70%). With chocolate you generally get what you pay for. There are, however, many single-origin chocolates available these days that can be as low as 64% and still have very good characteristics and flavour. They are usually pretty expensive, but they're a nice treat.

Storing

Heat and water are the enemies of chocolate. A damp climate draws the sugar out and produces that white coating on the surface called bloom. Bloom does not affect the taste of chocolate, it just looks bad. If chocolate melts slightly and resets, it can lose the 'temper' which gives it its lovely finish and that satisfying 'snap' when you break it. It will keep for ages somewhere airtight and coolish (but not in the fridge, which tends to be damp and therefore encourages bloom).

Melting

As we say above, chocolate hates heat. It will melt at a temperature of 34°C, just under body temperature (which is why it literally melts in the mouth so deliciously). If you heat it over 50°C, the emulsifiers become damaged and it starts to split into its constituent parts – fats and solids. So heat it carefully in a saucepan suspended over another saucepan containing very gently simmering water. (Be careful not to get any drops of water into the melting chocolate, as these can cause hard lumps to form.) You can melt large quantities of chocolate in an accurate oven set at under 50°C – this may take a couple of hours. It is possible to melt chocolate in a pan over a very gentle heat, stirring consistently, but it's not advised.

You can also use a microwave to melt the chocolate in 30-second blasts, stirring in between the blasts.

⑤ CREAM

Types of cream

Creams are named according to the amount of fat they contain. Broadly speaking, creams with a higher fat percentage will be richer and thicker, and easier to whip. The higher fat content creams are also more stable, and therefore less prone to curdling when heated or when acid is added to them. For example, a double cream (which is high in fat) can be boiled quite happily, whereas a single cream might split under the same treatment. Likewise, you can squeeze lemon juice into double cream with abandon, but you might want to be careful with single.

The naming of creams varies by country. In the UK the main types are:

Single cream

Contains no less than 18% fat by law, and normally around 20%. Splits easily, so is generally used cold to pour onto puddings. It won't whip up, no matter how hard you go at it.

Soured cream

A single cream that has been soured using a bacterial culture to produce lactic acid. It has a distinctive tang. As well as being used in some baking recipes, it is often used as a condiment where richness and sharpness are sought (e.g. to top fresh berries or baked potatoes or in burritos).

Whipping cream

Contains no less than 35% fat and can be quickly whipped and holds it shape. It will not curdle when you add acid or heat it.

Double cream

Contains no less than 48% fat. Will whip very readily and does not curdle. It is easy to over-whip it and set it far too hard. Sometimes it comes as an almost set cream (when it is called something like extra thick). You won't be able to whip this.

Crème fraîche

The double cream version of soured cream. It has a lovely tang to it. Good for spooning on puddings or using in sauces. Doesn't split easily.

Clotted cream

A high-fat cream that has been slowly heated and cooled until thickly set. Contains over 55% fat. For spooning on puddings (clotted cream scooped on to ice cream is a rare summer treat). Don't heat it, as it will melt and split like butter.

UHT/sterilized cream

This cream is sterilized for longer life and doesn't taste as good as fresh cream. However, in extremis (when the corner shop had nothing else) Henry has made ice cream with it – it was ice cream, not as we know it, but strangely good.

Best for whipping

Use whipping cream or double cream. Make sure it's cold (if it's warm it can turn into butter). Cream is much easier to whip than egg whites – and also easier to over-whip. For that reason it's safest to use a hand whisk, rather than anything electric. A hand whisk will also create the lightest foam. If you are making it in advance and putting it back in the fridge, always under-whisk it as it will harden a little while resting.

Whipping: the fun method

If you want to make a really classic banana split and generally be childish with cream, you can buy a cream squirter. This looks a bit like an old-fashioned soda fountain, and is powered by tiny canisters of nitrous oxide. Use it to whip the cream up into foamy swirled peaks – and to squirt cream directly into your mouth, like when you were eight. We use them for our Leon Salted Caramel Banana Split (see page 281)

Warning 1: This cream is unstable and will turn back to liquid within half an hour (unlike cream whipped with a whisk) so squirt it at the last minute.

Warning 2: Nitrous oxide is commonly known as laughing gas (or, on the labour ward, as 'gas and air') and can produce a euphoric effect if inhaled directly from the whipper. Do not try this unless you are giving birth and there is a midwife present.

⑥ PASTRY – BASIC

General tips

When making most pastries the trick is to trap little pieces of butter within a dough, which melt when you cook it and create something flaky and delicious as the water from the butter evaporates and turns to steam, which rises, pushing up the layers. Unless otherwise stated, therefore, make sure that all your ingredients are cold and that you make it in a cold room (if the butter melts before you cook it you will get something dense rather than light and flaky).

Always rest a dough in the fridge for at least half an hour before rolling it out. (This allows the gluten to relax, which will make the task much easier).

When rolling out pastry for a tart tin, lift the pressure as you get to the edge of the dough to avoid making it too thin.

Your pastry will vary depending on the type of flour you use, the fats, the humidity, the temperature etc. If you are keen to perfect the art, observe closely what happens each time you make a certain type of pastry and take notes. Over time you will learn when an extra splash of water or a sift of flour are required.

Basic pastries

The basic kinds of pastries that we use in this book are flaky, shortcrust and pressed-crust. Flaky pastry has thin layers of fat separating thin layers of dough and will break into thin flakes. Shortcrust and pressed-crust pastries crumble into small pieces, as the fat has been worked through the flour. We provide recipes for these with the main recipes as appropriate, but thought it would be useful to give the basics here for easy reference. (In addition to these you can find a hot water crust recipe with the pork pie on page 284).

Henry thinks life is a bit too short to be making your own puff pastry – you can now buy some very good all-butter versions from the supermarket.

Pressed-crust pastry

Makes enough for
a 20–23cm flan tin

140g **plain flour**
2 tablespoons **caster sugar**
100g **unsalted butter**, melted
1 tablespoon **white vinegar**

1. Blend the ingredients briefly in a food processor and pat into a tart tin.

Shortcrust pastry

Makes: 300g

200g **plain flour**
a pinch of **salt**
75g **unsalted butter**, cut into rough 1cm cubes
2½ tablespoons **cold water**

1. Sift the flour and salt and add the butter. Mix gently until the mixture resembles coarse sand.

2. Sprinkle the water over the mixture and mix until it forms a cohesive ball of dough.

3. Wrap the pastry in clingfilm and allow to rest in the fridge for at least 30 minutes before using.

Flaky pastry

The same ingredients as above but keep the pieces of butter larger and don't mix them in all the way.

⑦ MAKING CAKES

Slow & low

If in doubt when making a cake, bake it slow and low for greater moistness throughout. The name of this method came from a rap song that Claire is particularly fond of. 'Slow and low that is the tempo' is the lyric, and it has become her baking mantra.

To test for doneness

There are three ways to test for doneness.

The skewer method: Good for denser cakes. Insert a skewer (or a long thin knife) into the centre of the cake, and when it pulls out clean, the cake is done.

The listening method: Henry's mother-in-law, Petra (see page 274), swears by this for fruit cakes. Open the oven door, take out the cake and listen to it. A fruit cake will 'hiss' gently while it cooks. When it stops hissing, it is done.

The pressing method: Good for lighter cakes such as sponges. Press down gently on the top of the cake: when it springs back, rather than leaving a slight dent, it is done.

⑧ ICING

There are three main icings that we use in this book – basic, buttercream and royal.

Basic is simply a mixture of water (or more often fruit juice or purée) and icing sugar, and forms a delicate, flat, slightly crispy coating when set.

Royal icing is similar to basic icing, but uses egg white to make it harden to a much more brittle texture (think Christmas cake).

Buttercream icing (think cupcakes) is a rich and creamy mixture of sugar, butter and flavourings. Claire has also come up with vegan vanilla icing – a version of buttercream icing using coconut oil, soya and agave nectar in place of butter and sugar. It rocks.

You can find recipes for icings on the pages below:

Vegan vanilla icing 97
Royal icing 179
Buttercream icing 187

9 STORING

Cakes, bread & biscuits

These should all be wrapped in greaseproof paper and kept in an airtight container at room temperature. Storing them in the fridge will make them go stale more quickly (starches crystallize faster at colder temperatures). Bread freezes well. Try slicing it and storing it in airtight bags, then toasting it straight from the freezer.

Baking ingredients

Any ingredients that live in the fridge are best kept in an airtight container to stop them picking up smells from other foods. It's also best to keep flour, sugar and other larder ingredients in airtight containers to keep the damp out.

10 DOUGH

Kneading

When kneading dough by hand, remember that you are trying to stretch the gluten. This requires energy. Henry likes to break a sweat when making and baking bread. He says if you are not breaking a sweat, you are not working it hard enough. Big long stretches with the ball of the hand are the thing. Claire is a fan of the slap and tickle method: stretching the dough up and out, then slapping it down on to a work surface rather than using the pushing method. The idea with this method is to incorporate air into the dough whilst kneading and to form the gluten so that you don't need to add as much flour to the bread. Both methods will produce equally beautiful bread.

11 FRUIT

Juicing

There are three ways to juice a fruit: using an electric juicer (for hard fruit such as apples); using a squeezer or reamer (citrus fruit); and using a sieve (for soft fruit, such as raspberries, which can easily be forced through a sieve with the back of a metal spoon).

Zesting

Make sure you don't zest any of the bitter pith. Also, zest over a bowl in order to catch the highly flavoured oils that squirt out during the process.

Preparing mango

Use a large knife to slice the mango in half (Fig. 1), cutting either side of the large flattish stone in the middle. With a smaller paring knife, score the flesh in lines and then crosswise (Fig. 2), so that you have a criss-cross pattern. Invert the slice of mango so that the cubes of flesh are sticking out (Fig. 3), and cut them into a bowl. So as not to waste any flesh, have a go at the stone – cut off any remaining flesh from the top and bottom and add to your stash.

Preparing pomegranates

Slice the top off the pomegranate (like taking the lid off a pumpkin at Halloween). Invert the pomegranate over a bowl and tap it with the back of a wooden spoon. The seeds will pop right out! Pomegranate juice is pretty squirty and deeply coloured, so protect your clothes and any porous surfaces.

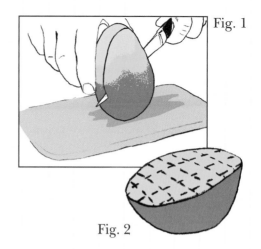

Fig. 1

Fig. 2

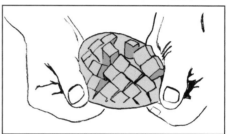

Fig. 3

Opening a coconut

Use a hammer and nail or an awl, and tap the tip of the sharp end into each of the three black 'eyes' in the end of a coconut. Invert the coconut over a glass and let the water drain out. Drink the water. It is so good for you. Once it has drained, place the coconut on its side on a tea towel that has been folded a few times.

One end of the coconut is slightly more bulbous. Use a hammer to tap the perimeter of the coconut at its fattest point. A natural fracture should occur. The coconut will then quite easily pop open.

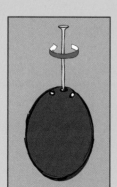

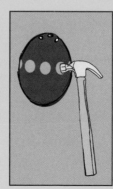
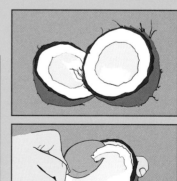

⑪ FIRST AID
WHAT TO DO WHEN IT GOES WRONG

Curdled butter & eggs

To help avoid curdling, always bring your ingredients to room temperature before you start. Your butter should be very, very soft. Whip the butter and sugar together with an electric hand whisk. It is so much easier than doing it by hand, and you will get enough air into the mixture to be able to hold the eggs. The butter and sugar mixture is ready when it has doubled in volume and turned almost white.

Add the eggs one by one, fully incorporating each addition.

If you're making a cake that has lots of eggs (such as a Victoria sponge), add a teaspoon or two of flour to help stabilize the mixture, but not too much or the cake may become tough.

Sunken cakes

If a cake has bicarbonate of soda in it and no acid (e.g. cream of tartar) to neutralize it, it can rise in the beginning and then fall down. (Note: if a recipe calls for baking powder, a mix of bicarbonate of soda and cream of tartar can be substituted.)

Always check the expiration dates on your leavening powders. They don't last for ever, and expired leavening powders are the source of many failed cakes.

Too much mixture in the cake tin can cause a cake to sink in the middle. When baking a sponge, always leave about a quarter of the tin unfilled to give the cake room to rise up. Fruit cakes won't rise as much, so you can fill the tin a bit more.

Sinking can also be a sign that your cake is under-baked. See Testing Doneness.

Testing doneness

Be sure to use the right method to test for doneness (see page 39), as not every method works for every cake.

Some cakes are meant to be moist, so the skewer test isn't foolproof. The spring-back-to-the-touch test is not always sufficient if a cake is supposed to be soft. The 'listening' method works best for fruit cakes, and the timer is never to be trusted.

Take notes on recipes – if you make a mistake the first time, you will know better next time round. It is important to learn to trust your instinct.

Try not to rush the cooling of a cake. As a cake cools, it continues to bake very slightly. Rushing it might mean it sinks instead.

Blind baking

Line your pastry tin with the dough, then be sure to chill it for at least 20 minutes in the fridge or 10 minutes in the freezer. This helps to keep the pastry from slumping down the sides.

Line the pastry with buttered baking parchment or a silicone-lined parchment paper that won't stick to it. Fill it right to the top of the case with baking beans or rice. Once the case has baked enough to hold its shape, remove the beans and paper and continue to bake until just golden.

If you want to keep the pastry on the lighter side, cover it loosely with foil or baking paper as it cooks. If you are using a fan-assisted oven this can be tricky, because the fan blows the paper around.

Fan-assisted ovens

Often cookbooks will ask you to put the cake in the middle of the oven, because heat rises and the top can be hotter than the bottom. Modern fan-assisted ovens are very efficient at circulating heat evenly around the oven, so there's no need to worry about positioning. Even if you have a few racks filled, the heat will be pushed by the fan all around the baking cakes.

All the recipes in this book have been tested without a fan, with the cakes positioned on the middle shelf of the oven. If you are using a fan-assisted oven, lower the given temperature by 20°C.

Meringues

The trick to making successful meringues is to open the oven door a few times during the baking to let condensation out. The idea is to dry out the exterior of the meringues while keeping the inside moist.

(The recipe for Pavlova on page 140 also adds cornflour and vinegar to help give that chewy centre.)

Baking powder & plain flour *v.* self-raising

If you only have plain flour on hand and a recipe calls for self-raising, you can add a teaspoon of baking powder for every 140g of plain flour.

Substitutes for buttermilk

Buttermilk and yoghurt make cakes soft and moist because of their acidity. Buttermilk is becoming more readily available in the UK, probably because of the fashion for American-style baking.

If you don't have buttermilk, you can use half plain yoghurt and half whole milk. Another alternative is to use 1 tablespoon of fresh lemon juice with 200ml milk – this will make the equivalent of 225ml of buttermilk.

Substitutes for brown sugar

If you have no brown sugar, add 1 tablespoon of molasses or black treacle to 200g of caster or granulated sugar to get the right flavour.

Rolling/patching pastry (when hot)

If you blind bake a pastry case and find it has small holes or cracks when it comes out of the oven, you can patch it while still hot with scraps left over from rolling. When the patches of raw pastry hit the hot pastry they cook and form little seals.

Domed cakes/muffins

There are two main reasons why cakes sometimes dome up in the middle.
(a) The metal on the outside of the pan conducts the heat faster. The sides of the cake set while the centre still continues to bake and rise.
(b) The structure of the cake is too strong, preventing the leavening gases from escaping until towards the end of baking, when they erupt through the centre in little tunnels. The mixture may have been mixed too much after the flour was added, and the air bubbles try to escape through the middle. When glutens form, the crumb becomes dry and tough.

ADVANCED TECHNIQUES

① STERILIZING JARS

To sterilize, put clean, washed and dried jam jars or bottles into a cold oven with the lids off. Turn the oven on to 170°C/340°F/gas mark 3½ and put the timer on for 20 minutes. When the bell goes, turn off the oven, leaving the jars inside. Pour in your jam, jelly, chutney or syrup while the jars are still hot.

② CHOCOLATE – ADVANCED

Tempering

Although it looks all smooth, the chocolate we eat is given its shine and 'snap' by the crystalline structure of cocoa butter. Unfortunately, the butter can crystallize in six ways and only one of them is the right kind. You will notice that if you take a bar of chocolate, melt it and then let it reset, it will be dull-coloured and soft, because the crystals have reformed the wrong way. This doesn't matter when you are using chocolate in cakes and so on. But if you want to make, say, an Easter egg with the proper shine and snap, you have to 'temper' it to ensure the crystals set right. There are three ways to do this.

Thermometer method

Requires concentration, but foolproof.

1. Place 150g chocolate in a bowl. Bring a pan of water to the boil and take it off the heat. Place the bowl of chocolate over the steaming water. Melt the chocolate, stirring, until it registers 46°C with a candy or chocolate thermometer.

2. Let it sit for 10 minutes and stir again. While it is sitting, chop another 50g of chocolate into finer pieces. Add this by spoonfuls to the melted chocolate, stirring until completely smooth each time.

3. You are trying to get the chocolate to 30°C. You may not need all the chocolate. (If you have lumps, use a hand-held blender to smooth it out).

4. Bring your pan back to the boil and remove it from the heat.

5. Place your bowl of chocolate over it for a few seconds to bring it up to 32°C.

Tempering machine

By far the easiest method. Just chuck the chocolate into the machine. It does the rest. If you live in a big city, you may find that you can rent one.

The marble slab method

This is how artisanal chocolate makers do it. It is good fun, really messy (see pictures on page 216), and quite hard. We would strongly recommend finding someone to teach you. You will need a marble or stone slab (at least 2.5cm thick). It must be uniformly cool, so make sure that you do not have a dishwasher on underneath it, and do not place anything hot (e.g. a cup of tea) on it.

Melt a large quantity of chocolate in the oven at 50°C maximum for dark chocolate, 40–45°C for white or milk chocolate (you will need an accurate oven to be sure of the temperature). Pour a quarter of the chocolate on to the slab. Swish it around using a dough scraper and a palette knife. It is important to keep the chocolate around the worktop so that none of it starts to set, and it all cools evenly. Periodically touch the chocolate to your lip. When it feels slightly cooler than body temperature (it will be the texture of cake batter), pour it back into the bowl and mix it into the remaining chocolate. Work fast.

BAKING WITH ALTERNATIVES

Baking with alternatives to wheat flour, butter and white sugar is easier than you might think. Think of these alternatives not as replacement ingredients but as new ones to experiment with. If you don't go in much for experimentation in the kitchen, don't worry, we have done most of the work for you already. All tried and tested, and this is one situation where curiosity definitely won't kill the cat.

If you want to be more experimental, try using these ingredients in your own recipes. You may need a bit of good old-fashioned trial and error before they work out, but to help you, here are some general rules that will let you predict how they may behave.

Flours

Rice flour is a great alternative to wheat if used in conjunction with a little xanthan gum, which is a good stand-in for gluten. Without it, cakes can crumble a bit too much. Rice flour has a slightly coarser texture to that of wheat flour. The finely ground rice has a crumbly texture which is similar to ground almonds and different from the light texture of wheat flour. It lies somewhere between wheat and maize flour.

Though corn and oats are OK for some people, they are not suitable for everyone with a wheat and gluten intolerance. We have tried to include recipes for everyone. Some ready-mixed gluten-free flours are an easy way to take your favourite recipe and make it suitable for you.

Sweeteners

Wherever caster sugar is called for, this is usually not just for sweetness but also for its structural qualities. For that reason, be cautious about using substitutes. You could, however, use a slightly less refined sugar such as golden caster sugar.

Agave nectar is a wonderful sweetener and much easier for our bodies to digest than sugar. It is also suitable for those who can't have sugar or honey. It takes longer to absorb into the bloodstream as well, so your blood sugar doesn't go haywire. We also love maple syrup, but it is very expensive.

Dairy & egg alternatives

Coconut oil is a very exciting discovery if you are staying away from dairy. It makes fantastic icing (though you'll need to chill it a bit, as it stays liquid at a lower temperature than butter). It also works very well baked in some cakes.

If soya milk agrees with you, you'll find it great to bake with. Rice milk and coconut milk are very good too, but a little different in texture. We use cashew nut butter in our vanilla icing, along with soy (or rice) milk and coconut oil, and the creamy texture is a dream.

Egg alternatives are easier to find than you might expect. A little ground flax meal or chia seed makes a great nutritional substitute. You can also use apple sauce to get the right texture in cakes. Commercial egg replacers are usually just soy and potato starch, which are thickeners.

RICE FLOUR

EVERY DAY

BREAKFAST • POWER SNACKS • TEA TIME
PUDDINGS • COOKING WITH CHILDREN
BREAD & SAVOURIES • SWEETS

BREAKFAST

READY TO SERVE

GRANOLAS • MILKS • NUT BUTTERS • MUFFINS • PANCAKES • BREADS

The idea of baking for breakfast probably seems little short of ludicrous.

Most of us are in such a hurry in the morning that it's all we can do to snatch a rusk from the baby's fist en route to the door. On the other hand, when you do have time to savour it, breakfast can be the most pleasurable meal of the day: your appetite is properly whetted by twelve hours without food, your tastebuds are firing on all cylinders, and you don't even need to get dressed for the feast.

The recipes that follow cover both kinds of breakfast. You can make the super-healthy granola and breakfast spreads at the weekend and then wolf them during the week, and we have also included some more indulgent weekend treats.

MADE AT HOME

Our Favourite Granola

A wonderful, rich, versatile granola. Eat it with milk or put some on yoghurt.

Makes: 1.6kg (a good amount)
Preparation time: 10 minutes
Cooking time: 1 hour 40 minutes
❤ WF GF DF V

600g **rolled oats**
125g **whole almonds** (skins on)
50g **ground flax seeds**
50g **sesame seeds**
50ml **maple syrup**
100ml **sunflower oil**
250ml **runny honey**
50g **dark brown sugar**
50ml **water**
1½ teaspoons **pure vanilla extract**
½ teaspoon **ground cinnamon**
a grating of **fresh nutmeg**
a pinch of **sea salt**
125g **dried apricots**, sliced
100g **sultanas**
50g **dried sour cherries**

1. Heat the oven to 150°C/300°F/gas mark 2. Line 2 baking trays with baking paper.

2. Put the oats, whole almonds, flax seeds and sesame seeds in a large bowl and set aside.

3. In a saucepan, combine the maple syrup, sunflower oil, runny honey, dark brown sugar and water. Place over a medium heat and whisk constantly to melt it all together without burning.

4. Remove the syrup mixture from the heat and stir in the vanilla, spices and salt. Pour the syrup over the oat mixture and stir well to completely coat the oats, nuts and seeds.

5. Spread the mixture out on the baking trays and bake in the oven for 1 hour.

6. Remove from the oven, toss the mixture well with a metal spatula and return to the oven. Lower the temperature to 140°C/275°F/gas mark 1 and bake for another 35–40 minutes, until the mixture is golden. Remove from the oven and allow to cool completely before stirring in the apricots, sultanas and sour cherries.

TIPS

✤ Granola will keep for weeks in an airtight container.

✤ You can replace the sugar and maple syrup with equal amounts of agave syrup for a low GI version.

Claire's Healthy Granola

You will not believe how good this tastes. It is light and clustery.

Makes: 1.5 kg (a good amount)
Preparation time: 10 minutes
Cooking time: 1 hour 40 minutes
♥ ✓ WF GF DF V

500g **buckwheat flakes**
125g **whole almonds** (skins on)
50g **ground flax seeds**
50g **sesame seeds**
50g **pumpkin seeds**
50g **amaranth**
250ml **agave syrup**
50ml **olive oil** (not extra virgin)
100g **coconut oil**
100ml **water**
1½ teaspoons **vanilla extract**
½ teaspoon **ground cinnamon**
a grating of **fresh nutmeg**
a pinch of **sea salt**
100g **sultanas**
50g **desiccated coconut**

I came up with this when I was on a cleanse, but I eat it all the time now. The buckwheat flakes have a wonderfully nutty flavour and the addition of coconut and olive oil makes it good for those avoiding certain fats. I love the crunch of amaranth too, another ancient grain.

CLAIRE

1. Heat the oven to 150°C/300°F/gas mark 2. Line 2 baking trays with baking paper.

2. Put the buckwheat flakes, whole almonds, flax seeds, sesame seeds, pumpkin seeds and amaranth into a large bowl and set aside.

3. In a saucepan, combine the agave syrup, olive oil, coconut oil and water. Place over a medium heat and whisk constantly to melt it all together without burning.

4. Remove the syrup mixture from the heat and stir in the vanilla, spices and salt. Pour the syrup over the dry ingredients and stir well to completely coat all the nuts and seeds.

5. Spread the mixture out on the baking trays and bake in the oven for approximately 1 hour.

6. Remove from the oven, toss the mixture well with a metal spatula and return to the oven. Lower the temperature to 140°C/275°F/gas mark 1 and bake for another 35–40 minutes, until the mixture is golden. Remove from the oven and allow to cool completely before stirring in the sultanas and desiccated coconut, then store in an airtight container.

TIPS

❖ Serve with fresh dates and low-fat natural yoghurt for a naturally sweet treat.

Luxury Granola

This one has white chocolate in it.

Makes: 1.9kg
Preparation time: 10 minutes
Cooking time: 1 hour 40 minutes
♥ WF GF V

600g **rolled oats**
125g **whole hazelnuts**
100g **pecan nuts**
50ml **maple syrup**
100ml **sunflower oil**
250ml **runny honey**
125g **brown sugar**
50ml **water**
1½ teaspoons **vanilla extract**
½ teaspoon **ground ginger**
a pinch of **sea salt**
3 tablespoons **golden syrup**
100g **jumbo flaked coconut**
200g **white chocolate pieces**
200g **dried blueberries**

1. Heat the oven to 150°C/300°F/gas mark 2. Line 2 baking trays with baking paper.

2. Put the oats, hazelnuts and pecans into a large bowl and set aside.

3. In a saucepan, combine the maple syrup, sunflower oil, runny honey, brown sugar and water. Place over a medium heat and whisk constantly to melt it all together without burning.

4. Remove the syrup mixture from the heat and stir in the vanilla, ground ginger and salt. Pour this over the oat mixture and stir well to completely coat the oats, nuts and seeds.

5. Spread the mixture out on the baking trays and cook in the oven for approximately 1 hour.

6. Remove from the oven, drizzle the mixture with golden syrup and add the coconut. Toss well with a metal spatula and return the trays to the oven. Lower the temperature to 140°C/275°F/gas mark 1 and bake for another 30 minutes, until the mixture is golden. Remove from the oven and stir in the white chocolate. Allow to cool completely before folding in the blueberries and storing in an airtight container.

TIPS

✤ Really good sprinkled on top of shop-bought vanilla ice cream for an easy pud.

Maggie's Milks

If milk doesn't agree with you, you're going to love these seed-based alternatives. Maggie (see page 232) taught Claire how to make them. Don't be put off because they sound a bit whacky. They are delicate, sweet and unbelievably good in their own right. Pour them on to your muesli or just glug them back from a glass.

Hazelnut Milk

Makes: about 650ml
Preparation time: 10 minutes +
soaking time overnight
Cooking time: none
♥ ✓ WF GF DF V

100g **hazelnuts**, soaked overnight or for 8 hours in chlorine-free water, drained and rinsed
seeds from ¼ of a **vanilla pod**
2 tablespoons **raw honey** (preferably crystallized)
600ml **water**
a tiny pinch of **sea salt**

1. In a blender, blend the soaked hazelnuts, vanilla seeds and honey with 200ml of the water until almost smooth.

2. Add the remaining water and blend to mix.

3. Strain through a nut milk bag, fine-mesh cheesecloth, or similar.

4. Chill and enjoy. Keeps for 6–8 days in the fridge.

Pumpkin Seed Milk

Makes: about 750ml
Preparation time: 15 minutes +
soaking time overnight
Cooking time: none
♥ ✓ WF GF DF V

300g **pumpkin seeds**, soaked overnight or for 6–8 hours in chlorine-free water, drained and rinsed
40g **cashews**, soaked overnight or for 6–8 hours in chlorine-free water, drained and rinsed
2 **dates**, pitted
1 tablespoon **maple syrup**
6 strokes of grated **nutmeg** (optional)
a pinch of **sea salt**
700ml **water**

1. In a blender, bend all the ingredients with 400ml of the water until almost smooth.

2. Add the remaining water and blend together.

3. Strain through a nut milk bag, fine-mesh cheesecloth, or similar.

4. Chill and enjoy. Keeps for 6–8 days in the fridge.

TIPS

❖   To make this milk 100% raw, omit the cashews, maple syrup and 100ml of water. Add 1 or 2 more dates.

Raw Nut & Seed Butters

One of the best things to spread on your bread first thing in the morning is a homemade nut butter. They are both indulgent and fantastically good for you.

Choose good-quality, very fresh raw walnuts, almonds, pumpkin seeds, hazelnuts, cashews or sunflower seeds.

1. If you like you can soak or sprout the nuts or seeds first. If you do this, make sure you dry them well before processing them.

2. Process the nuts or seeds in a food processor for several minutes to extract all the oil. As the nuts and seeds are whizzing round, you can drizzle in a little raw honey or water to help turn it into an emulsified butter.

3. Store in the fridge.

Salmon & Dill Muffins

A savoury breakfast muffin.

Makes: 6
Preparation time: 15 minutes
Cooking time: 20 minutes

240g **plain flour**
2 teaspoons **baking powder**
165g **grated cheese**
50g chopped **smoked salmon**
20g chopped **fresh dill**
1 **free-range egg**
180ml **buttermilk**
75ml **vegetable** or **sunflower oil**
100g **cream cheese**

Our friend Rebecca used to make these for us painstakingly every day at home and then drive them to the restaurants daily. Sadly (for us) she is now the proud mother of two and the muffins are no longer to be found in Leon. If you liked them, here they are.

HENRY

1. Heat the oven to 180°/350°F/gas mark 4, and line a 6-hole muffin tin with paper cases.

2. Mix the flour and baking powder together in a large bowl. Add the grated cheese, smoked salmon and dill.

3. In a separate bowl beat together the egg, buttermilk and oil.

4. Place half the wet ingredients into the dry ingredients and stir well. Then add the rest of the wet ingredients and mix until completely combined.

5. Spoon into the muffin cases until each is half full, then place a heaped teaspoon of cream cheese in the middle of each muffin. Top them up until they are full with mixture.

6. Cook for 10 minutes, then take the tin out and turn it around so the muffins cook evenly. Put the tin back into the oven and continue to cook for a further 10 minutes, or until the muffins are just browning on top.

FRIENDS & FAMILY RECIPES

Rebecca on her 9th birthday at home, 1982

Almond Date Oat Muffins

A nutty, semi-sweet breakfast muffin made with spelt flour, which is not only better for you than other varieties of wheat, but gives it its distinctive texture and flavour.

Makes: 12
Preparation time: 20 minutes
Cooking time: 25 minutes
♥ ✓ V

100g **whole almonds**, skins on
200g **unsalted butter**, melted
75g **light brown sugar**
200g **oat bran**
100g **rolled oats**, plus more to sprinkle the tops with
200g **fine spelt flour**
½ teaspoon **salt**
1½ teaspoons **bicarbonate of soda**
2 **free-range eggs**
350ml **natural yoghurt**
250g **pitted chopped dates**
zest from 1 **orange**

This muffin is inspired by one I learned to make at the wonderful Bovine Bakery, in Point Reyes, California. I started my career there, aged fifteen, under the tutelage of Deborah Ruff and Bridget Devlin. I learned so much from them, not only about baking but about running a small business. This muffin is my homage to them.

CLAIRE

1. Heat the oven to 170°C/340°F/gas mark 3½. Butter a muffin tin or line it with paper cases.

2. Spread the almonds out on a baking sheet and toast in the oven for 5–7 minutes, or until golden.

3. Melt the butter and sugar in a small saucepan and set aside to cool slightly.

4. In a large bowl, mix together the oat bran, rolled oats, spelt flour, salt and bicarbonate of soda. Roughly chop the toasted almonds and stir them into the dry ingredients.

5. In a new bowl, whisk together the eggs and yoghurt and stir in the dates and orange zest. Whisk in the melted butter and sugar and pour all of this over the dry ingredients. Mix just until combined.

6. Spoon the mix into the muffin tin and bake in the oven for 20–25 minutes.

TIPS

❖ You could also make these muffins with dates that have been soaked in juice or alcohol.

Saturday Pancakes

A little bit of Saturday morning indulgence.

Makes: about 12, enough for 4 people
Preparation time: 10 minutes
Cooking time: 5 minutes
V

For the pancakes
150g **plain flour**
75g **sugar**
1½ teaspoons **baking powder**
¾ teaspoon **bicarbonate of soda**
a pinch of **sea salt**
200ml **natural yoghurt**
200ml **milk**
3 **free-range eggs**
75g **melted butter**

For the topping
maple syrup
berries

1. Combine the dry ingredients and set aside.

2. Combine the yoghurt and milk and set aside.

3. Separate the eggs, adding the yolks to the yoghurt-milk mixture and stir to combine. Set the egg whites aside in a large clean bowl.

4. In a steady stream, add the yoghurt mixture to the flour and whisk until smooth. Whisk in the melted butter.

5. Whisk the egg whites to stiff but not dry peaks and fold them into the batter.

6. Pour a pancake-sized amount on to a hot griddle and cook for a couple of minutes on either side.

7. Stack them up and top with the syrup and the berries.

TIPS

✤ You can substitute buckwheat flour for the plain flour if you want your pancakes to be gluten free.

Eggy Bread

For a rainy Saturday, when you want to stay in your pyjamas all day.

Serves 4–6
Preparation time: 10 minutes
Cooking time: 15 minutes

V

2 tablespoons **unsalted butter**,
   plus extra to serve
5 **free-range eggs**
400ml **whole milk**
1 tablespoon pure **vanilla extract**
75g **caster sugar**
½ teaspoon **ground cinnamon**
8–12 slices of good **stale bread**
icing sugar, for dusting the top
maple syrup, to serve

This way of using up stale bread is almost as old as civilization itself (it features in a cookbook from fourth-century Rome). Every nation has a different name for it. The Americans call it French toast; the French *pain perdu*, the Czechs *chleba v kozíšku* ('bread in the little coat'). In Sri Lanka it's called Bombay toast, and in Germany *armer Ritter*, meaning 'poor knights' – presumably because it was eaten by impoverished noblemen who couldn't afford fresh bread. This dish is a universal classic for a reason – it has been tried and tested and found to be absolutely delicious.

HENRY

1. Heat a large heavy frying pan and drop in a little of the butter.

2. In a large shallow bowl, whisk together the eggs, milk, vanilla, sugar and cinnamon.

3. Place a couple of slices of bread in the eggy mixture and dunk it down, piercing the slices with tiny holes. Once the bread seems saturated, flip the slices over.

4. The pan should now be ready and the butter sizzling.

5. Carefully lift the slices of bread from the eggy mixture and place in the frying pan.

6. Brown the bread well on both sides, meanwhile repeating the dunking process with the remaining slices of bread.

7. Place on a plate, set in a warm place and butter the slices.

8. Dust the finished slices of buttered eggy bread with icing sugar and serve with maple syrup.

TIPS

❖ You can use all types of white crusty bread, as well as sourdough if you fancy it.

❖ Be sure to soak the bread with lots of eggy mixture. And don't be shy with the butter in the pan. You want a moist, custard-like middle and a crisp exterior.

❖ Serve with fresh berries in the summer.

❖ Try slices of ripe bananas with a pinch of cinnamon.

❖ Add orange or lemon zest to the eggy mixture for a nice bright flavour.

Hannah's* Banana Bread

A version of the classic bread made with spelt flour and a banana that sinks into the bread during cooking. This is the best banana bread we have tasted.

Serves: 8–10
Preparation time: 25 minutes
Cooking time: 50 minutes
♥ ✓ V

50g **pecan nuts**

150ml **vegetable oil**

200g **dark brown sugar**

1 teaspoon **vanilla extract**

2 **free-range eggs**

350g ripe skinned **bananas**

75g **natural yoghurt**

1 teaspoon **bicarbonate of soda**

1 teaspoon **baking powder**

½ teaspoon **ground cinnamon**

¼ teaspoon **salt**

225g **wholemeal spelt flour**

1 **banana**, peeled and 3 tablespoons **caster sugar**, for the top

I invented this for Leon, when they were looking for a spelt version of this classic fruit bread. The texture of the spelt flour and the nutty taste it imparts work so well with banana.

CLAIRE

*Some time ago people started leaving wishes on pieces of paper in a drawer in the Ludgate Circus branch of Leon. We celebrated this by granting the wishes of people who came to one of our parties. Hannah's wish was to have a cake named after her. Hence the name.

HENRY

1. Heat the oven to 170°C/340°F/gas mark 3½. Butter a 900g/2lb loaf tin and line it with baking paper. Line a baking sheet with baking paper as well.

2. Spread the pecans out over the lined baking sheet and toast them in the oven for about 5–7 minutes, or until lightly golden and fragrant. Set aside to cool.

3. In a large bowl, whisk together the oil, dark brown sugar, vanilla and eggs.

4. In a separate bowl, roughly mash up the bananas. Add the yoghurt and mix well. Sift the bicarbonate of soda, baking powder and cinnamon over the yoghurt mixture, add the salt and stir well to combine.

5. Now add the banana mixture to the egg mixture and stir to combine. Chop the pecans into small pieces and add them with the flour, stirring just until incorporated. Spoon the mixture into the prepared loaf tin.

6. Carefully slice the remaining banana in half lengthwise. Place one half, cut side up, on top of the bread and sprinkle with the caster sugar. (Eat the other half.)

7. Bake in the oven for 45–50 minutes, or until the bread is springy to the touch and a skewer inserted comes out clean. Cool in the tin for at least 10 minutes before turning it out on to a wire rack to cool.

TIPS

❖ Never over-mix the batter for quick breads like this, as they can easily go tough and rubbery. In fact, I have a tendency to under-mix them. The sugar on top makes a nice crunchy crust, but if you want to cut the sugar, just leave it out.

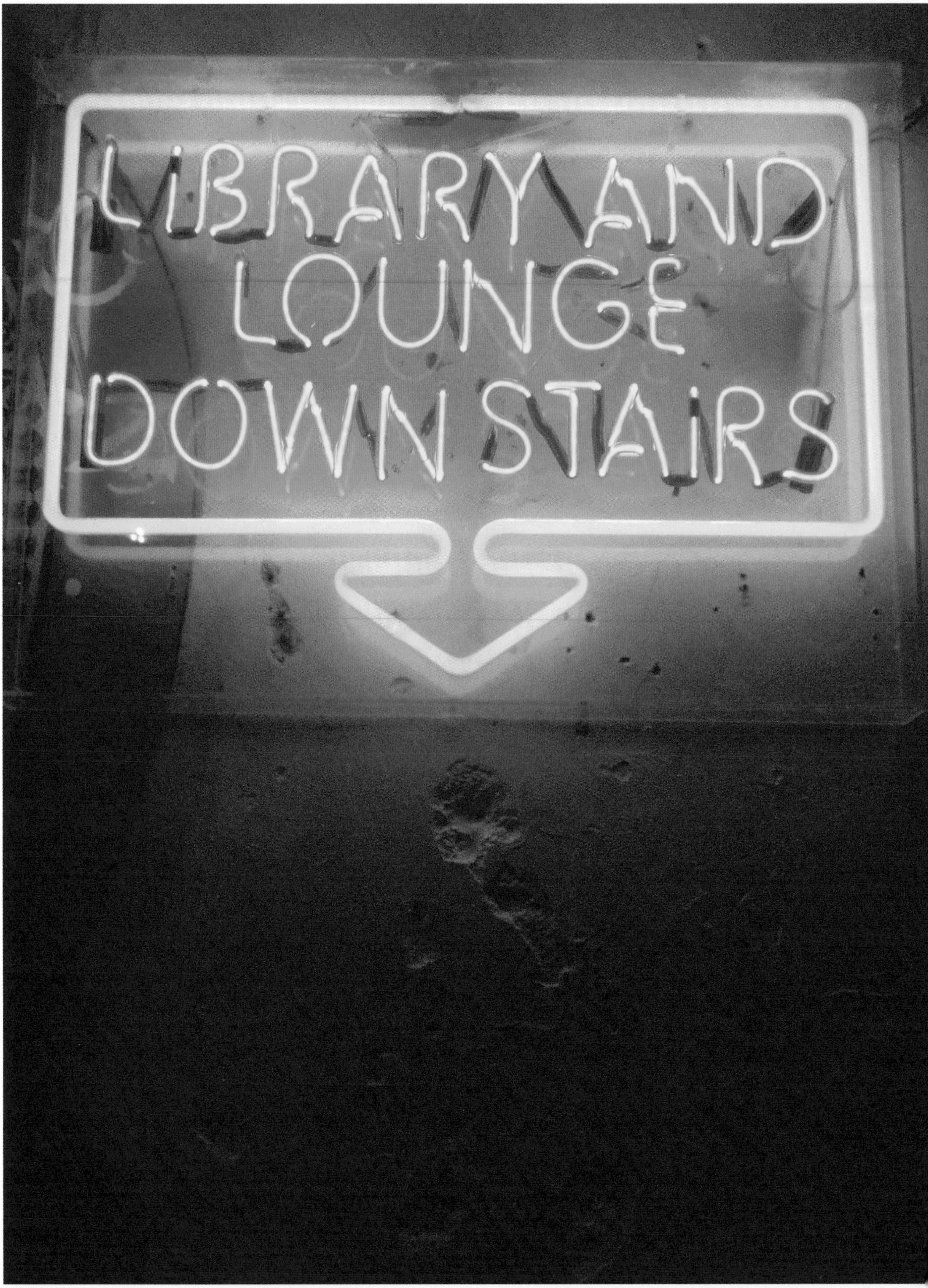
LIBRARY AND
LOUNGE
DOWN STAIRS

When we were putting together the first menus for Leon, we were aware that a lot of fast food, although superficially satisfying, actually makes you even hungrier. Foods that are full of refined carbohydrates make your blood sugar soar and then crash, leaving you craving more of the same.

Processed snacks tend to be particularly villainous in this respect. You want something wholesome to tide you over between lunch and supper – something that will release energy slowly, instead of making you fall asleep at your desk – but you end up buying a slab of wheat and white rice glued together with corn sugar and marketed as a healthy 'cereal bar'.

Not so with these homemade power snacks. Low GI and stuffed full of good things, they will keep well in an airtight container, so you can make batches in advance to keep your lunchbox interesting for a good couple of weeks.

POWER SNACKS

BARS * BISCUITS
BALLS * BROWNIES

FREE FROM GUILT

Claire's Chocolate Hazelnut Power Pills

These pocketable snacks taste sensational and give you a powerful burst of energy. Make a massive batch and give some to your friends.

Makes: 12 balls or 24 power 'pills'
Preparation time: 15 minutes
Cooking time: none
♥ ✓ WF GF DF V

125g **raw hazelnut butter**
100g **Brazil nuts**, finely chopped
50g **dried cherries**, preferably without oil or sweetener added, finely chopped
2 tablespoons **shelled hemp seeds**
1 tablespoon **chia seeds**, ground in a mortar
3 teaspoons **cacao nibs**, chopped
2 teaspoons **raw cacao powder**
3 teaspoons **raw honey**
1 teaspoon **maca root powder**
1 teaspoon **coconut oil**
½ teaspoon **blue green algae, spirulina**, or **other source of chlorophyll**
seeds from ¼ of a **vanilla pod**
extra **cacao powder, hemp seeds, chia seeds** or **coconut shreds**, for coating

The Americas are a very fertile land, and the ancient civilizations that lived there knew of the many health properties of the roots, fruits, seeds and herbs that grew there. Some of these plants – like chia seeds and maca root – are being rediscovered, and many of them are becoming widely available. There is good information on the internet if you want to learn more about their health benefits. Be brave and experiment with them. The flavours and textures are fascinating.

CLAIRE

1. Mix all the ingredients together in a bowl (easiest done using your hands).

2. Shape the paste into balls or pills and gently roll them in the extra cacao powder, hemp seeds, chia seeds, coconut shreds, or a combination of any of these.

3. Chill for 15 minutes. Keep refrigerated.

Lise's Cherry Almond Cookies with Chocolate Chips

The recipe below is based on Lise's oat and raisin cookie, which we serve in the restaurant, but with a sweet summer twist to it. If you want to make a version of the original, just replace the choc chips, cherries and almonds with raisins (see picture).

Makes: 15–20 cookies
Preparation time: 20 minutes
Cooking time: 10–12 minutes

V

200g **salted butter**, softened
235g **soft brown sugar**
2 small **free-range eggs**
130g **plain flour**
½ teaspoon **bicarbonate of soda**
185g **rolled oats**
150g **dried sour cherries**
50g **flaked almonds**
75g **chocolate chips**

Lise learned to love baking in her mother's kitchen. Her mother had a fruit and vegetable garden outside her kitchen in the Danish countryside, next to the wild pine forests that sloped gently down to the sea. Everything was organic in her mother's kitchen, and still is now, in Lise's Honeyrose Bakery.

1. Heat the oven to 180°C/350°F/gas mark 4. Oil several large baking sheets or line them with baking paper.

2. Cream together the butter and the sugar, then add the eggs, one at a time, and beat until light and fluffy.

3. In another bowl, combine the flour, bicarbonate of soda, oats, cherries, flaked almonds and chocolate chips. Add to the butter mixture, taking care not to over-mix the dough.

4. Scoop the dough into balls about 5cm in diameter, using an ice cream scoop (about 50–60g each). You can also use 2 tablespoons. Place the dough balls on the prepared baking sheets 25cm apart. Each cookie will spread to about 10cm. If your dough is cold, the cookies will not spread as well, in which case you will need to press them with the palm of your hand before baking.

5. Bake in the oven for 10–12 minutes, or until golden (you may need to bake them in batches). The cookies will be very soft when you take them out, but will become firmer as they cool down. Leave them on the baking sheets for a few minutes before transferring them to a wire rack to cool completely. Store in an airtight container.

Lise Madsen, Denmark, 1977

Nana Goy's Cranberry Flapjacks

These are moist and deliciously oaty like a good flapjack should be. We love them with dried cranberries but you could use any dried fruits (see tips below).

Makes: 16
Preparation time: 10 minutes
Cook time: 30–35 minutes

V

225g **dried cranberries**

55g **golden syrup**

170g **butter**

100g **caster sugar**

250g **rolled oats**

1. Heat the oven to 170°C/340°F/gas mark 3½, and butter a 20 x 20cm baking dish.

2. Put the cranberries into a bowl and cover with boiling water for a few minutes to rehydrate them. Drain away the water and roughly chop any that are particularly large.

3. Melt the syrup, butter and sugar together in a large pan over a gentle heat until the sugar has dissolved, then stir in the oats. Add all but a small handful of the cranberries and stir thoroughly.

4. Tip the flapjack mixture into the tin and smooth it down with a spatula. Sprinkle the remaining cranberries on top. Bake in the oven for 30–35 minutes until golden. Mark into squares while still warm, and remove from the tin once cool.

TIPS

❖ Add a handful of nuts and seeds to the mixture if you want to add another dimensions to your flapjacks.

❖ For a fruity hit, try making them with dates instead of cranberries. If you choose to do this alternative, chop the dates roughly before adding to the flapjack mix.

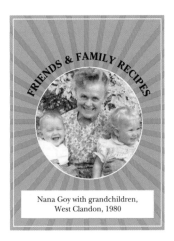

Nana Goy with grandchildren,
West Clandon, 1980

Better Brownie

We have been selling these brownies at Leon since we opened our first restaurant in London's Carnaby Street in 2004. Made in Dorset by one of our favourite bakers, Emma Goss-Custard, it is sugar- and wheat-free, but incredibly luxurious. Emma's stroke of genius was to add the little chunks of chocolate, providing the perfect contrast to the rich, gooey interior.

Makes: 12 large brownies
Preparation time: 25 minutes
Cooking time: 25 minutes
✓ WF GF

180g **unsalted butter**, plus extra for greasing
200g **dark chocolate** (54% cocoa solids)
1 **orange**
2 teaspoons **espresso** or **strong coffee**
80g whole **almonds (skins on)**
4 free-range **eggs**
100g **ground almonds**
160g **dark chocolate** (54% cocoa solids), in chunks
160g **very dark chocolate** (70% cocoa solids), in chunks
150g **fructose**
a pinch of **sea salt**
3–4 drops of **vanilla extract**

1. Heat the oven to 180°C/350°F/gas mark 4. Generously butter a 30 x 20 x 5cm baking tray, or one of similar dimensions.

2. Melt the butter in a small pan, and allow it to cool slightly.

3. In a separate bowl, melt the 200g of chocolate over a pan of hot water, stirring well to make sure that it is properly melted, and being careful not to burn it. Finely grate the orange zest directly into the melted chocolate to catch the oils that are released during the zesting process.

4. Add the coffee to the melted butter.

5. On another baking tray spread out the almonds and toast in the oven for 10 minutes, then roughly chop.

6. Crack the eggs into a large mixing bowl. Add the ground almonds, the chopped almonds, all the chocolate chunks and lastly the fructose. Stir in the salt and vanilla, followed by the butter mixture.

7. Mix well until creamy and thickened, but do not over-mix, as too much air will cause the brownie to crumble when baked.

8. Spoon the mixture into the prepared baking tray and place in the oven for approximately 20–25 minutes. Take great care not to over-bake the brownies. They are ready when the edges are slightly crusty but the middle is still soft.

9. Remove from the oven and allow to cool in the tin.

✤ Fructose turns a much darker colour when baked than sugar. The brownie develops a glossy sheen and will not look cooked, when in fact it is. Resist the temptation to cook it for too long.

✤ You can replace the fructose with 180g of sugar.

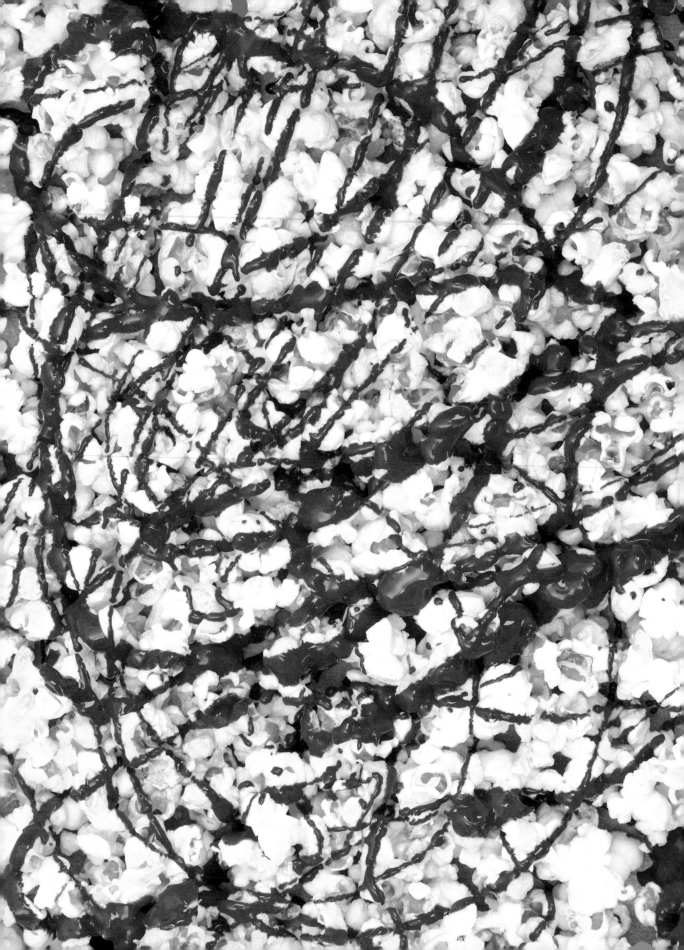

Sweet Popcorn with Chocolate Drizzle

A rainy Sunday afternoon snack that's almost as much fun to make as it is to eat. Make it alongside a salty popcorn and settle down on the sofa with a good movie.

Serves: 4
Preparation time: 20 minutes
Cooking time: 10 minutes
♥ ✓ WF GF

2 tablespoons **vegetable oil**
100g **popcorn**
100g **dark chocolate**, broken into pieces
75g **salted butter**
50g **golden syrup**

1. In a large saucepan with a tight-fitting lid, warm the oil over a medium heat. Pour the popcorn into the saucepan and cover it with the lid. The corn will begin to pop quite quickly. When the popping slows down, by which time most of the kernels should have popped, remove the pan from the heat and open the lid to release the steam. Set aside.

2. Melt the chocolate in a small heatproof bowl over a pan of barely simmering water, making sure the water does not touch the surface of the bowl. Stir occasionally. Meanwhile line a baking sheet with baking paper.

3. Melt the butter and golden syrup together in another saucepan, stirring continuously.

4. Fold the popped corn into the syrup and stir well to coat. Spread the popcorn out to cool on the baking sheet.

5. When the chocolate has melted, drizzle it over the sweet popcorn.

TIPS

❖ Don't worry about shaking the pan around on the stovetop. Use a good heavy-bottomed pot with a tight-fitting lid and you will get perfectly popped corn every time.

❖ Leave out the golden syrup if you want something less sugary.

Bar of Good Things

This recipe makes a healthy bar, and will keep you going on a long hike or make a great recharger after exercising.

Makes: 8 bars
Preparation time: 20 minutes
+ soaking time for seeds
Cooking time: 2 hours
♥ ✓ WF GF DF V

175g **sesame seeds**, preferably soaked and dried
110g **cashew nuts**, finely chopped
a pinch of **sea salt**
2 tablespoons **brown rice syrup**
2 tablespoons **tahini**
2 tablespoons **yacon syrup**
2 teaspoons **lemon zest**
60g **roasted, salted pistachios**, shelled and roughly chopped
80g **dried apricots**, chopped

For the fig paste
60ml **water**
1 teaspoon **vanilla extract**
80g **dried figs**
1¼ teaspoons **ground ginger**
¼ teaspoon **ground cumin**

For the coating
80g **sesame seeds**, lightly toasted

1. Heat the oven to 110°C/225°F/gas ¼. Line a 30 x 20cm baking tin with baking paper.

2. Heat the water with the vanilla in a small pan and pour over the dried figs. Allow to rest for 15 minutes, then blend with the ginger and cumin to form a paste.

3. Meanwhile, mix the sesame seeds, cashews and salt in a medium bowl.

4. Mix the brown rice syrup, tahini, yacon and lemon zest in a small bowl and stir in the fig paste.

5. Add the wet ingredients to the dry ingredients and mix well (this is easiest done with your hands, as the mixture should be quite stiff). Then fold in the pistachios and apricots.

6. Sprinkle half the sesame seeds for the coating into the prepared roasting tin and then press the mixture evenly on top so it is 1–1.5cm in thickness. Sprinkle over the remaining seeds.

7. Bake in the oven for 1 hour, then flip it over, put it back in the tin and bake for 1 more hour. Allow to cool in the tin. Cut into bars and keep in an airtight container.

TIPS

✚ The yacon syrup can be replaced by more brown rice syrup or agave nectar.

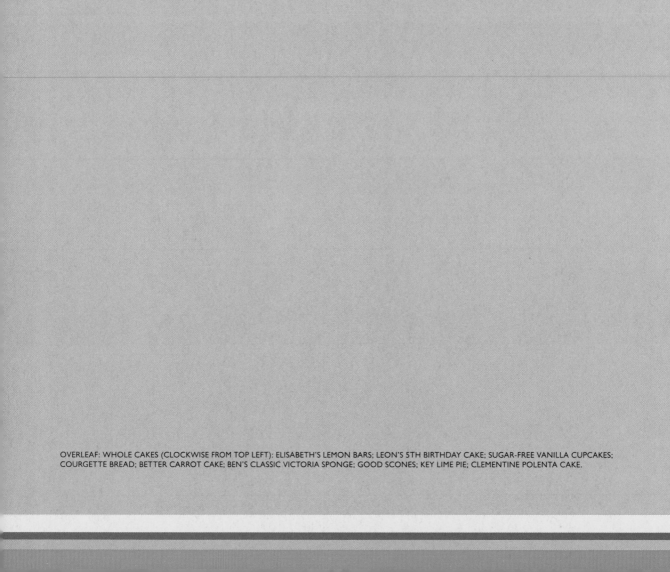

OVERLEAF: WHOLE CAKES (CLOCKWISE FROM TOP LEFT): ELISABETH'S LEMON BARS; LEON'S 5TH BIRTHDAY CAKE; SUGAR-FREE VANILLA CUPCAKES; COURGETTE BREAD; BETTER CARROT CAKE; BEN'S CLASSIC VICTORIA SPONGE; GOOD SCONES; KEY LIME PIE; CLEMENTINE POLENTA CAKE.

TEA TIME

Cakes, Tarts & Breads

DELICATELY SCENTED

Ben's Classic Victoria Sponge

Classic recipes are classic because they have stood the test of time. This is the mother of all teatime cakes.

Serves: 8
Preparation time: 25 minutes
Cooking time: 40 minutes

330g **unsalted butter**, very soft

330g **caster sugar**, plus more to finish

1 teaspoon **vanilla extract**

6 **free-range eggs**

330g **self-raising flour**

150g homemade or good-quality bought **raspberry jam**

2 punnets of **fresh raspberries** (if in season)

350ml **double cream**

1. Heat the oven to 160°C/325°F/gas mark 3. Butter two 25cm round cake tins and line them with baking paper.

2. In a large mixing bowl, beat together the soft butter and the sugar until very pale and fluffy. Add the vanilla extract and the eggs one at a time, alternating with 1 tablespoon of flour and beating well after each addition. Once all the eggs have been added, add the remaining flour and mix well.

3. Divide the mixture between the two tins and bake in the oven for about 40 minutes, or until a skewer inserted in the centre comes out clean.

4. Cool the cakes for at least 10 minutes in the tins before turning out on to a wire rack to cool completely.

5. Just before serving, place one cake on a serving plate and slather it with the raspberry jam. Whip the cream to very soft peaks – just stiff enough to start to hold a shape – and layer that over the jam, reserving a good dollop for the top of the cake. Scatter the raspberries over the cream (saving two or three for decoration) and finish with the second cake layer. Sprinkle with caster sugar and put the last dollop of cream on top of the cake. Finish with the raspberries.

TIPS

❖ This cake is best eaten right away, but it can be kept in the fridge in an airtight container for up to 3 days.

❖ Clearly you can experiment with all sorts of different fruit fillings. Also try using thick yoghurt or soured cream instead of double cream.

Our friend the actor Ben Miller was invited on to one of Gordon Ramsay's shows to compete against him in a bake-off. To prepare himself, Ben had a day of intensive training with Claire, perfecting this cake. The key, Claire told him, was to bake it 'slow and low' for a soft, yielding texture. The result? Ben beat Ramsay by a unanimous vote. Done.

WHEN WE ASKED BEN FOR A PICTURE OF HIMSELF AS A BOY, HE SENT US THIS...

Clementine Polenta Cake

This moist flourless cake is perfect for teatime, but also makes a beautiful pudding when drizzled with a little cream or topped with a blob of yoghurt.

Serves: 12
Preparation time: 25 minutes
Cooking time: 50 minutes
WF GF

For the cake

250g **unsalted butter**, very soft

250g **caster sugar**

2 **free-range eggs**

200g **fine polenta**

100g **ground almonds**

1 teaspoon **baking powder**

zest and juice of 3 **clementines**

2 tablespoons **lemon juice**

For the syrup

50ml **runny honey**

juice of 1 **clementine** and 1 **lemon**

1. Heat the oven to 170°C/340°F/gas mark 3½. Butter a 25cm round cake tin and line it with baking paper.

2. In a large mixing bowl, beat the soft butter and sugar until very pale and fluffy. Add the eggs one at a time, beating well after each addition.

3. In a separate bowl, whisk together by hand the polenta, ground almonds and baking powder. Add to the butter mixture and beat well. Fold in the clementine zest and juice and lemon juice before scraping the mixture into your prepared tin.

4. Bake in the oven for 50 minutes, or until a skewer inserted comes out clean.

5. To make the syrup, heat the honey with the clementine and lemon juice in a small pan over a gentle heat until runny, then pour over the cake whilst its still hot. Leave to cool in the tin.

TIPS

❖ Wonderful served with Greek yoghurt or double cream.

❖ You can experiment with other kinds of citrus in this recipe as well. It works very well with lemon.

❖ You can also use agave nectar instead of honey for the syrup (this would go nicely with lime juice in place of the clemetines).

Petra's Fruit Cake

Serves: 12–15

Preparation time: 40 minutes + soaking time

Cooking time: 3½–4 hours

V

225g **golden sultanas**

50ml **brandy**

225g good-quality **glacé cherries**, quartered

200g good-quality **candied peel**

125g **crystallized pineapple** or **papaya**, chopped

60g **crystallized ginger**, chopped into very small pieces

60g **candied angelica**, chopped into small pieces

125g **walnuts**

zest and juice of 1 **lemon**

225g **unsalted butter**, softened

225g **caster sugar**

4 **free-range eggs**, at room temperature

225g **plain flour**

½ teaspoon **salt**

1. Soak the sultanas in the brandy for several hours or overnight. Chop the fruits and the walnuts, and mix with the sultanas in a bowl.

2. Prepare a deep 23–25cm cake tin – one with a loose bottom is best. Butter it and line it with 2 layers of baking paper. Round the outside of the tin, tie a band of paper that sticks up 2.5cm or so above the rim to give the cake extra protection.

3. Just before you are ready to start making the cake, add the lemon zest and juice to the fruit.

4. Heat the oven to 160°C/325°F/gas mark 3.

5. In a large bowl, cream the butter and sugar until pale and fluffy. In a separate bowl, beat the eggs really well with an electric hand whisk until foamy, thick and have increased in volume – this may take up to 10 minutes but it is worth it to get the right texture. Add the beaten eggs to the butter mixture a little at a time, beating well after each addition. (If the mixture shows any sign of curdling, beat in a tablespoon of the flour.) Stir in the remaining flour and then the salt.

6. Now you can stir in the prepared fruit and walnuts, a little at a time.

7. Turn the mixture into the prepared tin and smooth it over with the back of a spoon or a small metal spatula. Put the cake into the oven. After 1½ hours reduce the temperature to 140°C/275°F/gas mark 1 and bake for a further 2 hours. After the cake has been in the oven for at least 2 hours you can look and see if the top is browning too much. If it is, cover it with a double thickness of greaseproof paper.

Petra & Hattie in Sussex, 1978

8. The cake is done when it is evenly risen and brown, and has shrunk from the sides of the tin.

9. Leave it in the tin to cool, away from draughts, for at least an hour before taking it out. Leave it to get quite cold before storing it in a large tin.

TIPS

❖ Petra describes the slight hissing noise the cake makes while it is cooking (if you put your ear close to the tin) as 'singing'. You will know when the cake is done when the 'singing' has stopped.

❖ This cake will work equally well as a christening or a wedding cake.

❖ Petra is a great cake baker, but not as great at icing, so she disguises this deficit with increasingly extravagant decoration.

❖ The higher the quality of the crystallized fruit the better. Petra buys the whole crystallized ones from Harrods and chops them up herself (which might be going a bit far).

❖ Petra varies the recipe a little each year, so as not to get bored. One of the nicest variations was the addition of 3 or 4 of the sugared apricots from Australia (not the ordinary dried ones). She cut down a little on the sugar and on the other fruit to compensate.

❖ Golden sultanas are essential, as they are so pretty. They can usually be found at Turkish shops.

Petra is my wife Mima's mum (and one of our baking heroes – see page 274). This is the cake that my wife and her sister had at their christenings, at their weddings and at the christenings of their own children. Word of its magnificence has spread, and with insane generosity Petra now seems to be in permanent production for friends and extended family.

HENRY

Tommi's More-fruit-than-cake Cake

Red wine and figs have a special affinity for one another and the spices in this recipe. The fig seeds create a wonderful popping sensation as they burst in your mouth.

Serves: 8
Preparation time: 25 minutes
Cooking time: 45 minutes
✓ V

375ml **red wine**
375g **dried figs**, chopped
1½ teaspoons **ground cinnamon**
1/4 teaspoon **ground cloves**
125g **unsalted butter**, cold
250g **honey**, plus extra for the top
1 **free-range egg**, briefly whisked
200g **spelt flour**
1½ teaspoons **baking powder**
1 teaspoon **bicarbonate of soda**

One of the great things about Claire is that her world is overflowing with cake. This cake got its name when she was round at dinner with our friend and fellow cook Tommi Miers. There wasn't any pudding, but Claire happened to have this experiment in her car outside. Tommi hasn't stopped talking about it since – 'Best cake I have ever had. Just sitting there. In her car!'

HENRY

1. Heat the oven to 160°C/325°F/gas mark 3. Line a 20cm square cake tin with baking paper.

2. Put the red wine, figs and spices into a medium saucepan and bring to the boil.

3. When the fruit has plumped up a little (about 5 minutes), remove the saucepan from the heat and allow to cool for 10 minutes. Stir in the butter and honey and leave for another 10 minutes. Stir in the egg.

4. Sift the flour, baking power and soda into a large mixing bowl. Pour the fig mixture over the flour mixture and stir just until mixed. Pour into the prepared tin.

5. Bake for about 45 minutes, or until a skewer inserted comes out clean. Allow to cool in the tin.

TIPS

❖ Serve with Greek yoghurt or soured cream.

❖ A great way to use up left over red wine.

❖ Can be served as a pud or at teatime. A chunk in the lunchbox also makes a great mid-morning snack.

Tommi in her modelling days, 1991

Elisabeth's Lemon Bars

Sweet and gooey, with a sharp finish. An indulgent treat.

Makes: 8–10
Preparation time: 30 minutes
Cooking time: 1 hour

280g **plain flour**, plus an extra 35g
80g **icing sugar**
1 teaspoon **salt**
225g **unsalted butter**
4 **free-range eggs**
350g **sugar**
120ml **fresh lemon juice** (Meyer or Amalfi if possible)
½ teaspoon grated **lemon zest** (Meyer or Amalfi if possible)
1 teaspoon **baking powder**
icing sugar to finish

1. Heat the oven to 170°C/340°F/gas mark 3½.

2. First you must make the shortbread base. Combine the 280g flour, icing sugar, salt and cold butter in a food processor and mix until crumbly. If you don't have a food processor, cut the butter up with two knives (though I always find this tricky), the back of a fork, or an old-fashioned pastry cutter (I prefer the latter).

3. Be careful not to let the butter get too warm either in the appliance or in your hands, as it changes the texture. Mix just until the dough forms a ball.

4. Press the dough into a 30 x 20cm baking tin.

5. Bake in the oven for 20–25 minutes or until golden and set, then leave to cool slightly while you get on with the topping.

6. Beat the eggs. Add the sugar, lemon juice and lemon zest. In a separate bowl, sift together the remaining 35g flour and the baking powder. Add to the egg mixture and stir to combine. Spread on to the cooled shortbread crust and return to the oven for 25–30 minutes, or until just set.

7. Cool completely in the tin. Sprinkle with icing sugar and cut into squares or diamonds. These will keep well in an airtight container for up to 3 days.

TIPS

❖ Sprinkle with lavender flowers if you have them growing in your garden.

My mom makes these for us with California Meyer lemons. I like to make them with Amalfi lemons because they have a similar sweetness, though the flavour is very different. They are my favourite treat. Judging by the speed at which they disappeared on the photo shoot for this book, I am not alone.

CLAIRE

Sugar-free Vanilla Cupcakes

A cupcake free of everything except indulgence. No one will ever believe they are so good for you.

Makes: 12
Preparation time: 15 minutes
Cooking time: 25 minutes
♥ ✓ WF GF DF V

280g **self-raising gluten-free flour**
100g **potato flour** (or **cornflour** if you can't find potato)
70g **coconut flour** (fine desiccated coconut)
1 tablespoon **flax meal** (optional)
1½ teaspoons **sea salt**
150g **coconut oil**, melted
250ml **agave nectar**
2 tablespoons **vanilla extract**
150ml **rice milk**
½ teaspoon **bicarbonate of soda**
100ml **boiling water**

There is a bit of a craze for healthy cupcakes and muffins at the moment, but the recipes in the books we have seen in the past either don't work or have too many ingredients. This one works. Magnificently. And is a tribute to the many hours Claire spent perfecting it.

HENRY

1. Heat the oven to 170°C/340°F/gas mark 3½, and line a 12-hole muffin tin with paper cases.

2. Put the gluten-free flour, potato flour, coconut flour, flax meal (if using) and sea salt into a large bowl. Use a balloon whisk or sieve to mix them together.

3. In another bowl, combine the melted coconut oil, agave nectar, vanilla extract and rice milk. In a small bowl, mix together the bicarbonate of soda and boiling water and then stir this into the other liquid ingredients.

4. Pour a third of the liquid ingredients into the dry and whisk together to make a batter, gradually adding the remaining liquid until all of it is incorporated.

5. Spoon the mixture into the paper cases and bake in the oven for 20–25 minutes, or until a skewer inserted in the centre of a cupcake comes out clean. These cakes are best eaten on the day they are made.

TIPS

✤ The flax meal can be left out if you can't find it at your local health food shop, but it adds nutrition and a nutty quality that we like, and also adds texture.

✤ If you don't like the flavour of coconut (you're crazy), you can replace the coconut flour with ground almonds.

✤ The coconut oil can be replaced with a good-quality tasteless oil such as sunflower, but only if you *really* must. Coconut oil is full of nutrition.

Vegan Vanilla Icing

We think this icing might be even better than the traditional butter and sugar version. It is the result of weeks spent by Claire testing different dairy- and allergen-free combinations. It is rich, but the coconut oil gives it a sublime melting consitency.

Makes: enough to ice 12 cupcakes
Preparation time: 15 minutes, plus cooling time in the fridge
Cooking time: none

♥ ✓ WF GF DF V

350ml **unsweetened soya milk**, preferably Bonsoy
100g **almond milk powder** (not ground almonds)
50ml **agave nectar**
2 teaspoons **vanilla extract**
1 **vanilla pod**, seeds scraped out
340g **coconut oil**, melted
2 tablespoons **fresh orange or clementine juice**
1 tablespoons **fresh lemon juice**
75g **cashew nut butter**

1. With a stick blender or in a food processor, combine the soya milk, almond milk powder, agave and vanilla. Blend until smooth.

2. Add the scraped seeds from the vanilla pod and keep the pod for another use.

3. Combine the melted coconut oil with the orange and lemon juice and add to the mixture gradually, blending until smooth. Add the cashew nut butter and again blend until smooth.

4. Chill overnight before using so that the coconut oil solidifies.

TIPS

✤ For pink icing replace 150ml of the soya milk with 150ml of puréed and strained raspberries or strawberries.

✤ You can play with other natural colours and flavours, as with Royal Icing (see page 189).

✤ If you can't do soya, substitute rice milk for the soya milk. The texture is not quite as smooth but the taste is great.

Better Carrot Cake

A beautiful carrot cake made without any dairy, wheat, gluten, soya or sugar. Baking with the ingredients below takes some getting used to – the mixture will have a different consistency from a traditional wheat-based cake – but the results are worth the effort. Coconut oil and boiling water make the cake very moist. The rice flour gives the cake a fine texture and the spices and mandarin oil impart a unique flavour.

Serves: 8–10
Preparation time: 30 minutes
Cooking time: 45 minutes
♥ ✓ WF GF DF V

250g **carrots** (unpeeled weight), peeled and grated
50g **apple** or **sweet potato**, grated
50g **desiccated coconut**
50g **coconut oil**, melted
50ml **sunflower oil**
120ml **agave nectar**
1½ teaspoons **yacon syrup** (optional)
2 teaspoons **vanilla extract**
70g **gram flour** or **polenta flour**
140g **gluten-free plain flour**
1 teaspoon **xanthan gum**
1 teaspoon **bicarbonate of soda**
½ teaspoon **sea salt**
1½ teaspoons **ground cinnamon**
1 teaspoon **ground ginger**
180ml **hot water**
½ teaspoon **mandarin, lemon** or **orange extract**
1 quantity **Vegan Vanilla Icing** (see page 97)

1. Heat the oven to 160°C/325°F/gas mark 3. Butter a 900g/2lb loaf tin and line it with baking paper.

2. Combine the carrots, apple or sweet potato, coconut, coconut oil, sunflower oil, agave, yacon syrup and vanilla in a bowl and set aside.

3. Combine the dry ingredients in a second bowl and whisk together to evenly distribute them. Whisk in the carrot mixture.

4. Gradually pour in the hot water and citrus extract and mix to a smooth batter. Pour into the prepared tin.

5. Bake in the oven for about 40–45 minutes, or until a skewer inserted comes out clean. Turn out of the loaf tin and allow to cool completely. Ice with vanilla icing.

TIPS

❖   Because there is no gluten in this recipe the cake mixture will look very different from the ones you are used to. The xanthan gum works as a binding agent to hold it all together, so make sure you don't leave it out. If you have trouble finding it, you might find a self-raising gluten-free flour blend that contains the ingredient already.

Courgette Bread

This sweet, dark bread is an American staple, but almost unknown in this country. They call it zucchini bread and eat it in the afternoon with a cup of coffee or tea. The cinnamon works very well with the courgette, and it's a great alternative to banana bread.

Almost every ingredient in this recipe is weighed to 200g, which makes it pleasingly simple to learn by heart.

Serves: 8–10
Preparation time: 20 minutes
Cooking time: 50 minutes

V

200g **butter**, plus a little extra for greasing the tin
200g **dark brown sugar**
3 **free-range eggs**
200g **courgettes**, washed and grated (skins left on)
200g **plain flour**
1 teaspoon **baking powder**
a pinch of **salt**
½ teaspoon **cinnamon**

1. Butter a 900g/2lb loaf tin and line it with baking paper. Heat the oven to 170°C/340°F/gas mark 3½.

2. Melt the butter in a small saucepan. Put the brown sugar into a large bowl and whisk in the eggs. Pour the melted butter into this in a steady stream until well mixed in. Stir in the grated courgettes.

3. Put the plain flour, baking powder, salt and cinnamon into another bowl and stir them together.

4. Add the wet ingredients to the dry ingredients and mix just until incorporated. Pour into the prepared loaf tin and bake for 40–50 minutes, or until springy and a skewer inserted in the centre comes out clean. Allow to cool in the tin.

VIOLET Coconut Macaroons

There is a sublime crispy gooiness to these biscuits that makes them like nothing else on earth. Warning: they are very addictive. Violet is the name of Claire's bakery and shop on Wilton Way and her stall at Broadway Market, both in Hackney, London.

Makes: 12
Preparation time: 5 minutes
Cooking time: 15 minutes
❤ WF GF DF

3 **free-range egg whites**
150g **caster sugar**
a pinch of **salt**
2 teaspoons **honey**
150g **desiccated coconut**
½ teaspoon **vanilla extract**

My friendship with Henry and Mima was ignited by their love of these macaroons, as they returned time and time again to my market stall to buy them.

CLAIRE

1. Heat the oven to 150°C/300°F/gas mark 2. Line a baking sheet with baking paper.

2. Combine the egg whites, sugar, salt, honey and coconut in a large pan over a medium heat.

3. Stir the mixture constantly until everything is dissolved and it just begins to scorch on the bottom.

4. Take the pan off the heat and stir in the vanilla.

5. Let the mixture cool completely, then use an ice cream scoop (about 50ml) to scoop out 12 even-sized macaroons, and place them on the baking sheet.

6. Bake in the oven for about 10–15 minutes, or until golden and set. Let the macaroons cool completely before peeling off the paper.

TIPS

❖ The key to getting these macaroons just right is to stir the ingredients in the pan until they begin to dry out.

❖ The vanilla extract isn't essential.

Leon Pecan Pie

A simple, rich, gluten-free pecan tart that has become a favourite in the restaurants. Baked by Craig Barton, one of our favourite bakers.

Serves: 8–10
Preparation time: 50 minutes
Cooking time: 1 hour 10 minutes
WF GF V

For the sweet pastry:

150g **butter**

100g **caster sugar**

1 **free-range egg**, plus 1 **yolk**

270g **gluten-free plain flour**

For the filling:

50g **butter**

225g **golden syrup**

2 tablespoons **caster sugar**

1 teaspoon **cornflour**

2 large free-range **eggs**

200g **pecan nut halves**

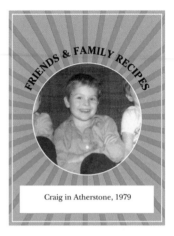

FRIENDS & FAMILY RECIPES

Craig in Atherstone, 1979

1. Cream together the butter and sugar with a wooden spoon or in a free-standing electric mixer until smooth.

2. Add the egg and egg yolk and mix until fully incorporated. Add the flour and quickly bring it together in a ball. Wrap the pastry in clingfilm and refrigerate for at least 30 minutes.

3. Butter a 23–25cm fluted flan tin. Roll the pastry out on a floured surface to about 3–5mm thick and line your tart case with it. Trim the edges and chill in the fridge for 30 minutes. Meanwhile, heat the oven to 160°C/325°F/gas mark 3.

4. Line the chilled pastry case with baking paper, and fill it with baking beans to stop it shrinking while it's being baked. Bake in the oven for 20 minutes then remove the baking beans. Return to the oven and bake for a further 5 minutes. The pastry should be a nice blonde colour. Set aside to cool.

5. Put the butter and golden syrup into a medium saucepan over a low heat. When it becomes runny, take it off the heat and whisk in the sugar.

6. In a small bowl, whisk the cornflour and eggs until smooth then add to the saucepan.

7. Fill the baked pastry with the pecan halves. Pour the golden syrup mixture on top and fill it up to just below the edge of the case. Put into the oven, taking great care not to spill any liquid over the sides, as this might make it difficult to remove it from the tin once it's baked.

8. Bake for about 40 minutes, or until the tart is a dark golden in colour and has slightly risen in the middle. Take out of the oven and leave to cool in the tin.

TIPS

❖ Serve cold for tea, or warm with Vanilla Ice Cream (see page 159).

Pecan Pie

Sweet and sticky and treacly and nutty

Petra's Honey Bread

A sweet, soft, wonderfully moreish tea bread. Dangerously addictive with a thick topping of butter.

Makes: 1 small (450g/1lb) loaf
Preparation time: 15 minutes
Cooking time: 1 hour
DF

225g **plain flour**
115g **caster sugar**
115g **honey**
250ml **hot water**
1 tsp **bicarbonate of soda**
zest of 1 **lemon**

1. Heat the oven to 160°C/325°F/gas mark 3. Butter a 450g/1lb loaf tin and line it with baking paper.

2. Mix together the flour and sugar in a large bowl.

3. In a small pan melt together the honey and the water.

4. Sprinkle the bicarbonate of soda over the water mixture and stir. Pour this over the dry ingredients and mix just until incorporated.

5. Turn the mixture into the prepared tin and bake in the oven for 50–60 minutes.

6. Remove from the tin and allow to cool, then serve thinly sliced, with butter.

TIPS

❖ You could brush the top of the warm bread with honey for a nice sticky finish.

❖ Try replacing the lemon zest with orange or clementine zest.

My mother-in-law, Petra, is the evil genius of teatime. Whenever we go to her house she plies us with homemade sweet treats: everything from millionaire's shortbread to fresh drop-scones, folded up warm in white damask napkins. This honey bread is one of her master strokes. Elegantly arranged in thin slices, it has a subtle flavour that demands a second helping. Next thing you know you've eaten the lot.

HENRY

Good Scones

These scones are made with lots of alternative ingredients that make them healthier. But we like the idea of eating them with clotted cream anyway.

Makes: 12
Preparation time: 25 minutes
Cooking time: 25 minutes
♥ ✓ DF V

100g **gluten-free self-raising flour**
100g **white spelt flour**
2 teaspoons **gluten-free baking powder**
a large pinch of **salt**
50g **coconut oil**, melted, or **sunflower oil**
2 tablespoons **maple syrup**
1 tablespoon **vanilla extract**
80ml **hot water**
50ml **rice milk**
clotted cream or **cream substitute**
   and **Fresh Strawberry Jam** (see page 226), to serve

1. Measure all the dry ingredients into a large bowl. In a small saucepan, melt the coconut oil and let it cool slightly. Pour the oil over the dry ingredients and toss together with a fork.

2. Mix the remaining ingredients except the cream and jam into the dry ingredients just until combined. Don't overwork it.

3. Let the dough rest for 10 minutes. Meanwhile line a baking sheet with baking paper, and heat the oven to 180°C/350°F/gas mark 4.

4. Roll out the dough 1.5–2cm thick. Use a biscuit cutter or a glass to cut out round discs.

5. Place the scones on the baking sheet and bake in the oven for 20–25 minutes.

6. When they are ready and firm to the touch, take them out of the oven and place on a cooling rack. Cool completely before splitting open and filling with cream and jam.

TIPS

You could make the scones wheat free by omitting the spelt flour and using either more of the gluten-free self-raising flour or substituting gram flour for the spelt.

Fruit puddings................................ 108

Fools & jellies.............................. 126

Cobblers, crisps & crumbles.............. 128

Meringues................................... 134

Chocolate.................................... 143

Granitas, sorbets & ice creams........... 150

Steamed puddings 162

FRUIT

Our UK climate and location means that we are blessed with a wonderful array of British fruit from spring (rhubarb), through high summer (berries, plums) and deep into autumn (quinces, pears, apples). Then, just when the cupboard is almost bare, the Spanish citrus fruits of midwinter come sailing to our rescue.

Most traditional English puddings feature one of these fruits in combination with flour, sugar and dairy. Delicious, but not always nutritious. The recipes that follow contain a few comforting favourites alongside some healthier alternatives.

The thing to remember with fruit is that it is eminently substitutable. Like the manager of a fantasy football team, once you have mastered the broad shape of a dish you can continually reinvent it by playing with another fruit.

GROWN AND PACKED BY

LEON

Roasted Peaches

Sometimes the best things are the simplest. Make sure you get the best peaches you can afford.

Serves: 4
Preparation time: 5 minutes
Cooking time: 15 minutes
WF GF (DF V if not using cream)

4 ripe **white** or **yellow peaches**
8 tablespoons **white wine**
100g **caster sugar**
double cream, to serve

1. Heat the oven to 180°C/350°F/gas mark 4.

2. Halve the peaches and remove the stones. Arrange the peach halves in a roasting tin, cut side up. Add the white wine and sprinkle over the caster sugar.

3. Bake in the oven for 12–15 minutes, until the fruit is bubbly and a little golden on the edges.

TIPS

❖ When the peaches come out of the oven, they will bubble as they start to cool down. Arrange them on small plates and pass the jug of cream.

❖ Use ripe delicious peaches. If they are underripe, no amount of cooking will be able to save them.

GEORGIA TAKING PICTURES OF BANANAS IN THE STREET

BBQ Chocolate Bananas

After the burgers and sausages have been made and the BBQ is cooling down, it is time to throw these babies on the grill. Easy and fun summer BBQ fare for the kids.

Serves: 6
Preparation time: 2 minutes
Cooking time: 10 minutes
✓ WF GF V

6 **bananas** in their skins
6 bars of your favourite **chocolate**, broken into pieces

1. Make a cut in the bananas from the stem to the opposite end through the peel and half way through the fruit.

2. Push in pieces of chocolate and place the bananas on the grill.

3. Cook until the chocolate starts to melt. The skins will blacken and not look very nice, but don't worry.

4. Serve.

 TIPS

❖ If you happen to have a little toffee sauce lingering in the fridge or want to make a quick caramel, it would be delicious drizzled over these.

❖ Sprinkle with a little flaky sea salt for lovely texture and flavour.

❖ You can serve them as they are in their skins, or carefully slip them out of the skins on to a plate and serve with a dollop of lightly whipped cream.

Baked Apples

Baked apples are easy and perfect for a chilly autumn night. They deserve to be more fashionable than they are.

Serves: 4
Preparation time: 15 minutes
Cooking time: approx. 1 hour
♥ ✓ DF V
(WF GF if you use gluten-free bread)

4 medium **apples**, such as Cox's or Braeburn
1 slice of stale **bread**, white or gluten-free
150g homemade or other good-quality **mincemeat**
a pinch of **sea salt**

1. Heat the oven to 180°C/350°F/gas mark 4. Line a baking tray with baking paper.

2. Dig out the cores of the apples without going all the way through to the bottom, then place them on individual squares of kitchen foil, big enough to wrap the apples, on the paper-lined baking tray.

3. Tear the bread into pea-sized pieces and mix with the mincemeat and salt. Pack the bread mixture into the apples. Bring the foil up and wrap it loosely around them, then bake in the oven for 45 minutes to an hour, until tender.

TIPS

✚ Serve with custard (see page 34) or double cream.

✚ Instead of mincemeat, the following work well as toppings:
• Raspberries, brown sugar and breadcrumbs, served with vanilla ice cream.
• Apricots, sultanas and sour cherries, plumped in red wine and sugar, drizzled with butter and served with double cream.

Pineapple Upside-down Cake

A carnival cake. Full of life. Full of flavour. A little bit kitsch. But deeply satisfying.

Serves: 6
Preparation time: 25 minutes
Cooking time: 40 minutes
V

For the caramel
100g **unsalted butter**
150g **light brown sugar**

For the cake
125g very soft **unsalted butter**
180g **caster sugar**
2 **free-range eggs**
1 teaspoon **vanilla extract**
1 teaspoon **salt**
100ml **whole milk**
210g **plain flour**
2 teaspoon **baking powder**
½ a **pineapple**, skin and core removed and cut into rings

1. Heat the oven to 170°C/340°F/gas mark 3½.

2. First make the caramel. Put the butter and brown sugar in the bottom of a deep 20cm cake tin and place the tin directly over a gentle heat on the hob. Stir constantly until the butter-sugar mixture comes together and bubbles. Set aside to cool.

3. Cream the butter and caster sugar until light and fluffy. Add the eggs one at a time and mix until incorporated. Add the vanilla and salt. Add half the milk and mix.

4. Sift together the flour and baking powder and add half to the mixture. Add the remaining milk and finally the rest of the flour.

5. Now that the caramel in the tin has cooled, cover it with the pineapple rings. Over that, pour the cake batter and smooth the surface. Bake in the oven for about 40 minutes. The top should spring back when cooked.

6. Let the cake sit in the tin for about 15 minutes before running a knife around the edge and inverting it onto a serving plate. If it is too hot, it can fall apart.

 TIPS

❖ If the cake sticks, you can either pop it back in the oven to melt the caramel a little, or place the cake tin directly on the heat of the hob for a minute (no longer, or it could burn), which will melt the caramel and help release the cake.

❖ You could substitute white spelt flour here, which would work very nicely. This is not a great place for gluten-free flour, however. The heavy fruit and caramel needs a stronger sponge than a gluten-free version could provide.

❖ You can use tinned pineapple.

Tarte Tatin

Crisp pastry and warm, soft caramelized apples in a pool of cream.

Serves: 8
Preparation time: 35 minutes
Cooking time: 40 minutes
V

250g frozen **puff pastry**
flour, for rolling
4–6 medium **apples** (Cox's and Granny
    Smiths are good)
juice of ½ a **lemon**
25g **unsalted butter**
75g **caster sugar**
pouring cream, to serve

1. Heat the oven to 200°C/400°F/gas mark 6. Line a baking tray with baking paper.

2. On a lightly floured surface, roll the pastry into a 30cm circle. Use a sharp knife to carefully trim the edge, making as perfect a circle as you can without losing too much of the diameter. Place the pastry circle carefully on the lined baking tray. Place it in the freezer if it will fit; if not, place it in the fridge.

3. Peel, quarter and core the apples, and coat in lemon juice to stop them turning brown.

4. Place a tatin dish – or a medium oven-proof frying pan – on a medium heat, and melt the butter until it foams. Add the sugar and allow it to dissolve. Turn up the heat and continue to cook until the sugar just starts to caramelize (goes light brown). Remove from the heat. The caramel will continue to darken as it cools, so take it off the heat well before it reaches a dark caramel.

5. Arrange the apples tightly in the pan in 2 layers.

6. Place the chilled circle of pastry over the top of the pan and tuck the edges down inside. Pierce the pastry with a knife to allow steam to escape during baking.

7. Place the pan in the oven and bake for about 30 minutes, or until the pastry is golden and the juices are bubbling at the sides. Remove from the oven and allow the tart to rest for 5 minutes.

8. Run a small knife around the edge of the pan to release the tart. Place a serving plate slightly larger than the tart pan over the tart, and quickly and carefully flip the tart over on to the plate. Drizzle any juices over the tart then serve hot and eat with plenty of pouring cream.

(TIPS)

❖ If you are unsure about when to stop cooking the caramel, you can take it as dark as you like it and then stop the cooking process by dunking the bottom of the pan in a sink full of ice-cold water. This will arrest the cooking so that the caramel does not burn.

❖ Try swapping the apples for pears or quinces.

Key Lime Pie

Key limes come from the Florida Keys (hence the name) and tend to be smaller and sweeter than conventional limes. If you can't get to Florida for your groceries, don't worry – the flavour will still be wonderful.

Serves: 6–8
Preparation time: 20 minutes
Cooking time: 35 minutes

V

200g crushed **digestive biscuits**

85g **unsalted butter,** melted

400g **sweetened condensed milk**

4 **large free-range egg yolks**

1 tablespoon **lime zest**, plus extra for garnish (about 3 limes)

120ml freshly squeezed **lime juice** (about 6 limes)

350ml **double cream**, chilled

1. Heat the oven to 180°C/350°F/gas mark 4.

2. Combine the crushed digestive biscuits and melted butter in a medium bowl and mix well. Press the mixture into a 23cm pie plate and bake in the oven until lightly browned. This will take about 12–15 minutes. Remove from the oven and transfer to a wire rack until completely cooled.

3. Lower the oven to 160°C/325°F/gas mark 3.

4. In a medium bowl, gently whisk together the condensed milk, egg yolks, lime zest and juice. Pour into the prepared, cooled crust.

5. Return the pie to the oven and bake until the centre is set but still quivers when the pan is nudged. This should take 15–20 minutes.

6. Let the pie cool completely in the tin on top of a wire rack.

7. Once the pie has cooled, place it in the fridge to chill until ready to serve.

8. Before serving, lightly whip the cream into soft peaks. Spread the cream over the chilled pie.

9. Garnish with a little more lime zest.

TIPS

❖ It is possible to buy digestive biscuits already crushed if you frequent a certain kind of cash-and-carry. Otherwise, simply put the biscuits into a thick plastic bag and smash them with a rolling pin.

Jossy's Jewelled Rhubarb & Mango

This is a simple but sublime combination, which also looks beautiful. The appearance of the deep yellow mango with the clear pink rhubarb, and the combination of their contrasting flavours, is wonderful.

Serves: 4
Preparation time: 20 minutes
Cooking time: 1 hour
♥ WF GF DF V

500g **early forced thin-stalked champagne rhubarb**

1.5cm piece of **fresh ginger**

2 or 3 **star anise**

150ml **cranberry juice**

juice of 2 **limes**

50g **caster sugar**

1 large or 2 small ripe **mangoes**

a few **mint leaves** to decorate

1. Heat the oven to 170°C/340°F/gas mark 3½.

2. Slice the rhubarb across on the diagonal into 5cm pieces. Peel the ginger, cut it in half and slice into small, very thin pieces.

3. Arrange the rhubarb, ginger and star anise in a wide ovenproof flan dish. Put the cranberry juice, lime juice and sugar into a saucepan and bring to the boil, stirring until the sugar has dissolved. Boil fiercely for 2 minutes, then pour on to the rhubarb.

4. Cover the dish tightly with foil and put it on the centre shelf of the oven for about 1 hour, until the rhubarb is very soft. Remove from the oven, take off the foil and leave to get cold.

5. Cut open the mangoes and cut the flesh off the stone, then skin them and slice into thin strips. Arrange the mango strips among the rhubarb, with the star anise dotted on top, then chill. Before serving, decorate with mint leaves.

Blueberry Cheesecake

A rich, creamy cheesecake cut by a sharper
fruit topping. Luxurious.

Serves: 8–10
Preparation time: 20 minutes
Cooking time: 45 minutes–1 hour

V

125g **digestive biscuits**
125g **gingernuts**
90g **unsalted butter**
550g **cream cheese**
125g **caster sugar**
2 teaspoons **lemon juice**
seeds from 1 **vanilla pod**
200g **crème fraîche** or **soured cream**
100g **thick Greek yoghurt**
3 **large free-range eggs**

For the blueberry topping
2 small punnets of **blueberries**
2 teaspoons **cornflour**
3 tablespoons **water**

There is a tradition at Leon
that if the team at one of the
restaurants does something
special, we bake them a cake.
I baked this one for Remi and
his team at our Cannon Street
branch after they posted record
sales. Putting the gingernuts in
the base is a trick I learned from
my mum. I figured they would
go well with the blueberries.

HENRY

1. Heat the oven to 160°C/325°F/gas mark 3.

2. Crush the biscuits to a fine powder in a food processor. Decant them into a bowl.
   Melt the butter and pour it over the biscuit crumbs, stirring to fully coat them.

3. Press the biscuit mixture into the base of a deep 20cm springform or loose-
   bottomed cake tin, then put it into the fridge to firm up.

4. Beat the cream cheese, caster sugar, lemon juice and vanilla seeds together until
   creamy. Mix in the crème fraîche and yoghurt, then the eggs and beat until smooth.

5. Spoon the filling over the chilled biscuit base. Smooth over the top and bake in the
   oven for 45 minutes, or until the filling has set (it may need a further 10 minutes).

6. Place the tin on a wire rack to cool completely, then run a small paring knife
   around the inside of the tin to help release the cheesecake from the tin.

7. Toss the blueberries in the cornflour and put them in a small saucepan with the
   water. Heat whilst stirring until the blueberries are bubbling and start to break
   up. Allow to cool then spoon over the top of the cheesecake.

TIPS

❖ Cherries are always welcome on a cheesecake, as are cranberries. Add a teaspoon
   of almond extract for the cherry version, and finely grated orange zest with the
   cranberry version.

Poached Pears

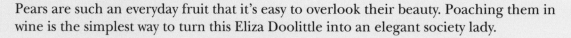

Pears are such an everyday fruit that it's easy to overlook their beauty. Poaching them in wine is the simplest way to turn this Eliza Doolittle into an elegant society lady.

Serves: 6
Preparation time: 10 minutes
Cooking time: approx. 20 minutes
♥ WF GF DF V

2 bottles of **white wine**
zest of 1 **lemon**
1 **vanilla pod**, split and the seeds scraped
300g **caster sugar**
300ml **water**
6 firm but ripe **pears**

1. Put all the ingredients except the pears into a pan large enough to hold all the pears and heat to dissolve the sugar, stirring occasionally.

2. Peel the pears and drop them into the poaching liquid.

3. Let the liquid come to a very light simmer, with bubbles the size of tiny shrimp eyes.

4. Cook until the pears are tender (about 20–30 minutes depending on ripeness).

5. Serve with cream, Sabayon (see below) or Quick Custard (see page 34).

TIPS

✤ Poach the pears in red wine instead of white, but change the lemon zest to orange zest, and the vanilla to a cinnamon stick. Or cut the recipe in half and make three red and three white wine pears.

✤ Save the poaching liquid and reduce it a little. This makes a wonderful sauce to drizzle over ice cream or a simple cake like Clementine Polenta Cake (page 89).

Sabayon

Sabayon, or zabaglione in Italian, is a perfect accompaniment to any poached fruit, but equally good with just a crispy sweet biscuit.

Serves: 4–6
Preparation time: 5 minutes
Cooking time: 35 minutes
WF GF V

75ml **Muscat, Sauternes** or **Marsala**
1 tablespoon **caster sugar**
4 **free-range egg yolks**
225ml **double cream**

1. Place the wine in a small pan on the stove and cook gently until it has reduced by half.

2. Using an electric hand mixer, whisk the caster sugar and egg yolks to thick ribbons.

3. In a steady stream, pour the hot reduced wine directly into the egg yolk mixture. Continue to whisk until cool to touch – it must be completely cool before you add the cream, otherwise the cream will melt and you will lose all the volume.

4. Lightly whip the cream, then fold it gently through the mixture.

Fools & Jellies

The simplest way to show off fruit in a pudding is either to set it into a jelly or fold it into whipped cream to make a fool. They are both very traditional English puddings.

Gooseberry Fool

Henry has a very small, slightly sad gooseberry bush at the bottom of his garden that produces about enough gooseberries each year to make one helping of fool. Here is the recipe.

Serves: 6
Preparation time: 10 minutes
Cooking time: 10 minutes
WF GF V

400g **gooseberries**
a couple of tablespoons of **water**
80g **caster sugar**
500ml **double cream**

1. Put the gooseberries and water into a pan over a medium heat and cook for 10 minutes, until the fruit is very soft.

2. Blitz briefly in a food processor with the sugar, checking for sweetness. Pass through a biggish sieve to get rid of the pips.

3. Whip the cream into soft peaks and loosely fold in the gooseberries so that there are still streaks of cream.

4. Serve in a large bowl, or in cold glasses if you want to be fancy.

TIPS

❖ Acidic northern fruits are best for fools if you fancy substituting something else for the gooseberries. Try rhubarb, plums, damsons or raspberries.

Blood Orange & White Wine Jelly

There is something about the limpid tremble of a lightly set jelly that is devilishly alluring. This one is based on a recipe from Richard Olney's 1970 classic *The French Menu Cookbook*. His recipe includes instructions on how to make the gelatine by boiling up calves' feet. Thankfully we can now buy perfectly good gelatine (from animal sources or vegetarian) in pristine transparent sheets.

Serves: 6
Preparation time: 10 minutes
Cooking time: 10 minutes
♥ WF GF DF
(V if you use vegetarian gelatine)

150ml **sweet white wine** (e.g. Muscat or Baumes de Venise)
50g **caster sugar**
1 stick of **cinnamon**
450ml fresh **blood orange juice** (5 or 6 oranges)
4 leaves of **gelatine** (about 40g)

1. Put the wine into a pan with the sugar, the cinnamon stick and 150ml of the orange juice. Bring to the boil, then take off the heat and remove the cinnamon. Melt the gelatine into the juice (following the instructions on the packet).

2. Pour the rest of the orange juice into a jug and pour in the liquid from the pan. Stir thoroughly, then pour into your mould. Allow to cool, then put into the fridge until set.

3. To turn out, loosen the edges of the jelly gently with your fingers. Dip the mould into a bowl of hot water for 1–2 seconds, place a plate on top, then invert the mould and shake. Serve with single cream or light double cream.

TIPS

❖ Richard Olney uses orange and lemon juice rather than blood orange juice. You can experiment with all sorts of liquids: white wines, elderflower cordial, pomegranate, grapefruit and lime juice are all good.

❖ Try flavouring the jelly with herbs and spices – rosemary with orange, for example, or cardamom with coconut milk.

❖ We prefer a lighter set. Use less gelatine where you can get away with it.

❖ Try putting whole fruit inside your jelly (grapes, peach slices, strawberries, currants, etc). Iou can make the fruit float if you set a layer of jelly first, then add the fruit followed by the rest of the jelly.

❖ Some fruits have enzymes that digest jelly, which will make it hard to set. These include: figs, kiwis, mango, melon, papaya, peach, pineapple and ginger.

COBBLERS, CRISPS & CRUMBLES

These are all ways to add a little sweet crunch to a dish of stewed fruit. The American cobbler has small, flat scones of pastry, like cobblestones, baked on top. The British crumble is covered completely with a ... well, crumbly top. Our crisps are like a crumble, but with a much thinner crispy layer. The good news is that all three form gooey caramelized bits around the side of the dish.

Strawberry & Blueberry Cobbler

Cobblers are the perfect summer pudding. (In fact, they make a damned good summer Sunday breakfast.) The cobbler topping is like a scone or American biscuit and melts into the jammy fruit. Serve this one with thick cream.

Serves: 6
Preparation time: 15 minutes
Cooking time: 40 minutes
WF GF V

250g **blueberries**

500g **strawberries**, hulled and quartered

50g **caster sugar**

4 tablespoons **cornflour**

200g **gluten-free self-raising flour**

2 teaspoons **gluten-free baking powder**

a large pinch of **salt**

50g **unsalted butter**, cut into small cubes

150ml **double cream**, plus extra to brush the topping

1. Heat the oven to 180°C/350°F/gas mark 4.

2. Combine the berries, sugar and cornflour and put into a deep 1–1.5 litre baking dish.

3. Put the flour, baking powder, salt and butter into a bowl and use the back of a fork or two knives to break up the chunks of butter into tiny pieces. Pour over the cream and mix until it all comes together.

4. Press the topping into a ball and place on a floured work surface. Let the mixture rest for 10 minutes. Then roll out to a 2cm thickness and cut out circles with a biscuit cutter.

5. Lay the circles flat over the fruit, brush with extra cream and place on a baking tray to catch any drips.

6. Bake in the oven for 35–40 minutes, or until the fruit is bubbly and the topping is golden brown.

TIPS

✤ You can also make this cobbler topping with regular self-raising flour.

✤ Experiment with different fruits: peaches and nectarines work well, with a little added lemon zest and juice.

Dittisham Plum Crumble

Crumbles are all about getting the balance right between sweet and sour and soft and crisp. This makes a lovely conclusion to a simple summer supper.

Serves: 6
Preparation time: 15 minutes
Cooking time: 45 minutes
WF GF V

1kg tart **plums** (Dittisham or Marjorie are good)
50g **caster sugar**
3 tablespoons **gluten-free plain flour**
1 tablespoon **sweet white wine**

For the crumble topping
100g **gluten-free plain flour**
100g **ground almonds**
50g **flaked almonds**
85g **brown sugar**
a pinch of **sea salt**
¼ teaspoon **ground cinnamon**
150g cold **unsalted butter**, cut into 1cm cubes

1. Heat the oven to 180°C/350°F/gas mark 4.

2. Halve and stone the plums and place in a bowl. Toss with the sugar, flour and wine and put into a deep 23–25cm square baking dish.

3. Put all the crumble topping ingredients into a bowl and use the back of a fork or two knives to break up the chunks of butter into tiny pieces.

4. Scatter the topping lightly over the fruit and place in the oven.

5. Bake for 40–45 minutes, or until the fruit is bubbly and the topping is golden.

TIPS

❖ Almonds and plums go nicely together here, but you could substitute hazelnuts and blueberries, or walnuts and apples.

The plums of Dittisham in Devon, have long been famous for their tart and deeply-fruity flavour. I developed this recipe when my husband and I went for a magical holiday in Dittisham with Henry's family. During the day, we were sailing and swimming and sunning ourselves; by the evening, everyone was ravenous. Henry's aunt brought us some plums from her garden, and we rustled up this crowd-pleasing crumble.

CLAIRE

Apple Crisp

A very easy pudding, and another great way to turn your stale bread into something delicious and sumptuous.

Serves: 6
Preparation time: 10 minutes
Cooking time: 35 minutes
V (WF GF if you use gluten-free bread)

1.5kg **apples**, peeled, quartered and cored

juice of 1 **lemon**

75g **caster sugar**, plus an extra 2 tablespoons for sprinkling

¼ teaspoon **ground cinnamon**

200g **stale**, **crusty white bread** crusts removed and torn into pieces

100g **salted butter**, melted

1. Heat the oven to 180°C/350°F/gas mark 4.

2. Combine the apples, lemon juice, sugar and cinnamon and put into a deep 1–1.5 litre baking dish.

3. In a bowl, toss the bread pieces in the melted butter and then arrange in a layer over the apples. Sprinkle sugar over the top and place on a baking tray to catch any drips.

4. Bake in the oven for 30–35 minutes, or ntil the fruit is bubbly and the topping is golden.

 TIPS

✛ Serve hot with pouring cream.

✛ Try using pears instead of apples and add a splash of white wine.

✛ Don't use sourdough or levain bread because it will be too sour. Use plain white bread or a French stick or baguette, nice and stale.

MERIN

/mə'raŋ/ *n.* a delicate confection the chief ingredients of which are pounded sugar and whites of eggs.

BAKING WITH MERINGUE CAN BE INTIMIDATING, BUT IT NEEDN'T BE WHEN YOU KNOW A FEW TRICKS AND YOU HAVE THE RIGHT TOOLS. AN ELECTRIC HAND WHISK OR FREE-STANDING MIXER IS ALWAYS GOING TO MAKE MERINGUE-MAKING EASIER. MERINGUE CAN TAKE AN INCREDIBLE AMOUNT OF BEATING (UNLIKE CREAM) SO IT IS HARD TO OVERDO IT. USING A PINCH OF SALT OR A PINCH OF CREAM OF TARTAR CAN HELP TO STABILIZE THE WHITES AND KEEP THEM FROM 'BREAKING'.

WHITES ARE 'BROKEN' WHEN THEY DEVELOP A SANDY TEXTURE AND DO NOT GO GLOSSY. ADDING SUGAR GRADUALLY AT THE BEGINNING OF THE WHISKING PROCESS IS A GOOD IDEA, TO STABILIZE. IF YOU ARE USING CASTER SUGAR (AS OPPOSED TO GRANULATED SUGAR) THE SECOND HALF OF IT CAN GO IN ALL AT ONCE WITHOUT CAUSING ANY PROBLEMS. THE FINE TEXTURE OF CASTER SUGAR MEANS IT DISSOLVES QUICKLY AND CAN BE INCORPORATED WITH NO PROBLEM.

Mont Blanc

Chestnuts are the unsung heroes of the winter table. Their subtle but rich flavour is enhanced when sweetened and combined with vanilla. This is one of the classic puddings – loved by the Italians and the French, named after their favourite mountain.

Serves: 6
Preparation time: 10 minutes
Cooking time: 2½ hours
WF GF V

For the meringue
3 **free-range egg whites**
¼ teaspoon **salt**
1 teaspoon **vanilla extract**
200g **caster sugar**

For the filling
1 x 435g tin **sweetened chestnut purée**
300ml **double cream**, lightly whipped

1. Preheat the oven to 120°C/250°F/gas mark ½. Line 2 baking sheets with baking paper.

2. Using an electric hand mixer, beat the egg whites, salt and vanilla on a high speed until soft peaks form.

3. Add half the sugar to the frothy egg whites. Whisk until very stiff, then add the remaining sugar. Whisk until smooth and glossy.

4. Portion out 6 large meringue circles about 4cm apart on the prepared baking sheets. Bake in the oven for about 2½ hours. Allow to cool on the baking sheet before peeling from the paper.

5. When ready to serve, spoon the chestnut purée over the meringues and top with lightly whipped cream.

TIPS

❖ Sweetened chestnut purée is available in lots of supermarkets. It is made from candied chestnuts and has a wonderful texture and translucence. If you can't find it ready-made, however, you have a number of options:

• Take an unsweetened chestnut purée and sweeten it to taste with icing sugar and vanilla essence, whizzing it all up in a food processor. Add cream or ricotta cheese if you want a softer texture.

• Buy crystallized chestnuts (marrons glacés) and purée them with a little vanilla extract, but no sugar.

• Make the purée from scratch. Buy fresh chestnuts, make a cut in each shell and boil them in water for about 10 minutes. Peel off the shells and skins and blitz the chestnuts in a food processor. Add just enough double cream to form a paste. Then add icing sugar and vanilla extract to taste.

Baked Alaska

This is fun to make, easier than you would think, and will make your guests squeal with nostalgic delight.

Serves: 8
Preparation time: 15 minutes +
3 hours freezing time
Cooking time: 5 minutes

V

500g **vanilla** or **strawberry ice cream** (or any favourite flavour, store-bought, or see pages 157–9)

1 x 20cm round of **sponge cake** (store-bought, or make it using ¼ recipe of Ben's Classic Victoria Sponge (see page 86)

4 **free-range egg whites**, at room temperature

¼ teaspoon **cream of tartar**

200g **caster sugar**

Thomas Jefferson is thought to have invented a version of this dish, but most people seem to agree that the credit should go to the eighteenth-century American physicist Benjamin Thompson. It's a stunt pudding made possible by scientific thinking: the ice cream is insulated by the air trapped in the sponge and meringue. Every time I attempt it I don't think it's going to work, but it always does.

CLAIRE

1. Line a 20cm diameter bowl with clingfilm.

2. Take the ice cream of your choice (we have some wonderful recipes in this book, see pages 157–9, either way, you will want a slightly softened ice cream to press into your prepared bowl). Pack the ice cream into the bowl very tightly and cover with more clingfilm. Place in the freezer for at least 3 hours.

3. Heat the oven to 220°C/425°F/gas mark 7. Place the cake sponge on a baking tray lined with paper and set aside.

4. Put the egg whites into a large clean bowl, and use an electric hand mixer to whisk them into soft peaks. Add the cream of tartar, then gradually add the sugar. Whisk until super stiff and glossy.

5. Take the ice cream out of the freezer and discard the top layer of clingfilm. Dunk the bottom of the bowl into a sink of hot water for a second. Invert the bowl over the sponge and use the clingfilm to help coax the ice cream from the bowl. Discard the clingfilm and immediately cover with the meringue. Use a knife to coax the meringue into peaks.

6. Bake in the oven for 5 minutes, until the peaks are golden.

7. Serve immediately!

(TIPS)

✣ Some say that using a Swiss meringue made with hot syrup (see steps 2–4 on page 157) will yield a stiffer Alaska that does not slide off the sides of the ice cream as you assemble it. We find that the real trick is to have very stiff meringue and very cold ice cream. A Swiss meringue is a lot more fussy, and the joy of this dessert is how easy it is, while being über-impressive.

Pavlova

There are hundreds of ways to dress a pavlova, but this is our favourite: simple and clean and drizzled with the sharp, juicy pulp of passion fruit. We like to serve it up on individual meringues, to make the recipients feel extra special.

Serves: 6
Preparation time: 20 minutes
Cooking time: 2 hours
WF GF V

3 **free-range egg whites**
¼ teaspoon **salt**
½ teaspoon **white wine vinegar**
½ teaspoon **pure vanilla extract**
200g **caster sugar**, plus an extra 2 tablespoons, to serve
1½ teaspoons **cornflour**
3 tablespoons **raspberry jam**, to serve
200ml **double cream**, lightly whipped, to serve
600g **strawberries**, to serve
3 **passion fruit**, to serve

1. Heat the oven to 120°C/250°F/gas mark ½. Line a baking sheet with baking paper.

2. Using an electric hand mixer, beat the egg whites, salt, vinegar and vanilla on a high speed until soft peaks form.

3. Whisk the 200g of sugar and the cornflour together by hand and add half to the frothy egg whites. Use the electric hand whisk to whip until very stiff, then add the remaining 100g of sugar. Whisk until smooth and glossy.

4. Spoon 6 large swoops of the meringue on to your baking sheet, 4cm apart.

5. Bake in the oven for about 2 hours, then check the meringues. Remove from the oven when dry and firm. It should be possible gently to peel them off the paper. If they stick to the paper they're not ready. Cool completely.

6. To assemble, place the meringues on a large serving plate or individual plates. Put a spoonful of raspberry jam on each and then a generous dollop of cream.

7. Cut and quarter the strawberries and toss with the 2 tablespoons of caster sugar. Leave to macerate for a few minutes while you halve the passion fruits.

8. Stir the strawberries and divide between the pavlovas. Scoop out half a passion fruit on to each and serve.

The Australians and the New Zealanders still squabble about who created the pavlova, which was named after the Russian ballerina Anna Pavlova after she had toured the Antipodes in 1926 (the meringue is meant to look like a tutu). It is a moot point really, as puddings made from combining fruit, cream and meringue had been popular for ages – it is just that somehow this name stuck.

TIPS

❖ You can prepare the strawberries up to 2 hours in advance and keep them in the fridge to save time.

❖ The meringues can be made up to 5 days in advance and kept in an airtight container.

Chocolate

Chocolate is the Casanova of the culinary world. Nothing else inspires such lust; such swivel-eyed devotion. Women, especially, go weak at the knees for it. There are all sorts of scientific theories about why this should be. Chocolate contains hundreds of mood-altering chemicals, including theobromine – a mildly addictive stimulant also found in caffeine. In a small way, it gets you high.

But even if it didn't, chocolate would still be one of the world's most sensuous foods. Hard and melting, bitter and sweet, it's like having a Mills & Boon hero in your mouth. The following recipes are designed to make the most of chocolate's seductive qualities – these are puddings so irresistible that your guests will be swooning over them for years to come. You weren't going to make them just for yourself now, were you?

Leon Chocolate Mousse

This is a recipe from the first cookbook (one of the magnificent creations of Leon co-founder Allegra McEvedy). We included it here because it is a favourite in the restaurants and we know there are lots of people who want to make it for themselves.

Serves: 4
Preparation time: 25 minutes
Cooking time: none
✓ WF GF V

100g **chocolate** (70% cocoa solids)

30g **unsalted butter**

2 **free-range egg yolks**

1 shot of **dark espresso**

a drop of **orange oil** or very finely grated
    zest of ½ orange (optional)

3 **free-range egg whites**

15g **fructose**

1. Melt the chocolate and butter until smooth in a large bowl in the microwave, or over a pan of simmering water, making sure the water does not touch the surface of the bowl.

2. Separately whisk the egg yolks until nearly white and thick in consistency. Gently stir the whisked yolks into the butter and chocolate, then stir in the coffee and the orangey bit, if you are adding it.

3. Use an electric hand whisk to whip the egg whites to soft peaks, then add the fructose and whisk for another minute just to get that shine.

4. Beat a third of the egg white into the chocolate mixture until smooth, then add the next third more gently, and the last with the strokes of an angel.

5. Neither over-mix nor leave white streaks, then divide the mousse into pretty things and leave in the fridge for an hour.

TIPS

❖ You can use Cointreau or Grand Marnier instead of orange oil or zest. Or you can leave out the orange flavour altogether.

❖ If you don't have fructose, you can use 20g of caster sugar (you need more because fructose is slightly sweeter).

Warm Gooey Chocolate Cakes

One of those chocolate-oozing-out-of-the-middle puddings that is not nearly as hard to make as your awestruck guests will assume.

Serves: 6–8
Preparation time: 10 minutes
Cooking time: 7 minutes
WF GF V

1 tablespoon **caster sugar**

85g **unsalted butter**

150g **dark chocolate**

a pinch of **salt**

5 tablespoons **cocoa powder**

100g **free-range egg whites** (about 2)

1. Heat the oven to 200°C/400°F/gas mark 6.

2. Butter individual mini pie dishes and sprinkle each one with some caster sugar.

3. Melt the butter, chocolate and salt in a large bowl over simmering water. When all is melted, sift in the cocoa powder.

4. In a separate bowl whisk together the egg whites and sugar until soft peaks form. Combine with the melted chocolate by folding gently and trying not to knock out too much air.

5. Spoon the mixture into the moulds and bake in the oven for just 7 minutes.

TIPS

❖ Whatever you do, do not over-bake these. They continue to bake slightly as they cool down, so take them out of the oven just before you think they are ready.

❖ Serve with pouring cream and a splash of Cognac if you have some around.

❖ You could also make a whipped Chantilly cream by adding a small amount of sugar and vanilla extract to whipping cream.

Life by Chocolate Cake

This fudgy flourless chocolate cake is SO rich, yet super-light, like a mousse. Once you have added it to your repertoire, you will make it again and again, not least because your friends and family will give you no choice. You have been warned.

Serves: 10–12
Preparation time: 20 minutes
Cooking time: 40 minutes
WF GF V

5 **free-range eggs**
200g **soft light brown sugar**
100ml **instant espresso**
350g **dark chocolate**, broken into pieces
250g **unsalted butter**, cut into small pieces
1 teaspoon **vanilla extract**
a pinch of **sea salt**

1. Heat the oven to 160°C/325°F/gas mark 3. Butter a 23cm cake tin, preferably not loose-bottomed, and line the base and sides with baking paper.

2. With an electric hand mixer, beat the eggs and 100g of the sugar to voluminous peaks.

3. In a saucepan, dissolve the remaining sugar with the coffee over a medium heat, then stir in the chocolate pieces and butter and take off the heat.

4. Add the vanilla and salt to the saucepan and stir occasionally until everything is completely melted.

5. In a steady stream, pour the melted chocolate mixture into the whisked eggs and stir just until combined.

6. Pour into the prepared cake tin, then place in a deep roasting tin and pour enough hot water into the roasting tin to reach almost to the top of the cake tin.

7. Bake in the oven for 35–40 minutes. The cake should be set but not solid. Leave to cool in the tin.

 TIPS

✤ This cake tastes even more beautiful with a little dollop of crème fraîche.

Line the tin

Whisk the eggs till they look like this

Butter, sugar, coffee and chocolate

Fold it in slowly

Be careful not to over mix

Pour in the water

GRANITAS, SORBETS & ICE CREAMS

Many people feel that to make ice creams, they need an ice cream machine. However – while the machines are a lovely gadget – you don't need to invest in expensive hardware to make beautiful frozen puds.

In this section we cover four techniques for making ice creams and the like. Two don't require a machine at all, while the other two are easier if you have one, but can be made without if you are prepared to put in the labour.

We have given one or two recipes for each technique and some suggestions for alternative flavours, so once you have mastered the basics you can experiment merrily.

The techniques are:

GRANITA

The simplest of all of the frozen puddings. A flavoured (cream-free) syrup is simply agitated throughout the freezing process with a whisk and forms lovely shards of ice as it freezes. The resulting pudding is crunchy, light and refreshing. If you are planning a multi-course banquet (and who isn't?), an alcoholic, citrusy granita is a lovely way to clear the palate between the starter and the main course.

SORBET

Similar to a granita, but churned – either in a machine or by hand – so that it has a very light, snowy texture. A protein of some sort is usually added to a sorbet to give it that fuller texture. Gelatine, egg whites or alcohol are usually used.

ICE CREAM
THE ITALIAN MERINGUE METHOD

Henry's mum, cookery writer Josceline Dimbleby, has never been one for kitchen gadgetry. She has therefore become an expert cheat at making ice cream. She has tried just about every method (her first book – *A Taste of Dreams*, published in 1976 – included a remarkably tasty ice cream made from a packet of Bird's Dream Topping), but her all-time favourite is the Italian meringue method.

This works by folding a meringue mixture into the whipped cream and fruit. You can then pop it into the freezer without churning it: the air bubbles in the meringue prevent any large ice crystals from forming. You are left with a wonderfully smooth, creamy ice cream. This same method can be applied when using egg yolks and whipping them up with sugar until they are voluminous and almost white. Richer but equally good.

ICE CREAM
THE TRADITIONAL CUSTARD METHOD

This is the classic method, in which egg yolk is used to make a rich custard base. It makes a dense, luxurious ice cream. You cannot simply leave it in the freezer, otherwise long, crunchy ice crystals will form. This is where an ice cream machine comes in useful. Otherwise, you'll need to freeze the mixture in a shallow, wide container, that will fit into your freezer. Every 30 minutes use a whisk to stir and break up the ice that has formed until it becomes a light ice cream.

Champagne Granita

A lovely light way to end a meal. Or, if you are feeling extravagant, to serve as a palate cleanser between the starter and the main course (see picture on page 151, top).

Serves: 4–6
Preparation time: 10 minutes
Freezing time: 3–4 hours
♥ WF GF DF V

100g **caster sugar**
200ml **water**
325ml **Champagne**
  (½ a bottle)
juice of 1 **lemon**

We originally wanted to do an absinthe granita, one that would make a party swing. Sadly the stuff was so alcoholic that we couldn't get it to freeze, leaving us with a lethal, ice-cold absinthe syrup. Best to stick to Champagne really.

CLAIRE

1. Dissolve the sugar and water together in a pan over a moderate heat. Stir in the Champagne. Add lemon juice to taste.

2. Freeze in a roasting tray or other container that is shallow and wide, but will fit into your freezer. Every 30 minutes, use a whisk to stir and break up the ice that has formed, until all the liquid has turned into paper-thin ice shards.

 TIPS

❖ You can play around with granitas as much as you want. Sharp rosé wine and fruit work well together, as do coffee, and vodka.

❖ Different alcohols also go well with different fruits. The alcohol can really bring out the flavour of a fruit, lifting it and making it more complex. Try Grand Marnier with orange, kirsch with cherries or pineapple. There are some wonderful small distilleries cropping up that are mixing fruits and alcohol. You can find pear, greengage, quince and others. They are worth seeking out.

Quince Granita

A more scented, full-bodied granita, and a lovely way to finish off an autumn dinner (see picture on page 151, below left).

Serves: 6
Preparation time: 25 minutes
Cooking time: 2 hours
Freezing time: 5 hours
♥ WF GF DF V

1½ **quinces**
300g **caster sugar**
700ml **water**
1 **vanilla pod**, split in half lengthwise
juice of ½ a **lemon**

1. Peel and quarter the quinces. Put the sugar, water and vanilla pod into a saucepan and stir to dissolve the sugar. Bring to the boil.

2. Add the quinces and the lemon juice. Simmer for 1–2 hours, or until the quinces are tender when pierced and rosy in colour.

3. Remove the quinces from the syrup and core them. Remove the vanilla pod.

4. Purée the quinces and syrup together, then add some water to adjust the consistency so it's less thick.

5. Freeze in a roasting tray or other container that is shallow and wide, but will fit into your freezer. Every 30 minutes, use a whisk to stir and break up the ice that has formed, until all the liquid has turned into paper-thin ice shards.

 TIPS

❖ Quinces are thick and fluffy when puréed and lend themselves very well to being frozen. Be sure to cook them long enough so that they are tender.

❖ Add a teaspoon or two of honey to the purée as a variation. Honey and quince have an affinity for each other.

Clementine Granita

A light, fruity granita for winter refreshment (see picture on page 151, below right).

Serves: 4–6
Preparation time: 5 minutes
Cooking time: 10 minutes
Freezing time: 3–4 hours
❤ WF GF DF V

100ml **water**
50g **caster sugar**
300ml **clementine juice**, strained

1. Combine the water and sugar over a low heat to make a syrup. Cool completely.

2. Stir in the strained clementine juice.

3. Freeze in a roasting tray or other container that is shallow and wide, but will fit into your freezer. Every 30 minutes, use a whisk to stir and break up the ice that has formed, until all the liquid has turned into paper-thin ice shards.

 TIPS

❖ Serve with grapefruit or orange sections, in pretty glass cups.

❖ It is also nice with a crisp buttery biscuit.

Apple Sorbet

We call this apple sorbet, but apple snow might be a better description. It is light and fluffy and pure as the driven … The egg white and gelatine add protein, which gives the sorbet its gorgeous texture.

Serves: 4–6
Preparation time: 25 minutes
Freezing time: up to 5 hours
♥ WF GF DF V

500ml cloudy **apple juice**
50g **caster sugar**
1 teaspoon **powdered gelatine**
1 **free-range egg white**
a splash of **apple brandy** (optional)

1. Gently heat 250ml of the apple juice with the sugar in a small saucepan.

2. In another pan, soften the gelatine with the remaining apple juice off the heat and then heat it gently to dissolve. Once dissolved, combine the two liquids and pour into a container to cool. When cooled, place in the fridge until ready to freeze.

3. Whisk the egg white to soft peaks and fold it into the chilled sorbet base. Add the apple brandy, if using, then pour into an ice cream machine and freeze according to the manufacturer's instructions.

TIPS

❖ Use a high-quality tart apple juice, or, even better, juice your own.

❖ Try substituting pear, peach, watermelon or grape juice for the apple. If they are very sweet you might need a squeeze of lemon to add some acidity.

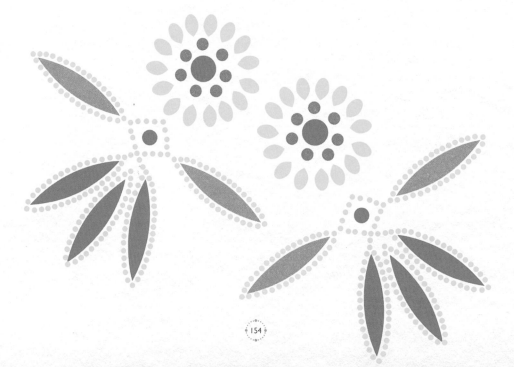

Plum Parfait (aka Jossy's Damson Ice Cream)

Fluffy and creamy at the same time, this is an easy ice cream that does not require an ice cream machine.

Serves: 6–8
Preparation time: 10 minutes
Cooking time: 20 minutes
Freezing time: 5 hours minimum
WF GF V

400–450g **plums** or **damsons** (not too ripe)
juice of 1 **lemon**
175g **caster sugar**
2 large **free-range egg whites**
a pinch of **salt**
200g golden **caster sugar**
6 tablespoons strained **lemon juice**
300ml **whipping cream**
2–3 tablespoons **plum** or other **fruit liqueur** (optional)

1. Cook the plums in advance: cut them in half, remove the stones and put the fruit into a large saucepan with the lemon juice and caster sugar. Cover the pan and put over a fairly low heat, stirring often until the sugar has dissolved. Cook gently until mushy. Then put into a food processor, whiz to a rough purée and leave until cold.

2. Now put the egg whites into a large clean bowl with the salt and use an electric hand mixer to whisk until they begin to stand in soft peaks.

3. Put the golden caster sugar into a saucepan with the lemon juice and stir over a low heat until dissolved. Then increase the heat and boil fiercely, without stirring, for 3 minutes.

4. Pour the syrup immediately on to the whisked egg whites from above in a thin stream, whisking all the time with the electric hand mixer until the mixture is thick and looks like uncooked meringue.

5. In a separate bowl, whisk the cream until thick but not stiff. Then, using a metal spoon, gently but thoroughly fold the cream into the egg white mixture, followed by the plum purée. If you are using fruit liqueur, gradually stir it in.

6. Finally, turn the mixture into a serving bowl – glass looks pretty, but make sure it's freezer-proof – and freeze for at least 5 hours before eating.

TIPS

✛ Add a blob of clotted cream on top of the parfait before serving.

✛ Try making this with puréed berries or mango for other delicious ice cream flavours.

This is a dish that my mum used to make for us every summer in Dittisham in Devon. The Dittisham Ploughman plum is found only in this village, and is thought to have been brought over here by German monks. These plums are particularly good for puddings, as they have great acidity. If yours are sweeter, add more lemon juice.

HENRY

Ice Cream Base

The base for almost all ice creams. Once you have mastered this, you can experiment by adding fruit purées, dried fruits, booze, candied nuts, or even caramelized days-old breadcrumbs. This base is made with both double cream and whole milk, making it a little lighter than usual and consequently a better vehicle for other flavours.

Makes: 900ml
Preparation time: 30 minutes
Freezing time: up to 5 hours
WF GF V

5 **free-range egg yolks**

300ml **double cream**

300ml **whole milk**

180g **caster sugar**

1. Make sure the eggs are at room temperature. Crack them into a large bowl and whisk them briefly to break up the yolks.

2. Pour the cream into a plastic container that will hold all the ingredients and also fit into your fridge. Place a fine sieve over this and then set aside.

3. Put the milk and caster sugar into a small pan. Bring to just under the boil, stirring to make sure the sugar dissolves.

4. Pour the hot milk slowly into the eggs, whisking as you go.

5. Pour the milk/egg mixture back into the pan and place back on the hob. Stir constantly with a wooden spoon or a heatproof plastic spatula. It is ready when you can swipe a finger through the custard and leave a trail on the back of a spoon. This should happen quite quickly.

6. Immediately pour the custard through the fine sieve into the reserved cream. Sieving removes any bits of cooked egg, and if you are flavouring the custard with vanilla or coffee beans, for example, they will be strained out here.

7. Give the ice cream base a good stir and taste. If it needs a pinch of salt or a teaspoon of vanilla extract or brandy, now is a good time to add it.

8. Chill the base until cold (it's a good idea to start the day before you're ready to freeze it, or early in the morning). Pour into an ice cream machine and freeze, according to the manufacturer's instructions.

TIPS

❖ When tasting your ice cream base, bear in mind that it will taste sweeter at room temperature than when it is frozen.

❖ Save your egg whites, as they will keep for up to 5 days in the fridge. You can use them in the Violet Coconut Macaroon recipe (see page 101), or in any of the meringue recipes (see pages 136–141).

❖ It is easy to flavour your ice cream base with vanilla beans or cinnamon sticks. Any of your favourite spices can make a delicious ice cream. Steep them like tea in with the milk in step 3 (opposite), then strain. Here are a few guidelines:

❖ For Coffee Ice Cream: 50g of freshly roasted whole coffee beans.

❖ For Vanilla Ice Cream: 1 vanilla pod, split, seeds scraped out.

❖ For Cinnamon Ice Cream: 1 short stick of soft Ceylon cinnamon.

❖ For Cardamom Ice Cream: 3 whole cardamom pods.

Raspberry Ripple Ice Cream

You can leave out the vodka if you are making this for children, but it really lifts the flavour of the raspberries (and the spirits).

Makes: 1.1 litres
Preparation time: 30 minutes
Freezing time: up to 5 hours
WF GF V

1 x quantity **Vanilla Ice Cream Base** (see above)
200g **raspberries**
4 tablespoons **icing sugar**
2 tablespoons **vodka**
2 teaspoons **vanilla extract**

1. Make the vanilla ice cream base.

2. Put the raspberries, icing sugar, vodka and vanilla extract into a blender or food processor and blitz to a thick purée. Push through a sieve to remove the seeds.

3. Before the ice cream is fully frozen (but when it's pretty stiff), stir in the raspberries in thick seams. Continue to freeze in the freezer (see page 150) or in your ice cream machine.

Henry's Chocolate & Salted Caramel Ice Cream Bombe

An outrageous pudding to show off with. Don't worry about the calories – it is scientifically proven that anything you eat after dark doesn't make you fat.

Serves: 8
Preparation time: 45 minutes
Freezing time: 45 minutes (first churn)
+ 5 hours
WF GF V

For the ice cream
400ml **double cream**
150ml **milk**
100g **chocolate** (70% cocoa solids)
5 **free-range egg yolks**
130g **caster sugar**
30g **cocoa powder**

For the caramel (crunchy nut toffee)
150g **caster sugar**
400ml **double cream**
juice of ½ a **lemon**

For the cracknel
200g **sugar**
80g **hazelnuts**

My mum always used to make ice cream bombes when we were children. I remember one in particular that had a lemon ice cream exterior and grated dark chocolate inside, which tumbled out of it when you cut into it. I concocted this homage to those childhood bombes one Saturday, after I had promised to bring pudding to a friend's dinner party. It took me all day, and was gone in five minutes. You could say it went down a bomb.

HENRY

1. To make the ice cream, bring the cream and milk to the boil. Stir in the chocolate.

2. Put the egg yolks into a large bowl. Add the sugar and cocoa powder and beat well. Whisk in a little of the hot cream/milk mix, then put everything into a pan and return it to the stove. Heat gently, stirring well, for 10 minutes, and allow to simmer. Pour through a sieve and leave to cool.

3. Freeze in an ice cream machine according to the manufacturer's instructions. Or by hand (see page 150). Leave the ice cream to rest in the freezer, but not for too long. You need it softish to put the whole thing together.

4. To make the caramel, melt the sugar in a pan until it's a warm brown syrup. Slowly add the cream – it will whoosh up in an exciting fashion but will eventually settle down. Add a good pinch of sea salt. When all the sugar has dissolved in the cream, add the lemon juice. Allow to cool, then put into the fridge.

5. To make the cracknel, dissolve the sugar in a non-stick pan. Toss in the hazelnuts and pour on to an oiled sheet of greaseproof paper. When it's cold, wrap the paper in a tea towel and give it a satisfying smash with a rolling pin.

6. To put it all together, line a pudding basin with clingfilm. Press three-quarters of the chocolate ice cream into the basin, leaving a well for the caramel. Scoop the fridge-cold caramel into the well. Seal the bombe with the remaining ice cream (this will be the base when you turn it out) Freeze for a good 5 hours or more.

7. Turn out on to a plate and sprinkle with the hazelnut cracknel.

❖ To serve, slice with a sharp knife dipped in hot water.

❖ This is not quite as hard to make as it sounds. The second one you make, however, is likely to be better than the first.

❖ Once you have got the hang of making bombes you can have a lot of fun with them: lemon ice cream with grated chocolate; vanilla ice cream with a raspberry middle; chocolate ice cream with fresh mint ice cream inside. Have fun.

STEAMED PUDDINGS

Let's not kid ourselves: there is nothing healthy about a steamed pudding. It is, however, one of the greatest comfort foods ever invented. Hot, stodgy, oozing sweetness, it can take the edge off the bitterest British winter. Ideally consumed after a long march through the frozen countryside, it may not do much for your arteries but it will certainly warm your soul.

Spotted Dick

A classic British pudding, with a classic British name.

Serves: 4–6
Preparation time: 20 minutes
Cooking time: 2½ hours

360g **plain flour**
a pinch of **salt**
2 teaspoons **baking powder**
180g **vegetable suet**
125g **soft brown sugar**
175g **currants**
grated zest of 1 **lemon**
½ teaspoon ground **mixed spice**
150ml **whole milk**
butter, to grease and serve
golden syrup, to serve

1. Sift the flour, salt and baking powder into a large mixing bowl. Stir in the suet, sugar, currants, lemon zest and mixed spice, then add just enough milk to make a soft dough.

2. Shape the dough into a log shape and wrap loosely in a sheet of buttered heavy-duty clingfilm. Wrap this loosely in muslin and secure with string.

3. Drop the log into a large pan of boiling water and simmer for 2 hours. If using a cylindrical mould, line it with buttered greaseproof paper, put the dough in the mould and steam for 2½ hours.

4. To serve, remove the wrappings and cut the pudding into 3cm slices. Serve with a knob of butter and drizzle with golden syrup.

TIPS

✣ You can substitute spelt flour for white flour if you prefer it.

✣ Serve with Quick Custard (see page 34), or double cream.

This dish was recently renamed 'Spotted Richard' and then 'Sultana Sponge' at a Welsh council canteen, after the catering staff complained of 'immature comments' from council staff. The move was proclaimed ludicrous by one councillor, who campaigned successfully to have the proper name reinstated. People will soon be 'frightened of their own shadow', he harrumphed. Makes you proud to be British.

HENRY

Jossy's Lemon Pudding Delicious

This pudding was one that Henry's great granny Enid handed down to his mother. It was cut out from a newspaper and was called 'Lemon Pudding' – next to it Enid had written 'delicious!'

Serves: 6
Preparation time: 20 minutes
Cooking time: 40 minutes
V

50g **unsalted butter**, at room temperature, plus extra for greasing
225g **golden caster sugar**
finely grated zest and juice of 2 large **lemons**
4 large **free-range eggs**, separated
50g **self-raising flour**
225ml **whole milk**
½ level teaspoon **cream of tartar**
icing sugar, for sprinkling

1. Heat the oven to 180°C/350°F/gas mark 4 and place a roasting tin half-filled with water on the centre shelf to warm up. Butter a 1.5–1.75 litre soufflé or other ovenproof dish.

2. Whisk the butter in a large bowl until soft, then add the sugar and whisk until fluffy. Gradually whisk in the lemon juice, followed by the grated lemon zest and the egg yolks.

3. Sift the flour on to the mixture and stir it in with a metal spoon, then gradually stir in the milk. Whisk thoroughly until very smooth.

4. In a clean bowl, whisk the egg whites with the cream of tartar using an electric hand mixer until they stand in soft peaks. Then, using a metal spoon, fold them gently into the pudding mixture, about a quarter at a time.

5. Pour the mixture into the soufflé dish and stand it in the roasting tin of water in the oven. Bake for 40 minutes, or slightly less in a fan oven, until risen and golden brown on top.

6. Serve hot or cold, with a little icing sugar sifted over the surface if you like.

Jossy in London, 1978

St Clement's Pudding

An old-fashioned steamed pudding with a sticky, gooey top and the flavour of clementines infused throughout.

Serves: 4–6
Preparation time: 30 minutes
Cooking time: 2 hours

V

1 **clementine**

1 **vanilla pod**

140g **unsalted butter**

125g **caster sugar**

3 **eggs**, lightly beaten

200g **plain flour**

1½ teaspoons **baking powder**

100–150ml **whole milk**

For the syrup
zest and juice of 2 **clementines**

200g **caster sugar**

150ml **water**

double cream, to serve

1. Heat the oven to 160°C/325°F/gas mark 3. Butter a medium-sized pudding basin.

2. Grate the zest from the clementine and scrape the seeds from the vanilla pod. Set the zested clementine and seeded vanilla pod aside for later.

3. Cream together the butter, sugar, clementine zest and vanilla seeds until light and fluffy, then gradually add the beaten eggs.

4. Sift in the flour and baking powder and fold in thoroughly. Add the milk and set aside.

5. To make the syrup, put the clementine juice and zest into a small pan with the sugar, water and the vanilla pod. Heat gently, stirring until the sugar has dissolved, then bring to the boil and simmer until the mixture has reduced to a syrup.

6. Cut the zested clementine in half and place in the pudding basin with the cut sides down. Pour over three-quarters of the syrup, reserving the rest for later.

7. Spoon in the sponge mix and place a round of baking paper on top, then cover the basin with a second larger piece of baking paper (with a generous pleat in the middle) and secure with an elastic band or string.

8. Put the basin into a deep roasting tin and pour enough hot water into the tin to come halfway up the sides of the basin. Steam for about 2 hours, or until well risen and firm to the touch (remember to keep the water topped up). Turn out on to a large serving dish deep enough to catch the syrup and pour the last of the syrup over the top. Serve with double cream.

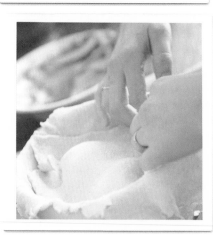

Sussex Pond Pudding

Suet, once a staple of the British larder, has fallen out of fashion in recent years. But it deserves its place in our culinary canon: nothing else can give a steamed pudding quite the same glossy, sticky crust. In this recipe the juice from the orange mixes with the butter and sugar to create a devilish pool of syrup inside.

Serves: 6
Preparation time: 35 minutes
Cooking time: 2½ hours

For the pastry
250g **self-raising flour**, plus extra for dusting
125g cold grated **suet** (or **unsalted butter**)
150ml **whole milk**

For the filling
300g **unsalted butter**, softened
200g **soft brown sugar**
100g **golden syrup**
1 large unwaxed **orange**, pricked with a fork

1. In a bowl, gently toss together the flour and the suet or butter. Place in the freezer while you get the remaining ingredients together and prepare a 1.5 litre pudding basin by buttering it and dusting it with flour.

2. Remove the flour mixture from the freezer and add the milk, stirring with your hands to form a dough. Work quickly and do not overwork the dough. Wrap in clingfilm and place in the fridge to rest.

3. To make the filling, beat the softened butter and soft brown sugar together well. Add the golden syrup and set aside.

4. Heat the oven to 160°C/325°F/gas mark 3. Take the dough out of the fridge and lightly dust a work surface with flour. Roll the dough out to a round that is large enough to fit your pudding basin. Use a paring knife to cut a wedge (about a quarter) out of the circle of pastry. This will make the top of the pudding.

5. Put the circle of dough (with the wedge removed) into your prepared basin and press the seams together where the wedge was removed to make a solid piece of pastry. There should be a centimeter or two of pastry hanging over the rim of the bowl. Fill with the brown sugar mixture and place the pricked orange on top of that. Cover with the reserved wedge of pastry. Take the excess pastry that is hanging over the rim of the bowl and fold it over, sealing the lid. Cover with pleated baking paper and tie with string or an elastic band.

6. Place the pudding in a deep roasting tin and pour enough hot water into the tin to come halfway up the sides of the basin. Bake in the oven for 2–2½ hours, until golden. Remove from the oven and let sit for 5 minutes before carefully inverting on to a large serving dish deep enough to catch any syrup.

TIPS

✦ You can replace the orange with the more traditional lemon if you fancy, or have both.

George's Ice Cream Sandwich

A dairy-free, sugar-free indulgent treat for you and any children in your life.

Makes: 12 discs
Preparation time: 10 minutes +
2 hours soaking
Cooking time: 2 hours
♥ ✓ WF GF DF V

200g **almonds**
50g **shelled hemp seeds**
150g **fresh dates**, chopped
seeds of ½ a **vanilla pod**
a pinch of **sea salt**

I like these chewy biscuits so much for their texture and lovely flavour. One of the wonderful benefits of eating sweets and cakes that are made with alternative ingredients is that they usually satisfy your cravings much better and you therefore eat less of them.

CLAIRE

1. Soak the almonds in water for 2 hours, drain then crush to a paste in a mortar, or a food processor.

2. Heat the oven to 110°C/225°F/gas mark ¼.

3. Add the hemp seeds, chopped dates, vanilla seeds and salt to the almonds and bring everything together by pounding or blitzing for a few seconds.

4. Press out on to baking paper and roll to 2mm thickness. Use cutters to cut 5cm discs. Re-roll any excess to get 12 discs. Dry out for 2 hours in the low oven.

5. To make the ice cream sandwich: take a scoop of Maggie's Coconut Kiss Ice Cream and sandwich it between 2 discs. Hand to small child. Be prepared to load washing machine (don't worry, it doesn't stain).

Maggie's Coconut Kiss Ice Cream

A rich, fruity, dairy-free and 'raw' ice cream.

Serves: 6–8
Preparation time: 20 minutes
Freezing time: overnight
♥ ✓ WF GF DF V

400ml whole-fat **coconut milk**
50ml **water**
250g **dried sour cherries**
50g + 2 teaspoons **palm sugar**
5 whole **cardamom pods**
zest of 2 **oranges**
a pinch of **sea salt**

Maggie worked as a raw chef and learned how to delicately balance the flavours inherent in some commonly used ingredients. The combination of coconut, cardamom and a tangy berry here works so well. Maggie originally used dried blackcurrants, but they can be difficult to track down so I made it with sour cherries.

CLAIRE

1. Heat the coconut milk and water in a pan over a low heat with the cherries, palm sugar and cardamom pods. Stir occasionally and crush the cherries with the back of the spoon until softened and a deep caramel colour is achieved. Remove from the heat and allow to cool. Remove and discard the cardamom pods.

2. Add the orange zest and sea salt. Pass the mixture through a fine mesh sieve. Thoroughly chill, then pour into an ice cream machine and freeze, according to the manufacturer's instructions (or see page 150 for manual method).

COOKIES

GOOEY

BISCUITS

4

DREAM CAKE

CHAOS

ICINGS

CHOCOLATE

COOKING WITH CHIL

DREN

All the neighbourhood kids love Claire. She worries that this is only because she is always carrying an enormous tower of cake boxes. Certainly my three-year-old son, George, has an unfortunate habit of greeting her with the words: 'Hello Claire. Can I have some cake?'

The truth is, he loves her because she is generous and funny – and she always has cake. Grown-ups don't come much better than that.

These are some of Claire's favourite recipes to cook with children.

HENRY

Cut-out Biscuits

You need the right kind of dough to make cut-out biscuits – one that holds its shape during cooking. This recipe should be a cornerstone of your baking repertoire, especially if you have young children. Make these crumbly, light biscuits for Christmas, children's parties, or just because it's a great way to keep the kids entertained.

Makes: 24, depending on size
Preparation time: 15 minutes +
2 hours chilling time
Cooking time: 15 minutes
V

225g **unsalted butter**, very soft
400g **caster sugar**
2 **free-range eggs**
1 teaspoon **vanilla extract**
560g **plain flour**
1 teaspoon **baking powder**
a pinch of **salt**
Royal Icing (see page 179)

1. With an electric hand mixer, beat the softened butter with the caster sugar until light, pale and fluffy.

2. Add the eggs, one by one, then the vanilla extract.

3. Weigh the flour into a separate bowl and whisk in the baking powder and salt. Add half of this to the creamed mixture and beat on a low speed until just combined.

4. Add the remaining flour mixture and beat again to combine well.

5. Divide the dough in half and wrap each ball in clingfilm. You could freeze one ball for another time if you like. Chill for about 2 hours or overnight before using.

6. When ready to make the biscuits, heat the oven to 160°C/325°F/gas mark 3. Line a couple of baking sheets with baking paper.

7. Lightly dust a surface with flour, then roll out the dough to about 5mm thick. Cut out shapes with your cutters and transfer the biscuits to your prepared baking sheets. Chill for 15–20 minutes, then bake for 15 minutes or until just starting to turn golden. Transfer to a wire rack and leave to cool completely.

8. Decorate the biscuits with royal icing and leave out overnight to dry.

9. Store in an airtight container for up to a week.

TIPS

❖ Try adding flavours to the biscuits for variation. Anita (who designed this book) put a ½ teaspoon of ground mixed spice into her Halloween Biscuits (see page 253), which made them deliciously autumnal. You could also add lemon zest, cinnamon or other spices you like. Henry is quite fond of ground cardamom seeds for a scented flavour.

❖ If you're making these with children, you really ought to let them do the decorating. Lay out lots of little bowls filled with sugary things to stick on to the icing – hundreds and thousands, silver sugar balls, Smarties, whatever – and let them go mental.

PURÉES

ICINGS

Greengage

Quince

Rhubarb

Raspberry

Strawberry

Turmeric

Royal Icing

Swooped over a fruit cake or drizzled on cut-out cookies, royal icing is an old-fashioned edible decoration that – although incredibly sugary – is as classy as the name suggests.

You don't need to reach for artificial colourings (although sometimes we think it's OK and sort of fun). Purée brightly coloured fruit to make natural colourings instead (see tips below), or try using powdered turmeric for a gorgeous yellow icing with a delicate aniseedy flavour.

Makes: about 800g,
or enough to cover a 20–25cm cake
Preparation time: 10 minutes
Cooking time: none
❤ WF GF DF V

4 **free-range egg whites**
660g **icing sugar**
125ml **water** or **fruit purée**

1. Put all the ingredients together in a bowl and use an electric mixer on a low speed to mix until combined. Then turn the speed up to medium for about 7 minutes, or until thick ribbons form.

2. You can make the icing softer or looser by adding a little more water.

 TIPS

✤ Purée fruits that are fresh, ripe and vibrant-coloured by simply blending them to a pulp in a blender. Strain the purée to remove seeds and skin (except in the case of strawberries, which seem to benefit from keeping their little seeds in).

S'mores

In America this is not a recipe as much as a part of growing up. Children learn to make s'mores – so named because everyone wants some more – from a very early age. They symbolize summer camp, ghost stories, and, in a way, independence. You are free to toast the marshmallows as much or as little as you like, creating a very personal treat.

Makes: enough for 6
Preparation time: 5 minutes
Cooking time: 2 minutes

 V

2 bags of **marshmallows**
6 bars of your favourite **chocolate**
2 packets of **digestive biscuits**
long skewers, for roasting

1. Build a campfire or bonfire, or have an adult build one.

2. Bring all the ingredients out to the campfire or bonfire.

3. Gather your own personal supply of marshmallows and digestive biscuits, and your chocolate bar.

4. Take 1 digestive biscuit and top it with a piece of chocolate. Set aside.

5. Get cosy.

6. Push 2 or 3 marshmallows on to a skewer while listening to ghost stories. Hold the end of the stick just above the flame to char the marshmallows. We like them golden but just starting to burn.

7. When you have charred them to your liking, quickly press the marshmallow on to the chocolate and sandwich with another biscuit.

8. Devour.

 TIPS

❖ Sometimes the marshmallows will go up in flames. This is OK, just blow out the flame.

A Good Chocolate Cake

A great cake for a children's party if you don't want your house terrorized by children high on sugar and food colouring. It is vegan, but they'll never know it. It also looks ravishing decorated with flowers from the garden.

Serves: 8
Preparation time: 30 minutes
Cooking time: 35 minutes
Cooling and decorating time: 2 hours
♥ ✓ DF V

For the cake
150ml hot **water**
80g **cocoa powder**
200ml **agave syrup**
200ml **coconut milk**
juice of ½ a **lemon**
80ml **sunflower oil**
2 teaspoons **vanilla extract**
180g **white spelt flour** or **plain flour**
½ teaspoon **baking powder**
1½ teaspoons **bicarbonate of soda**
a pinch of **salt**

For the icing
50g **coconut oil**
200g **dark chocolate**
1 teaspoon **vanilla extract**
50ml **agave syrup**

flowers from the garden, to decorate (optional)

1. Heat the oven to 160°C/325°F/gas mark 3. Grease and line a 20–23cm cake tin with baking paper.

2. Whisk together the hot water and cocoa powder until smooth. Add the remaining wet ingredients and set aside.

3. In a large bowl, sift together the flour, baking powder, bicarbonate of soda and salt. Pour the wet mixture over the dry and whisk in a circular motion from the centre of the bowl, moving outwards to combine. Pour the mixture into the cake tin.

4. Bake in the oven for about 35 minutes, or until a skewer inserted comes out clean and the cake is springy to the touch. Let the cake cool for 10 minutes before turning it out on to a wire rack to cool completely.

5. For the icing, put all the ingredients into a heatproof bowl and place over a pan of barely simmering water to melt, and stir. Move the cake to a serving plate and drizzle the chocolate icing over it. If you like, decorate with flowers from the garden.

TIPS

❖ Instead of flowers, you could add some raspberries to the cake and arrange a few on top for decoration.

Maggie's Best Chocolate Chip Cookies

Gooey, chocolatey, but without the flour or sugar.

Makes: 24
Preparation time: 15 minutes
Cooking time: 11 minutes
WF GF V

280g **gluten-free flour**

2 teaspoons **baking soda**

½ teaspoon **sea salt**

200g **dark chocolate chips** or chunks

50ml **agave nectar**

200ml **maple syrup**

125g **unsalted butter**, melted

1 tablespoon **vanilla extract**

sea salt, for sprinkling (optional)

1. Heat the oven to 180°C/350°F/gas mark 4. Line a baking tray with baking paper.

2. Mix together all the dry ingredients in a medium bowl (including the chocolate chips or chunks).

3. Mix together all the wet ingredients in a small bowl.

4. Add the wet ingredients to the dry ingredients, and stir until they are well combined, but do not over-mix.

5. Drop spoonfuls of the cookie dough on to the prepared baking tray. Lightly sprinkle with sea salt if desired.

6. Bake in the oven for only 11 minutes, and allow the biscuits to cool on the tray for 1 minute before transferring to a cooling rack.

TIPS

❖ These are even better the next day. Enjoy with a glass of cold Hazelnut Milk (see page 56).

❖ Following the baking time instructions will give you the perfect gooey texture.

❖ If you can't get hold of gluten-free flour and you don't mind the gluten, normal flour can be substituted.

Once you have got the hang of these, you can obviously play around with the recipe. We like to substitute white chocolate and dried blueberries for the dark chocolate, and add milk chocolate and toasted pecans, or walnuts or hazelnuts in with the dark chocolate in the original recipe. Maggie is one of the bakers we love (see page 232). In her original recipe, she uses plain flour, not gluten-free, and maple sugar instead of agave syrup. I have substituted agave syrup here because maple sugar is difficult to find in the UK. She also sometimes adds a ½ teaspoon of molasses, which sounds divine.
CLAIRE

Technicolor Dreamcake

A really fun cake to make, and lurid enough – despite the natural colours – to satisfy any child. The idea came from an old cake book Claire picked up at a charity shop.

Serves: 10–12
Preparation time: 25 minutes
Cooking time: 50 minutes

V

For the cake

300g **plain flour**
½ teaspoon **salt**
4 teaspoons **baking powder**
200g **unsalted butter**, very soft
400g **sugar**
1 teaspoon **vanilla extract**
4 **free-range eggs**, separated
225ml **milk**

For EACH of the three layers of icing:

15ml **fresh fruit purée** for each layer, strained (we used raspberry, quince, turmeric and strawberry)
30g **unsalted butter**, softened
150g **icing sugar**
lemon juice or **vanilla extract**

1. Heat the oven to 160°C/325°F/gas mark 3. Grease 2 x 23cm cake tins and line them with baking paper.

2. In a large bowl, sift together the flour, salt and baking powder and set aside.

3. Cream the butter and sugar until fluffy. Add the vanilla, then the egg yolks one at a time, mixing well after each addition. Add half the milk and mix well. Add half the flour mixture and combine. Repeat with the remaining milk and flour.

4. Whisk the egg whites in a separate bowl until soft peaks form. Stir a third of the egg whites into the cake mixture to lighten the batter and then fold in the remainder, taking care not to knock out too much air in the process.

5. Carefully spoon the mixture equally into the tins and bake in the oven for 45–50 minutes, or until a skewer inserted comes out clean. Leave the cakes to cool for 10 minutes before taking them out of the tins and letting them cool completely on a wire rack.

6. Split each layer in two and place the bottom of one on a cake stand. Slather with your favourite buttercream icing flavours (see page 178 for inspiraton), then continue to stack up the layers. The top layer looks great with a buttercream icing or Royal Icing (see page 179) that drizzles down the sides. Top with fresh fruit.

To make the buttercream icing, strain the fruit purée and set aside. In a medium bowl, beat the butter and sugar until light and fluffy. Add the fruit purée, then taste. A little lemon juice or vanilla can balance the flavours of your icing nicely.

SPELT LOAF • SOURDOUGH • GLUTEN-FREE BREAD
RYE BREAD • CRUSTY WHITE ROLLS • SODA BREAD

BREAD

& SAVOURIES

FLATBREAD • PIZZA • OATMEAL BISCUITS

WITHOUT BREAD, WE WOULD HAVE NO CIVILIZATION.

Civilization requires surplus. When man worked out how to exploit wild grains – to store them during the winter months and multiply them again during the summer – he no longer needed to spend his life roaming about in search of food. He finally had a modicum of time on his hands, which he spent learning new skills such as writing, architecture, making music and generally starting down the long road towards culture. Thanks to bread, we have *The X Factor* and Morris dancing.

The early breads – first made about 12,000 years ago in the Fertile Crescent of the Middle East – were solid cakes made from ground pastes of barley and the earliest strains of wheat, einkorn and emmer. These dense patties still have their descendants around the globe – in Indian chapatis, Mexican tortillas and crumbly Scottish oatmeal biscuits (see recipe on page 212).

But breadmaking was transformed when yeast was first introduced to raise the dough and make lighter, softer loaves. Yeasted breads are first mentioned in the literature of the Egyptians, but the chances are that this breakthrough was made much earlier, as any mixture of wheat

and water, left out, will turn spontaneously into bubbling sourdough, powered by the natural yeasts that live on the grains. You can repeat this experiment – as wondrous as any in gastronomy – by following the recipe on page 195–7.

Sadly, over the last century many of the supposed advances in bread-making have in fact stripped the goodness from this elemental food. Ancient strains of wheat have been selectively bred to increase yields and gluten content. This has had two unwelcome side effects: modern wheat contains fewer nutrients and far more of the proteins that trigger inflammatory reactions. Hence the massive increase in wheat intolerance and allergy. Most bread is also now made using the Chorleywood process, which was introduced in the Sixties and uses hardened vegetable fat, intense energy, very high volumes of yeast and many additives to reduce the time required to make bread (and therefore its cost). A traditional loaf of bread contains four ingredients: water, salt, wheat and yeast. A typical Chorleywood loaf contains more than 20 ingredients.*

The bread recipes in this book all use traditional methods. We favour ancient grains such as spelt and rye, and there's even an entirely gluten-free loaf. None of which, incidentally, means that these loaves are remotely academic or complicated to make. Homemade bread is in fact one of the easiest ways to put the goodness – and the pleasure – back into your daily diet.

*For further reading on this, see Andrew Whitley's excellent book *Bread Matters*.

Bread – The Basics

TYPES OF BREAD

All breads fall into four main categories, defined by what makes them rise:

SOURDOUGH

Sourdough is the most ancient form of leavened bread. It is made with a sourdough starter (see page 195), which can either be taken from someone else's existing starter or created by leaving wheat and water to ferment naturally. The starter contains a symbiotic combination of natural yeasts and lactobacillus culture. It is the culture that creates the lactic acid that gives this bread its distinctive sour taste.

Sourdough has a reputation for being frustrating and unpredictable if you don't make it all the time, because the starter needs attention. But starters are surprisingly robust – Henry, being chaotic and absent-minded, has had to bring many a forgotten and slimy starter back to life.

The thing that takes a bit of getting used to is the timing – the cycle for making a loaf is a minimum of twelve hours, and typically twenty-four. But the actual work involved is minimal (most of that time is spent waiting for the dough to rise), and the reward is a uniquely flavoured loaf that stays fresh for over a week.

YEASTED BREADS

Most bread is risen using baker's yeast, a species of *Saccharomyces Cerevisiae*. It is the same yeast that is used to brew alcohol. It feeds on the sugars in the wheat and converts them into carbon dioxide, the gas that causes the bread to rise. It is easier to use than a sourdough because it does not require looking after and it is a good deal more vigorous – a loaf can rise in a couple of hours in a warm room. You can buy yeast fresh in blocks or dried in granules.

If you have not made bread before, this is the way to start. The simple spelt loaf on page 193 is outrageously easy to make and equally impressive. You can also experiment with different flour mixtures and flavourings to create your own signature loaf.

If you have some sourdough in the fridge, you can add a little to traditionally yeasted breads to get a touch of the flavour in under half the time.

SODA BREAD

This bread uses bicarbonate of soda as its raising agent. Wheatflour is mixed with buttermilk (or sometimes yoghurt) and the lactic acid reacts with the soda to create bubbles of carbon dioxide, which raise the bread.

It is a relatively modern bread, having become popular in Ireland in the mid-nineteenth century as a cheaper and faster alternative to yeast. It has a wonderful soft, cakey texture and a distinctive taste.

UNLEAVENED BREAD

This is a dough that requires no raising agent at all. It is the easiest of all breads to make.

A few RULES of thumb

Whichever of the above breads you are attempting, there are a few rules worth remembering:

BREAD BAKING IS NOT AN EXACT SCIENCE

The specific batch of flour you are using, the quality of the yeast and water, atmospheric temperature and humidity, and the foibles of your oven will all affect how your loaf turns out.

BE PREPARED TO FOLLOW YOUR INSTINCTS

That might mean leaving it to rise a little longer on a cold day, adding some more water if the dough feels dry.

IT CAN'T GO THAT WRONG

Don't worry about creating the perfect loaf. You will learn more from experimenting than from doing it the same way every time. Even the ugliest-looking efforts generally taste good.

WETTER IS BETTER

If you are wondering whether your bread is too wet, don't automatically add more flour. It is almost always better wetter.

ADD STEAM FOR THE PERFECT CRUST

Putting a cup of water in a baking tray at the bottom of the oven works wonders to create a glossy crust.

WRITE IT DOWN

There are few things more maddening than creating a great loaf and not being able to remember quite how you tweaked the recipe. Take notes.

Spelt Bread & variations

This is a bread that Henry has been baking for years, at his wife's insistence.
It is very easy to make and impossible to get wrong. It is also a great recipe to
play with – adding nuts and seeds, mixing in spices, and using different flours.

Makes: 3 loaves
Preparation time: 10 minutes
+ 2 hours rising time
Cooking time: 40 minutes
♥ ✓ V
(DF if you use oil for greasing)

soft **butter**, for greasing
1.5kg **strong wholemeal spelt flour**
2 x 7g sachets of **dried quick yeast**
2 tablespoons **sea salt**, crushed
125g **pine nuts**
125g **pumpkin seeds**
125g **sunflower seeds**
125ml **extra virgin olive oil**
900ml–1 litre warm **water**
50g **sunflower seeds** and **nuts**, to
sprinkle on top

When Henry's wife gave birth
to each of their sons, he baked
her a version of this bread full
of the spices that are said to
encourage lactation. It seems to
work. To make bread that will
fill your breasts with milk add
1 tablespoon each of aniseed,
caraway seeds, fennel seeds
and fenugreek (ground in a
pestle and mortar or coffee
grinder). This has no impact
on men or woman who aren't
breastfeeding, and we think it
is the most delicious of all.

1. Grease 3 x 900g/2lb loaf tins with butter.

2. Mix all the dry ingredients (except the seeds for the top)
   together in a bowl large enough to knead the dough in.

3. Add the oil, then the water, stirring until the mixture sticks together. Knead in the
   bowl for a few minutes, until smooth. You can add a little flour if it is too sticky, but
   remember the maxim – wetter is better. It doesn't matter if a little sticks to your hands.

4. Cut into 3 pieces, shape into vague ovals, then put into the loaf tins. Cut a
   pattern in deep gashes on the top and sprinkle the reserved seeds into the
   gashes, sprinkling a little spelt flour (or bran if you have some to hand) all over.

5. Put the tins into a large plastic bin bag and tuck the ends of the bag under the
   tins, leaving them enclosed with plenty of air. Leave until the dough has doubled
   in size. This will take about 2 hours in a warm kitchen.

6. Bake at 230°C/450°F/gas mark 8 for 20 minutes, then turn down to 200°C/
   400°F/gas mark 6 for a further 20 minutes. Turn out and cool on a rack.

TIPS

❖ These freeze really well in freezer bags, but don't keep bread in the fridge as it
   goes stale more quickly.

❖ You can use normal wholemeal flour if you can't get hold of spelt. Or if you like
   your loaf lighter you can replace 500g of the wholemeal with strong white flour.

❖ Experiment with all sorts of additions. Breads with nuts and fruit in can be
   amazing. Try date and almond, or apricot and walnut.

❖ Play with herbs and spices: rosemary, dill and oregano are all interesting.

SOURDOUGH STARTER

If you can't find a kindly soul to give you some starter, here are tips on how to make one – courtesy of master baker Tom Herbert, of Hobbs House Bakery in Gloucestershire, who gave Henry a piece of the starter that has been handed down in his family for 55 years.

STARTING A SOURDOUGH

Find a suitable container to house your sourdough – a kilner jar is ideal. Clean it well and weigh it while empty, noting the weight on an address tag or label (this will save you having to empty it out to know how much you have left in the future).

Weigh 100g of organic wholemeal/dark rye/wholemeal spelt flour (these all work really well) and 100g of warm water into your jar and stir. Leave the jar in a prominent and warm place in your kitchen (this will be its second home), with the lid sealed.

Each day for a week repeat the feeding process. Put 100g of the starter in a bowl (you can use the surplus to flavour cakes, buns, pancakes and pizza dough), add 100g of water and 100g of flour and stir vigorously to remove all floury lumps with a clean finger or a fork. Return it to the jar.

After about 5 days you'll notice bubbles in the dough – like the first windy smile of a baby. You can start to use it after a week, but it'll be slow, weak and infantile. From now on, you can keep it in the fridge (its first home), removing it a couple of days before use to feed it back into full bubbly liveliness (using 100g of starter, 100g of flour and 100g of water as before). After a month, the dough will have matured and you'll get a better, more even flavour and rising performance.

If it is not performing well enough, try taking it out of the fridge and giving it an extra feed. Remember that it is a living culture – if it's not hibernating in the fridge where it can survive for several months – and it likes to be fed, warm and aerated (stirred/whisked). If it dies you'll know because it'll smell like a dead dog on a hot day. Bin the lot and start again.

I'm the custodian of our family sourdough, which has been raising award-winning loaves at Hobbs House Bakery for over fifty-five years. Who will you leave your sourdough to in your will?

Peace and loaf,
Tom Herbert

Opposite: Wholemeal spelt starter (above), white wheat starter (below).

TOM (RIGHT) AND BROTHER GEORGE, MONTE CARLO, 1981

Sourdough bread

There are two stages to making a sourdough: the 'sponge' – a reinvigorated starter – and the 'dough'.

Makes: 1 loaf
Preparation time: 14 hours
(including rising)
Cooking time: 35–40 minutes
♥ DF V

For the sponge
180ml **water** at about 27°C/80°F
100g **sourdough starter** (see page 195) brought to room temperature
340g **strong white flour** (organic here makes a big difference. The chemicals used to kill pests on the growing wheat will also kill the good organisms needed for the bread to rise properly when using a natural yeast)
½ teaspoon **fine sea salt**

For the dough:
90ml **water** at 27°C/80°F
400g **strong white bread flour**
1 tablespoon **fine sea salt**

1. **The sponge:** In a medium-sized bowl or container that will fit into your fridge, combine the water, starter, and strong white flour with a wooden spoon.

2. It is fine if there are lumps of flour or starter because as the sponge starts working it will all meld together. It will have a wonderfully soft and bouncy consistency – too wet to form a dough at this stage.

3. Set this aside in a warm area of your kitchen, draped with a clean cloth or clingfilm. Ideally the temperature should be in the upper 20's°C. This is easy on a hot summer's day, but in the winter or spring, you might put it near the radiator or the oven while doing other cooking. Let this rise for 4 hours.

4. **The dough:** Put the sponge into a mixing bowl. You can mix by hand, of course, but if you have a free-standing mixer with a dough hook, it will make the job easier. Add all of the dough ingredients and mix for about 8–10 minutes. You should end up with a smooth and elastic dough that is just slightly tacky.

5. If you must knead by hand to feel like you are really making bread, then now is your chance (see page 40). You really don't need to put flour down on your work surface, so avoid this temptation. Put the dough back in the bowl and cover it again and place it back in its warm spot for 3–4 hours.

6. Line a bowl with a muslin cloth or a clean tea towel and generously dust it with flour. Turn the dough out on to your work surface and bash it around a bit to knock some of the air out. This also gets the yeasts acting again. Then shape it into a round loaf shape. Plop the dough into the flour-lined bowl and cover it with another cloth. Let it sit in the warm spot for about 5 hours.

7. This is very important: turn your oven on a good 45 minutes before you are ready to put the dough inside it. Get it good and hot, as hot as your oven will go. Claire uses an oven thermometer to check that it is at its maximum before proceeding.

8. Put a baking sheet into the oven and get it really hot, and place a baking tray with a rimmed edge (to hold a shallow depth of water) on the floor of your oven. Prepare a jug of water next to the oven, ready to pour into the tray. Now, uncover your loaf.

9. When everything is ready, remove the hot baking sheet from the oven and quickly close the door. It is so important to keep the heat in there. Now, turn the dough out onto the baking sheet and slice four slits into the top in the shape of a square (or you can develop your own signature cut).

10. Quickly open the oven, slide the baking sheet in, and pour a few glugs of water into the tray on the floor of your oven (be careful the steam does not burn your hand) and slam the door fast.

11. Set your timer for 20 minutes, and don't peek. Then take a look and you may find it will need 15–20 minutes more. Claire likes her loaf to get nice and dark, even burnt in places. Cool on a wire rack.

Gluten-free Bread

The gluten in a loaf gives it that chewy interior and tender crumb. Take the gluten out and you get something a little denser of crumb and a bit more cake-like. In its own right, however, it is very satisfying.

Makes: 1 loaf
Preparation time: 20 minutes
+ 1 hour rising time
Cooking time: 55 minutes
♥ WF GF V

500g **gluten-free brown bread flour**
½ teaspoon **sea salt**
2 x 7g sachets **dried quick yeast**
2 tablespoons **honey**
325ml **milk**
1 tablespoon **cider vinegar**
2 tablespoons **olive oil**
2 **free-range eggs**
poppy seeds, to sprinkle

1. Grease a 450g/1lb loaf tin.

2. Combine the flour, salt and yeast and set aside.

3. Warm the honey and milk slightly and remove from the heat. Add the vinegar and oil and whisk in the eggs.

4. Add the wet ingredients to the dry ingredients and bring together to form a dough. Then shape the dough into a log. Place it in your prepared tin, sprinkle with water and then scatter poppy seeds over the top, to cover. Put the dough in a warm place and leave to rise for 1 hour.

5. Heat the oven to 200°C/400°F/gas mark 6 and bake for 45–55 minutes.

6. Leave to cool in the tin for 5 minutes before turning out on to a wire rack to cool completely.

TIPS

✤ Try adding some seeds to the dough to vary the texture and flavour of this loaf. It is always a good idea to soak the seeds overnight before adding them to the bread mixture, because soaking the seeds increases the amount of vitamins your body can absorb from them.

Flour Station Rye Bread

We use this bread at Leon to make the New York-style open sandwiches we serve for breakfast. It is baked for us by the magnificent bakers at London's Flour Station, who add baked potatoes to the dough to keep it moist. It has a lovely springy texture, with nutty sunflower seeds adding bite.

Makes: 1 loaf
Preparation time: 1 hour
+ resting and proving time
Cooking time: 55 minutes
♥ ✓ WF DF V

25g **rye starter** (50% water/50% rye flour)
100g **baking potatoes**
1½ teaspoons **water**
100g **rye flour**, plus extra for dusting
10g **dried yeast**
2 teaspoons **salt**
100g **sunflower seeds**
2 tablespoons **molasses** or **black treacle**

1. First make your rye starter as you would a wheat or spelt starter (see page 195).

2. Bake the potatoes and allow them to cool, then peel them.

3. Put all the ingredients into a mixing bowl (avoiding direct contact between the fresh yeast and the salt).

4. In a free-standing mixer with a dough hook, mix on a slow speed until everything is blended, or mix by hand. The dough will be very wet and sticky, but after a while the colour will change slightly from brown to a lighter, more yellow colour.

5. Cover the bowl with a damp cloth and leave the dough to rest for approximately 3 hours, or until the dough is 'active' or bubbling.

6. Butter a 900g/2lb loaf tin and dust it with rye flour.

7. Dust the table with rye flour and turn out the dough. Shape and place in the prepared loaf tin. Press down lightly and dust the top with rye flour.

8. Leave in a warm, draught-free place to 'prove' (or rise), until you see cracks appearing on the surface of the dough. It should increase in size by approximately 50%.

9. Heat the oven to 220°C/425°F/gas mark 7. Dust the dough with rye flour again and bake in the oven for 55 minutes, or until the loaf has a rich dark crust.

TIPS

✤ This bread actually improves with age and is best enjoyed the day after baking. It will stay fresh for at least a week, as the potatoes attract moisture and therefore keep the bread moist for longer.

✤ Toast thin slices of this bread and top with butter or coconut oil and a Nut Butter (see page 57).

Raab the Baker's Crusty White Rolls

Sometimes there's nothing to compare with a bit of crusty white bread – despite its shortcomings in the nutrition department. Mima and Henry recently spit-roasted a lamb for a birthday party in their garden (the lamb took up about a third of the garden). We served it with mint sauce, and Claire suggested crispy white rolls from this family baker in Islington, London. She was spot on.

Makes: 10–12
Preparation time: 30 minutes +
1½ hours resting time
Cooking time: 20 minutes
♥ V

20g **fresh yeast**
150–200ml **warm water**
100ml warm **milk**
a pinch of **sugar**
450g **strong white flour**
1 teaspoon **salt**
50g **white vegetable shortening** or **vegetable oil**
ice cubes

1. Put the water into a bowl, add the yeast, and stir to dissolve. Add the milk and a pinch of sugar to help activate the yeast.

2. Place the flour, salt and shortening on a work surface, making a well in the middle (if using vegetable oil, add it in the next step).

3. Pour the liquid yeast mixture into the well and gradually blend it into the flour to form a dough, mixing it all together with your hands. Add a little more flour to prevent sticking and knead for 10–12 minutes, until a smooth elastic dough is achieved.

4. Place the dough in an oiled bowl, cover it with a damp tea towel, and leave it to rest in a warm place for an hour, or until it has doubled in size.

5. Tip the dough on to a floured work surface and divide it into 10–12 pieces, approximately 50g each. Shape them into rounds, pressing down with your hands using a circular motion.

6. Place the rolls on a baking tray lined with silicone paper or oiled well, leaving enough room for the rolls not to touch once they have risen. Cut a slit in the top of each roll with a sharp knife. Cover with a tea towel.

7. Preheat the oven to 220°C/425°F/gas mark 7 and place an empty baking tray at the bottom of the oven.

8. When the rolls have doubled in size, place the tray in the oven. At the same time as the rolls go in, throw approximately 10 ice cubes on to the hot empty baking tray at the bottom of the oven and shut the oven door. This will create steam, which is essential for a crusty roll. Bake for 15–20 minutes, or until golden brown.

NO CHILDREN WERE HARMED IN THE TAKING OF THESE PHOTOGRAPHS

Ballymaloe Brown Soda Bread

A classic version of this yeast-free, cakey, breakfast bread.

Makes: 1 large loaf or 2 small loaves
Preparation time: 10 minutes
Cooking time: 40 minutes

♥ ✓ V

300g **brown wholemeal flour**
  (preferably **stone-ground**)
300g **plain flour**
2 teaspoons **sea salt**
2 teaspoons **bicarbonate of soda**, sieved
550ml **buttermilk** or **sour milk**

1. Heat the oven to 230°C/450°F/gas mark 8.

2. Mix all the dry ingredients together in a large wide bowl, then make a well in the centre and pour in all the buttermilk or sour milk.

3. Using one hand, stir in a full circle, starting in the centre and working towards the outside of the bowl until all the flour is incorporated. The dough should be soft but not too wet and sticky. When it all comes together, in a matter of seconds, turn it out on to a well-floured board.

4. WASH AND DRY YOUR HANDS.

5. Roll the dough around gently with floury hands for a second, just enough to tidy it up. Flip it over and flatten slightly, to about 5cm.

6. Sprinkle a little flour on to a baking sheet and place the loaf on top of the flour.

7. Make a deep cross with a knife on top of the loaf and bake in the oven for 15–20 minutes. Reduce the heat to 200°C/400°F/gas mark 6 and bake for approximately 15–20 minutes more, or until the bread is cooked (in some ovens it may be necessary to turn the bread upside down on the baking sheet for 5–10 minutes before the end of baking).

8. When the bread is ready it will sound hollow when tapped. Cool on a wire rack.

TIPS

❖ You can add 12g of fine oatmeal, 1 egg and 12g of butter to the above to make a richer soda bread dough.

Darina Allen and her family have been running the Ballymaloe Cookery School in East Cork, Ireland, for nearly thirty years. The school is set within ten acres of market gardens, greenhouses and orchards – themselves set in hundreds of acres of organic farmland. Stepping through the little wooden gate into the courtyard of the school is like entering another world. I have been lucky enough to have been invited over there a number of times to give cooking demos, and the thing I most look forward to is the breakfast, especially when the previous day's lesson included making soda bread.

CLAIRE

This recipe is from *Ballymaloe Cookery Course* by Darina Allen (Kyle Cathie, 2001)

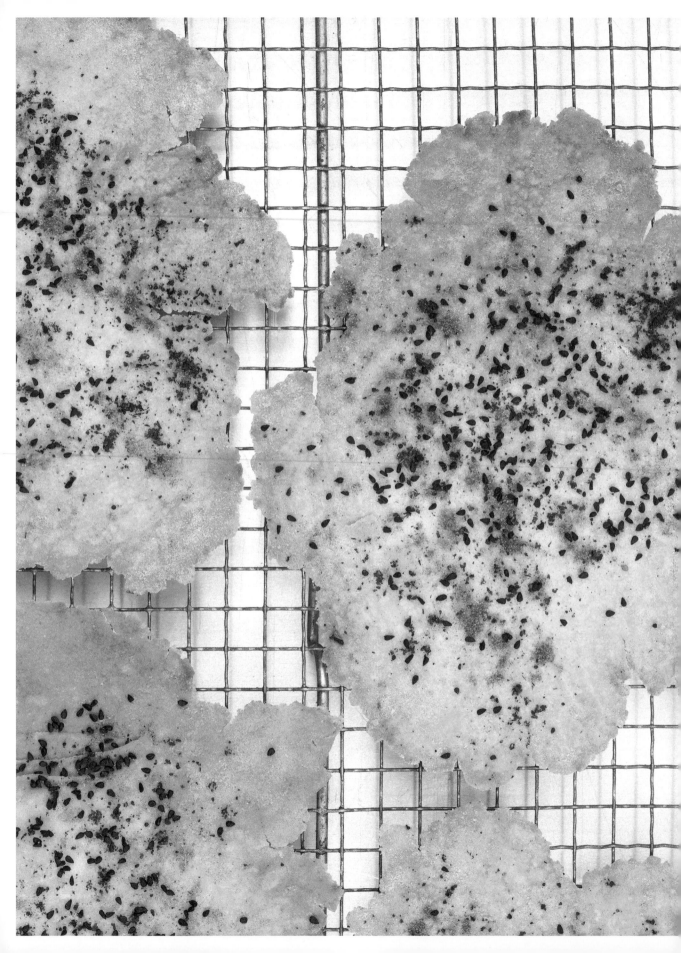

Flatbread with Zatar

This flatbread actually contains a small amount of yeast, which gives it a little lift. The texture of the dough is very dry while you are making it and feels similar to a pasta dough. Both of the flours below are available in many supermarkets and small delis. They are worth seeking out for their unique texture.

Makes: 10
Preparation time: 2 hours
Cooking time: 10 minutes
♥ DF V

1 x 7g sachet **dried quick yeast**
100ml warm **water**
3 tablespoons **olive oil**
280g **fine semolina**
70g '**00**' **flour**
1 teaspoon **sea salt**
10 teaspoons **zatar**

1. Dissolve the yeast in the warm water in the bottom of a large mixing bowl. Pour in the olive oil, add the semolina, flour and salt, and mix it all together roughly with your hands or a wooden spoon to make a dough.

2. Cover the bowl and set the dough in a warm place to rise for about 1½ hours.

3. When the dough has rested, divide it into 10 pieces and roll each piece into a ball. Let the dough rest again for 10 minutes.

4. Heat the oven to 230°C/450°F/gas mark 8.

5. Flatten each ball of dough with your hands and cover with a damp towel for about 30 minutes.

6. Sprinkle the flatbreads with zatar and place on baking trays in the oven for about 10 minutes, until crisp and golden. Cool on a wire rack.

TIPS

❖ Zatar is a flavouring which can be found in larger supermarkets, Middle Eastern shops or delis. If you can't find it you can make your own, by mixing together ground spices – typically thyme, sesame seeds and sumac. Cumin, coriander and nigella seeds also work well.

❖ You could also make it without zatar – sprinkle with a little flaky sea salt once cooked and serve with really good green olive oil.

French Onion Tart

This recipe is an adaptation of the French classic *pissaladiere*, but made with spelt flour. It is very simple and very versatile. The possibilities for alternative toppings are endless.

Serves: 8 as a canapé or 4 for lunch
Preparation time: 30 minutes
Cooking time: 30 minutes

♥ V

Spelt pastry:
125g **plain spelt flour**
pinch of **salt**
pinch of **sugar**
100g cold **unsalted butter**, cut into pieces
4 tablespoons **iced water**

Topping:
3 tablespoons **olive oil**
2 **onions**, thinly sliced
1 teaspoon **vinegar**
50g **black** or **niçoise olives**
6 **anchovies**
small bunch of **thyme**
1 **free-range egg**, beaten
salt and **black pepper**

To make the spelt pastry:

1. Combine the spelt flour, salt and sugar in a bowl and cut in the butter with a knife. Leave larger chunks of butter than you would think (about the size of a garlic clove) to make the pastry more flaky.

2. Drizzle in the water and bring it all together in a ball.

3. Wrap in clingfilm, and let it rest in the fridge for at least 30 minutes.

Meanwhile, make the topping:

4. Heat the oil in a heavy-based saucepan and add the sliced onions. Stir occasionally to be sure they don't burn. You are looking for a caramelized but soft onion.

5. Once cooked (about 7 or 8 minutes) add the vinegar and 2 teaspoons of water. Sprinkle with thyme leaves and transfer into a bowl to cool.

6. Heat oven to 160°C/325°C/gas mark 3.

7. Pit and break up the olives a little. On a floured surface roll out the dough to approximately 3mm thick and transfer to a baking sheet. Arrange the cooled onions, anchovies and olives over the dough, leaving a small boarder, and season with salt and pepper.

8. Brush the edges with beaten egg, then bake in the oven for 25–30 minutes.

(TIPS)

✢ These are some of our favourite alternative toppings:

- **BUFFALO** Onions, slices of buffalo mozzarella and tomato. Basil. Drizzle of olive oil.

- **SAUSAGE & SAGE** Onions and bits of sausage and chopped sage.

- **TOMATO & THYME** Fine layer of Dijon mustard. Onions and slices of tomato. Thyme.

- **BROCCOLI & GOATS' CHEESE** Onions. Finely chopped pieces of broccoli. Crumble on goats' cheese after cooking.

Pizza Dough

This is a softer, thicker version of pizza dough than the thin-crust pizzas that are everywhere at the moment. It is super-easy to make and super-comforting to eat.

Makes: 2 pizzas
Preparation time: 4 hours
Cooking time: 30 minutes
♥ DF V

1 teaspoon **dried yeast**
300–350ml **water**
500g **'00' flour**
olive oil

1. In a large bowl dissolve the yeast in 100ml of the water. You can use water slightly warm from the tap for this, but use cold water for the rest of the dough.

2. Once the yeast has dissolved, add the flour and then up to 300ml of water. The dough should be soft and pliable. Allow it to rest for 10 minutes, and decide at that point whether or not to add the remaining 50ml of cold water.

3. Knead the dough in the bowl until it is smooth and soft. Rub a little oil on the dough and cover the bowl with a cloth for 30 minutes.

4. Once the dough has rested you need to add air by kneading it for 5 minutes every 30 minutes. Do this three times.

5. At this stage leave the dough to rise without touching it for 90 minutes in a warmish place in your kitchen.

6. Heat the oven to 200°C/400°F/gas mark 6. Dust 2 baking sheets with flour or line them with baking paper. Divide the dough into 2 pieces and gently press each piece out into a rectangular shape. Don't roll the dough or you will squeeze the air out of it. Irregularity in the dough is what you are striving for.

7. Drizzle the dough with olive oil and cover it with the topping of your choice – see some suggestions below. Bake for about 15 minutes, or until golden.

- Our favourite topping at the moment is potato & rosemary (pictured opposite). You will need olive oil, 2 baking potatoes (peeled and sliced 2mm thick), 200g mascarpone cheese, 200ml double cream, a sprig of fresh rosemary and salt and pepper to taste. Rub the dough with oil, arrange the potato slices on top, dot with the cheese and pour over the cream. Scatter rosemary leaves over the top and season with salt and pepper.

- Other toppings we like:

    • Prosciutto, crème fraîche, sage
    • Halved cherry tomatoes, salami, mozzarella, finely chopped dried chilli
    • Sausagemeat, fennel seed, crème fraîche, blanched broccoli
    • Stilton, walnut, endive or other chicory

- Add about 100g sourdough starter (see page 195) to the dough to give it a lovely sour flavour.

Oatmeal Biscuits

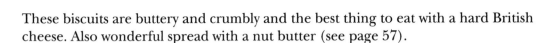

These biscuits are buttery and crumbly and the best thing to eat with a hard British cheese. Also wonderful spread with a nut butter (see page 57).

Makes: 12
Preparation time: 15 minutes +
30 minutes chilling time
Cooking time: 10 minutes
✓ V

250g **oatmeal**, stone-ground or fine
150g **spelt flour**, plus extra for dusting
100g **wholemeal spelt flour**
½ teaspoon **bicarbonate of soda**
1 teaspoon **salt**
250g **unsalted butter**
1 free-range **egg**

1. Mix together the oatmeal, spelt flours and bicarbonate of soda. Rub the butter into the oatmeal mix between your fingertips until it just about disappears.

2. Add the salt and egg to bring the dough together, then chill for at least 30 minutes.

3. Meanwhile heat the oven to 180°C/350°F/gas mark 4 and line a baking tray with baking paper.

4. Roll out the dough to about 3mm thickness on a lightly floured surface. Cut out the biscuits with a round cutter, or cut a circle of dough 18cm in diameter and then cut that into 4 wedges.

5. Place the biscuits on the baking tray and cook in the oven for 8–10 minutes. They will crisp up as they cool. They should be eaten fresh or kept in a tin for up to a week.

TIPS

❖ These biscuits will absorb moisture and become soft if left out, but they can be re-crisped (as can any biscuits containing butter) by laying them out on a baking sheet lined with baking paper and popping them into a preheated oven at 160°C/325°F/gas mark 3 for 5 minutes.

❖ A Christmas essential with Stilton cheese.

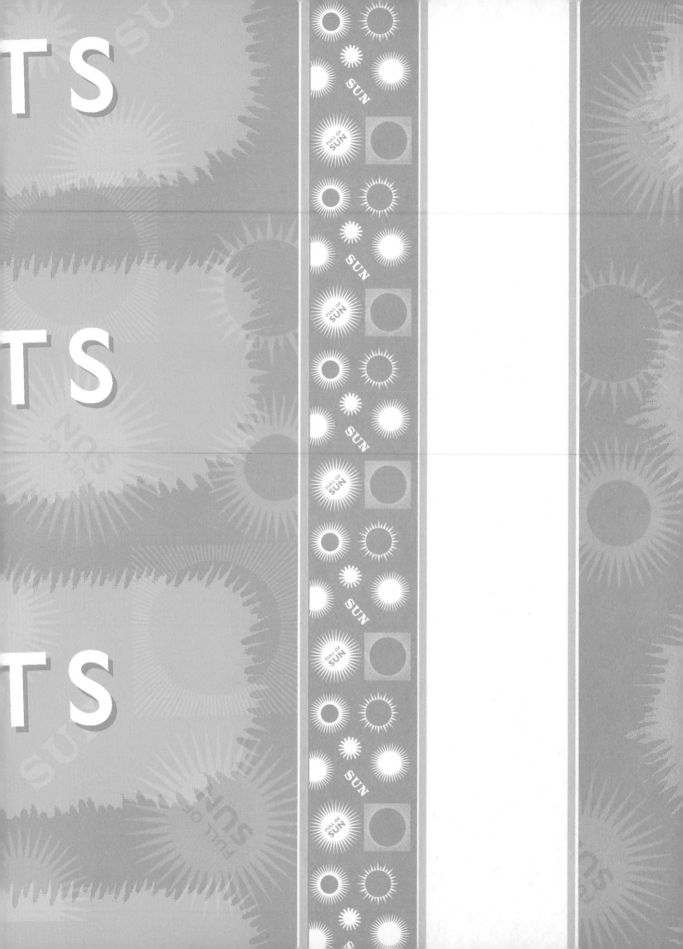

SWEETS

Rather like bread, mass-produced sweets have become so cheap and commonplace that people no longer even think of making them at home. This is a shame. There is a delicacy to the flavour of homemade sweets and a beauty to their irregularity that cannot be reproduced in a factory. It is also a particular thrill to learn how to magic up your favourite confections: like becoming Willy Wonka for a day.

These recipes are simpler than they look but leave yourself plenty of time to experiment. The alchemy of making your own sweets deserves to be savoured.

CHOCOLATE MAKING DAY

 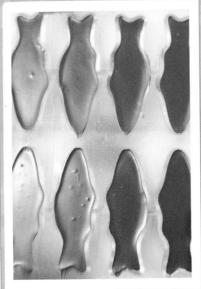 

Strawberry Marshmallows

Homemade marshmallows – soft, oozing mouthfuls with little resemblance to the dried-out, spongy things you can buy in the supermarket. You don't have to use a sugar thermometer, but it makes things much simpler (and they are easy to buy online).

Makes: 20 marshmallows
Preparation time: 20 minutes
Cooking time: 30 minutes
♥ WF GF
(V if you use vegetarian geletine)

25g **icing sugar**
25g **cornflour**
2 tablespoons **powdered gelatine**
90ml **water**
200g **caster sugar**
1½ teaspoons **golden syrup**
1 **free-range egg white**
100ml puréed **strawberries**, strained (about 200g whole berries)
1 teaspoon **vanilla extract**

1. Oil a 7cm deep 23–25cm roasting tin. Sift together the icing sugar and cornflour. Then, using about half the mixture, sift it over your oiled tin to coat.

2. Soften the gelatine in 50ml of cold water in a small saucepan, off the heat.

3. In another small saucepan, combine the caster sugar, golden syrup and the remaining water and place over a low heat. Stir to dissolve the sugar. Bring the syrup to a boil and insert a sugar thermometer. You want to heat the syrup to 'hard-ball' stage, 127°C.

4. While the sugar boils, work quickly and whisk the egg white in a large bowl with an electric hand mixer. Set aside.

5. Just before the syrup reaches hard-ball stage, place the softened gelatine in its water over a low heat until it is dissolved. Now, with your syrup at hard-ball stage and the gelatine dissolved, remove from the heat and combine the two by pouring the gelatine mixture into the syrup and whisking by hand.

6. Add the strawberry purée and the vanilla extract to the gelatine and sugar mixture.

7. Now pour the strawberry mixture into the egg whites in a slow, steady stream, whisking as you pour, until all the mixture has been incorporated.

8. Whisk on medium-high speed for 5 minutes, or until the mixture is thick and billowy. Pour into the prepared tin and smooth the top. Allow to set for about an hour.

9. Dust your work surface with more cornflour and icing sugar and turn the marshmallow out on to it. Cut into cubes and serve. Store in an airtight container for up to a week. (Dust again to stop the marshmallows from sticking together.)

TIPS

❖ These would be perfect to add to S'mores (see page 180).

Honeycomb

Essentially, we're talking about making your own Crunchie. And if that doesn't get your inner child hopping up and down with excitement, wait until you see what happens at the critical moment in this recipe. It's like the best chemistry lesson you never had.

Makes: a 20 x 20cm tin
Preparation time: 5 minutes
Cooking time: 15 minutes
♥ WF GF V

100g **unsalted butter**
1 tablespoon **white wine vinegar**
300ml **golden syrup**
400g **caster sugar**
1 teaspoon **bicarbonate of soda**, sifted

1. Butter a 20cm-square cake tin and line it with baking paper.

2. Put a LARGE heavy pan (the size is very important) over a low heat and melt the butter. Add the vinegar, golden syrup and caster sugar, letting the syrup and sugar melt into the butter. Turn the heat up to medium without stirring the mixture. Insert a sugar thermometer and heat the syrup until it reaches the 'hard-crack' stage (149°C/300°F).

3. Remove the pan from the heat and immediately stir in the bicarbonate of soda. The baking soda will fill the mixture with air bubbles of carbon dioxide so that it foams up dramatically, threatening to overflow and engulf your kitchen. That's why you make it in a LARGE pan.

4. Pour the mixture into your prepared cake tin and leave it to cool. When it begins to set, score the toffee with a knife into bite-sized pieces. Once it is completely cooled it can be broken into pieces along the score lines and stored in an airtight container.

 TIPS

❖ Coat the honeycomb with chocolate (see page 44 for how to temper it) to make your own Crunchie.

❖ Otherwise, it's great crunched up into cake icings, or sprinkled on top of a cake to give it a golden sparkle.

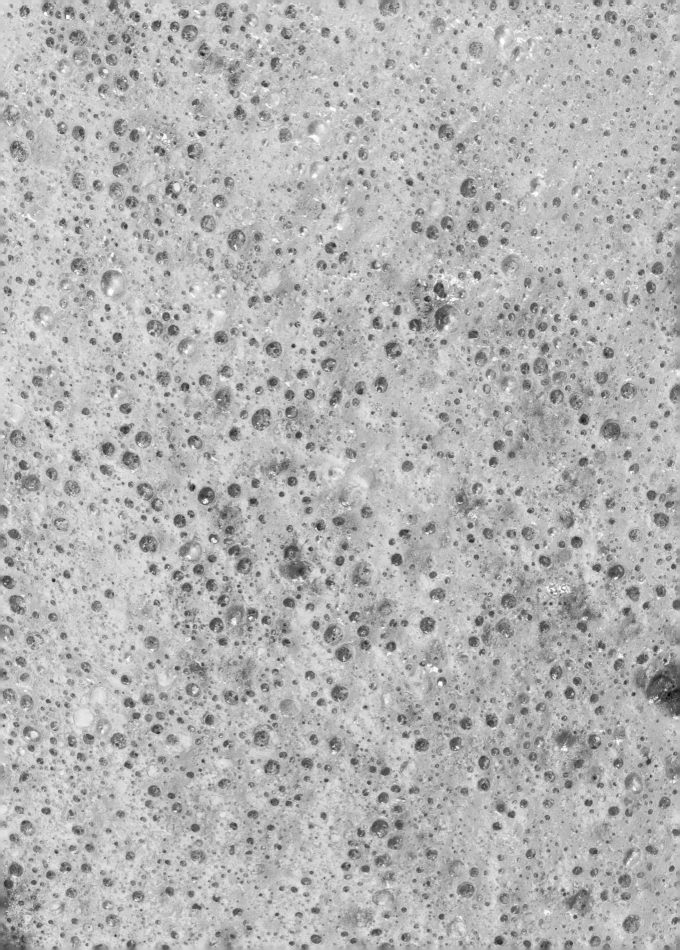

Soli's Floral Persian Dates (with Burnt Almonds & Pistachios)

These are the daintiest treats you've ever seen: each one a beautifully wrapped parcel of sweetness. Popular all over the Middle East, they have been perfected by Claire's Iranian friend Soli.

Makes 25 (enough for about 8 people)
Preparation time: 30 minutes
Cooking time: none
♥ ✓ WF GF V

25 **Persian dates** (Medjool will do, but Persian dates are juicier)
13–14 **almonds**, cut in half lengthwise
60g **mascarpone**
1½ teaspoons **icing sugar**
3 tablespoons **orange blossom water**
25 **whole unsalted pistachios** (nice green ones!)
a handful of **dried rose petals**, to decorate

1. Start with the dates. Using a sharp knife, cut them lengthwise. Remove the stone from each one and gently push the cavity open.

2. Brown the almonds in a heavy-based frying pan until they turn a nice smoky dark brown (but are not quite burnt), then set aside.

3. Spoon the mascarpone into a small bowl. Gradually combine with the icing sugar and orange blossom water, adding a little at a time, and pushing down with the back of the spoon till you have a smooth and fluffy mixture.

4. Using your smallest teaspoon, carefully stuff the cavity in each date with the orange blossom mascarpone.

5. Press half an almond and a whole pistachio into the top of each stuffed date, arrange on a platter and scatter with rose petals. Serve with Persian black cardamom tea. Bah bah! (Persian for: yum yum!).

FRIENDS & FAMILY RECIPES

Soli in Dubai, 1988

Soli Zardosht has an adorable stall at Broadway Market in Hackney, east London, called Black Lime, named for the Persian spice that features heavily in the cooking of that region. She is a wonderful cook and wonderful host.

CLAIRE

JAMS & COMPOTES

SPECIAL FRUIT STANDARD

STRAWBERRY, RASPBERRY, QUINCE, DRIED FRUIT

From our first day at Leon we have made our own jams and compotes, because most commercial ones contain ridiculous amounts of sugar. We blend the compotes into our power smoothies as well as adding them to our yoghurts for breakfast.

Compote is much the same as jam but the fruit tends to be less broken down and, unlike jam, it does not set. Both are great methods for making ripe fruit last a little bit longer. Compote will keep for a couple of weeks in an airtight jar in the fridge; jam should keep for a year at room temperature and then for a couple of months in the fridge once it is opened.

SERVE THE COMPOTES WITH CHEESE, OR WITH YOGHURT FOR A LIGHT EVENING DESSERT; SPOON THEM OVER ICE CREAM; MIX A LITTLE INTO FRUIT SALAD; OR USE THEM JUST LIKE JAM – ON TOAST.

Fresh Strawberry Jam

Fresh jams like this one are so easy to make and taste wonderful. They are a very good way to use up over-ripe fruit.

Makes: 550ml
Preparation time: 3 hours
Cooking time: 10 minutes
❤ ✓ WF GF DF V

500g **strawberries**, hulled and quartered
120ml **agave nectar**

1. Soak the strawberries in the agave syrup for about 3 hours.

2. Place in a small non-reactive saucepan and bring to the boil. Boil for 7 minutes and then pour into a container. Allow to cool completely, then store in the fridge.

Fresh Raspberry Jam

This jam takes a mere 10 minutes to cook, but the fruit and sugar must macerate overnight to get the right consistency.

Makes: about 1 litre
Preparation time: 5 minutes
+ overnight macerating
Cooking time: 10 minutes
❤ WF GF DF V

500g **raspberries**
500g **granulated** or **preserving sugar** (no pectin added)
juice of 1 **lemon**

> Irish chef Darina Allen taught me that jam should take only 5–7 minutes to cook on the stove in order that it should taste of the fresh fruit. It was an invaluable lesson and has changed the way I make jams.
> CLAIRE

1. Place the raspberries and sugar in a bowl. Toss and leave to macerate overnight.

2. Place the mixture in a warm pan on the stove and stir gently. Once the fruit comes up to the boil, cook for 5–7 minutes only.

3. Decant into a bowl or a couple of sterilized jars.

4. The jam will set as it cools.

TIPS

✤ Because of the high seed content in raspberries, they have a lot of natural pectin, which allows the jam to set so beautifully. Other fruits can be made to this method but may need added pectin. You can also use preserving sugar, or 'jam sugar', which has added pectin.

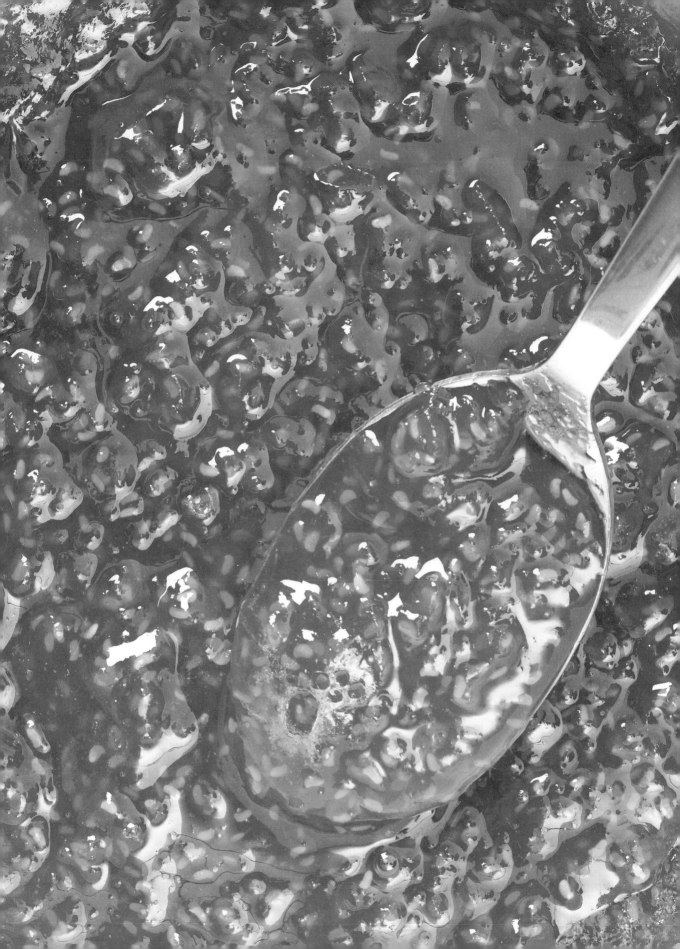

Roasted Quince Compote

Lovely with cheese after dinner, and an awful lot easier than making membrillo (a traditional Spanish quince paste boiled for hours).

Makes: 1 litre
Preparation time: 15 minutes
Cooking time: approx. 1 hour 40 minutes
♥ WF GF DF V

3 **quinces**
1 **bay leaf**
1 large strip of **lemon peel**
½ a **vanilla pod**, split in half lengthwise
250ml **water**
250g **granulated sugar**

1. Heat the oven to 200°C/400°F/gas mark 6.

2. Peel and quarter the quinces (don't worry about coring them until after they have been baked, when they are soft and easier to manage). Arrange them in a roasting tin large enough so that they have a little room.

3. Add the bay leaf, lemon peel and vanilla pod and cover with water and sugar. Cover tightly with foil and bake for 1 hour.

4. Remove the foil, then turn the heat down to 170°C/340°F/gas mark 3½, toss the quinces in the juices and put the tin back in the oven for another 35–40 minutes. The compote is ready when it is a deep pinky-red and the sugar syrup is thick.

5. Remove the cores from the quince when they have cooled and before you serve the compote.

TIPS

✤ Small pieces of the cooked quince can also be added to crisps and crumbles (see pages 128–133), or thinly sliced on a tart.

✤ Make a panna cotta or other creamy pudding and serve with the compote.

✤ Serve on top of a good yoghurt for breakfast.

Dried Fruit Compote

Dried sour cherries and apricots provide a lovely way to spruce up a winter pudding when other fruits are out of season. This compote is spicy, tart and sweet. Use it alongside the Clementine Polenta Cake (page 89), or with a dollop of Greek yoghurt for a simple pudding fit for a king.

Makes: 1 litre
Preparation time: 5 minutes
Cooking time: 10 minutes,
plus 30 minutes resting time
♥ WF GF DF V

200g **caster sugar**

100ml **water**

½ a stick of **cinnamon**

½ a **vanilla pod**, split in half lengthwise, seeds scraped

1 **orange**

200g **dried apricots**, cut into quarters

100g **dried sour cherries**

1. In a medium pan, combine the sugar, water, cinnamon, vanilla pod and seeds and the zest of half the orange. Bring the mixture slowly to the boil, stirring occasionally to dissolve the sugar.

2. Add the quartered apricots and the sour cherries to the boiling syrup. Add the juice of the whole orange. Stir, then remove the pan from the heat. Place a lid or plate over the pan and allow the fruit to steep for half an hour.

TIPS

✤ This compote is also great with porridge at breakfast.

✤ You could make this without the cinnamon and cherries for a vanilla and apricot compote.

✤ Add yellow sultanas and a cardamom pod for variation.

Dried Fruit Compote (above) and
Roasted Quince Compote (below)

A BAKER WE LOVE

MAGGIE LEVINGER

Maggie Levinger and I are from the same small town in Northern California. She comes from a huge family (she has seven brothers and sisters), and I spent a lot of time at her house when I was growing up. One of Maggie's main hobbies was having bake sales in the village (something I also did). At a tender age, Maggie was already famous locally for her blackberry crisps and huckleberry pies.

Years later, after her mother was diagnosed with cancer, Maggie began to look for healthier alternatives to the sweet things that she grew up with. She studied wholegrain nutrition and worked as a chef at revolutionary raw food restaurants in California. She now runs Wild West Ferments in Marin County with her partner Luke – growing food, making sauerkraut, brining vegetables, and perfecting wild fermented fruit sodas.

They both visited London recently and parked their camper van outside our flat for a week. It was perfect timing: I was in the middle of a 'cleanse', and her knowledge of alternative foods, and 'live' and raw food preparation, was a revelation. As they drove around Europe, they were growing sprouts and making wild-fermented fruit sodas right in their vans.

Maggie has been a great help with some of the recipes in this book. She excels at baking and has an extensive knowledge of healthy, whole ingredients.

Maggie either conceived and/or contributed to Hazelnut and Pumpkin Seed Milks (page 56), Chocolate Hazelnut Power Pills (page 71), the Bar of Good Things (page 80), Chocolate Chip Cookies (page 184) and Coconut Kiss Ice Cream (page 170).

CLAIRE

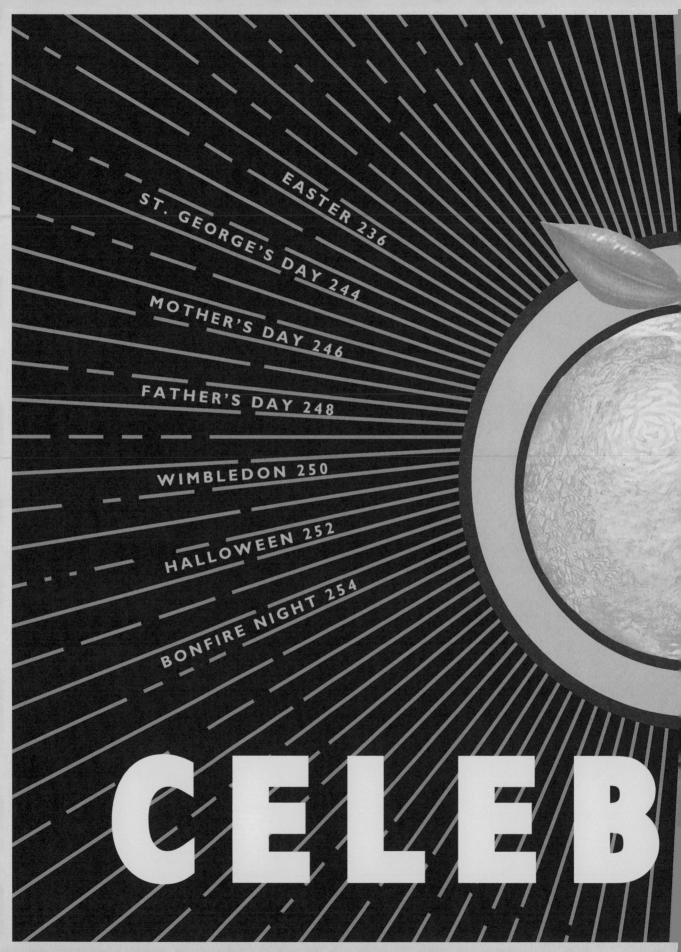

EASTER 236

ST. GEORGE'S DAY 244

MOTHER'S DAY 246

FATHER'S DAY 248

WIMBLEDON 250

HALLOWEEN 252

BONFIRE NIGHT 254

CELEB

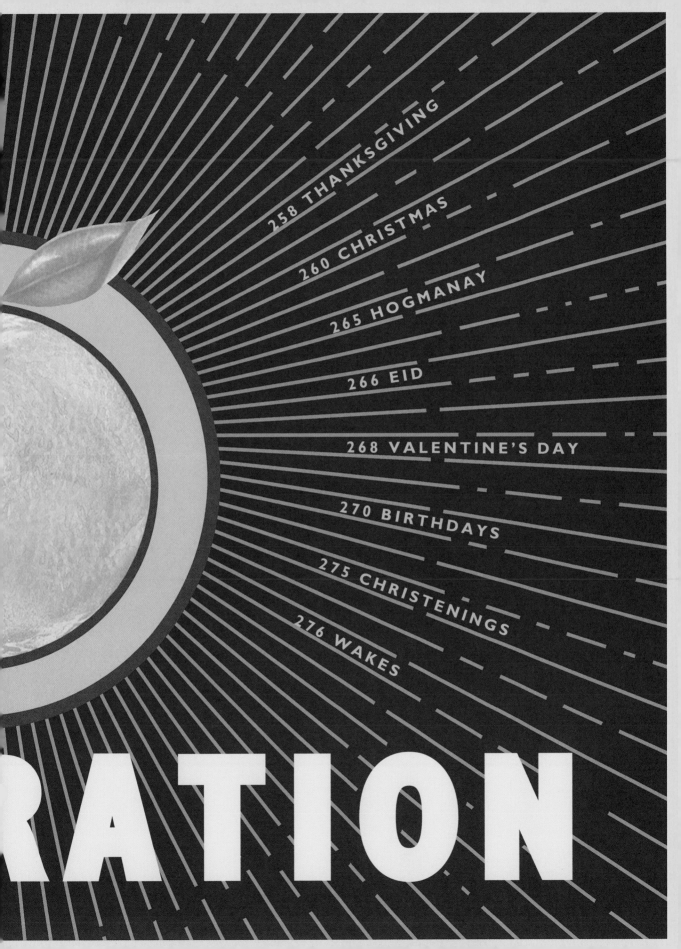

258 THANKSGIVING

260 CHRISTMAS

265 HOGMANAY

266 EID

268 VALENTINE'S DAY

270 BIRTHDAYS

275 CHRISTENINGS

276 WAKES

RATION

Spelt Pancakes

The key is to throw the pancakes as high as you can without getting them stuck to the ceiling.

Makes: approx. 20 pancakes
Preparation time: 1 hour 10 minutes
Cooking time: 3 minutes
♥ ✓ V

100g **white spelt flour**
a pinch of **salt**
1 **free-range egg**
200ml **whole milk**
50ml **ale** or **lager**
butter, for the pan
lemon juice and **caster sugar**, to serve

1. Measure the flour into a large bowl and add the salt.

2. Whisk in the egg from the centre, moving outwards in a clockwise motion.

3. Add the milk and whisk to a smooth batter.

4. Strain the batter into a measuring jug and stir in the beer. Chill the pancake batter for at least an hour.

5. Heat a non-stick frying pan or iron crêpe pan until hot, then add a little butter. Stir the batter a little before pouring a small amount into the pan. Swirl the batter quickly around the pan to coat in a thin, even layer.

6. Cook for a minute or so, until it starts to bubble, then slide a thin spatula beneath the pancake to loosen it and flip it over. Flip 'em high – that is the fun bit. Cook for another minute or so before piling the pancakes up on a plate to cool.

7. To serve, squeeze lemon juice over the pancakes, sprinkle with sugar, then fold into triangles or roll into scrolls.

 (TIPS)

❖ Allowing the batter to rest makes all the difference. Don't be tempted to skip that step.

❖ You can use agave nectar instead of caster sugar. You can also substitute white flour for the spelt flour if you want to. And of course you can use water instead of beer.

Simnel Cake

This is another cake from the wonderful Petra (see page 274). Simnel cake is a British Easter tradition. It is widely accepted that the balls of marzipan on top are meant to represent the disciples, but there is some debate as to how many there should be: eleven if you exclude the traitor Judas, twelve if you count him in, or thirteen to include Jesus. Petra's home-made marzipan is so good that we recommend thirteen: every time you leave the room you will return to find that another ball has mysteriously vanished.

Serves: 10–12
Preparation time: 1 hour
Cooking time: 3½ hours

For the marzipan
450g **icing sugar**
450g **ground almonds**
2 **free-range eggs**
1 teaspoon **lemon juice**
1 teaspoon **almond extract**

For the cake
225g **plain flour**
½ teaspoon **salt**
¼ teaspoon freshly grated **nutmeg**
½ teaspoon **ground cinnamon**
¼ teaspoon **allspice**
175g **unsalted butter**
175g **demerara sugar**
2 tablespoons **dark treacle** or **molasses**
3 **free-range eggs**
450g **currants**
300g **sultanas**
120g good-quality **candied peel**
zest and juice of 1 **lemon**
50g **ground almonds**
150ml **whole milk**
a little **apricot jam**
1 **free-range egg**, slightly beaten (for an egg wash)

1. First make the marzipan. Sift the icing sugar into a bowl, then add the ground almonds, eggs, lemon juice and almond extract to taste. Add the extract slowly, and keep tasting as some brands are stronger than others. Form into a ball and knead lightly. Divide into 3 pieces and wrap each one tightly in clingfilm until ready to use.

2. Heat the oven to 150°C/300°F/gas mark 2. Butter and line a deep 20cm cake tin with baking paper.

3. Sift the flour, salt and spices together and set aside.

4. In another bowl cream the butter, sugar and black treacle or molasses until very light and fluffy. Add the eggs one at a time, sprinkling in a little of the sifted flour and beating well after each addition. Stir in the remaining flour, then the fruit, peel, zest, juice and ground almonds. Add the milk and mix until all the ingredients are well combined.

5. Roll out one of the pieces of marzipan into a 20cm disc. Turn half the cake mixture into the tin, level it out and cover it with this circle of marzipan. Then cover with the rest of the cake mixture and smooth the top.

6. Bake in the oven for about 3½ hours, or until a skewer inserted comes out clean. The top of the cake should be dull, not shiny.

7. When the cake is completely cooled, brush the top with a little warmed jam, sieved if necessary. Roll out another ball of marzipan and place it on top of the cake, pressing it down well. Score the top in a cross-hatch pattern. Brush with egg wash.

8. Turn the grill or oven to high. Divide the remaining ball of marzipan into 11 balls (representing the 12 apostles less Judas) and arrange them round the edge of the cake. Brush each ball with the egg wash and put the cake into the oven or under the grill for a few minutes to give it that attractive, toasted appearance.

TIPS

❖ Petra says the bore of Simnel cake is twiggy currants. She always picks them over to remove the little twigs.

❖ If your oven runs hot, wrap a second layer of paper around the perimeter of the cake tin to keep it from getting too dark.

❖ If you are serving the cake to the infirm, try to find pasteurized eggs – or eggs from flocks you trust (the ones with Lion marks are good)– for making the marzipan.

Spelt Hot Cross Buns

Wholesome and delicious. These buns are a little less sweet than most hot cross buns but just as festive. Toast them and slather with butter – or coconut oil if you don't do dairy. You can make the dough the day before, pop them into the fridge overnight, and bake them fresh in the morning on Easter Day.

Makes: 12
Preparation time: 50 minutes +
3½–3¾ hours rising time
Cooking time: 15 minutes
♥ ✓ DF V

2 x 7g sachets of **dried quick yeast**
200ml **rice milk**, warmed slightly, plus extra to
    brush the tops
200ml **agave nectar**
250g **strong wholemeal spelt flour**
250g **plain spelt flour**
1 teaspoon **salt**
½ teaspoon **ground allspice**
½ teaspoon freshly grated **nutmeg**
1 teaspoon **ground cinnamon**
75g **currants**
75g **sultanas**
zest of 1 **orange**
1 **free-range egg** or **egg substitute**
50g **coconut oil**, melted

For the crosses:
70g **strong spelt flour**
1 tablespoon **water**

For the bun wash:
75ml **water**
100ml **agave nectar**

One a penny,
two a penny...

1. Preheat the oven to 220°C/425°F/gas mark 7 and line 2 baking trays with baking paper.

2. Dissolve the yeast in the warm rice milk with the agave nectar and set aside.

3. In a separate bowl, combine the flours, salt, spices, currants and sultanas and orange zest.

4. Add the egg or egg substitute and the coconut oil to the milk mixture, then pour all of this over the dry ingredients. Stir the dough to combine and then allow it to rest for about 20 minutes.

5. Turn the dough out on to a floured surface and knead it for 10–12 minutes, until it becomes silky. Put it back into the bowl and cover with a clean cloth. Leave in a warm place until the dough has nearly doubled in bulk. This should take about 3 hours.

6. Divide the dough into 12 pieces. Form each piece into a ball and place on the prepared baking sheets, about 2cm apart. Allow the buns to rise on trays for about 30–45 minutes, while you prepare the crosses.

7. When the buns have risen, brush them with a little rice milk. Put the 70g of flour for the crosses into a small bowl and add about 1 tablespoon of water to make a paste. Use a piping bag with a small round nozzle (or make one out of paper), to pipe the paste in crosses over each bun. Bake in the oven for about 15 minutes, or until golden brown.

8. While the rolls are baking, make the 'bun wash' by heating the water and agave nectar in a small pan.

9. As soon as the buns come out of the oven, brush them with the bun wash. Serve warm or toasted, with your favourite spreads.

EASTER EGGS

Mastering the art of tempering chocolate (see page 44) opens up a whole new world of Easter activities.

If you have the time and the resources, it is an easy next step to invest in a few moulds and colourings and spend a day making your own Easter eggs. You can paint patterns or pictures on to the moulds before filling them with chocolate. Children, especially, love designing their own eggs.

WARNING: IT CAN GET VERY MESSY.

Eccles Cakes

These Lancashire currant cakes are a quintessentially English treat. But only eat one: they are so rich that they were banned by the Puritans lest they agitate ungodly humours.

Makes: 12
Preparation time: 15 minutes +
1 hour chilling
Cooking time: 25 minutes

V

125g **unsalted butter**

320g **dark brown sugar**

450g **currants**

2 teaspoons **ground cinnamon**

½ teaspoon **nutmeg**, freshly grated

zest of 1 **orange**

1 x 375g packet of **puff pastry**

1 **free-range egg** or **egg yolk**, for glazing

1 tablespoon **single cream**

1. Melt the butter with the sugar, currants, cinnamon, nutmeg and orange zest.

2. Chill for at least 1 hour, then divide the mixture into 12 balls.

3. Roll out the pastry and cut into 10 x 10cm squares. Place a ball of filling on each one, then bring the edges together around the ball of filling and pinch to seal so the filling does not escape when cooking.

4. Place, seam side down, on a lined baking sheet and chill for 10 minutes. Heat the oven to 180°C/350°F/gas mark 4.

5. In a small bowl, mix the egg or egg yolk and cream together with a fork, to make an egg wash. Brush the cakes with the egg wash, then use scissors to snip 3 small holes in the top of each pastry. Bake in the oven for about 20–25 minutes until golden and risen. Transfer to a wire rack to cool.

TIPS

❖ These are amazing served with a crumbly, mild Lancashire cheese. Hence the saying taught to us by Fred (below): 'An Eccles cake without the cheese is like a kiss without the squeeze.'

❖ Try adding a drop of rum to the currant mixture – a trick apparently used to help preserve them when the Lancastrians exported them in the early nineteenth century.

FRED LOSES HIS FIRST TOOTH, 1975

It isn't just the English who celebrate St George's day. He also happens to be the patron saint of Malta, Ethiopia, Georgia and Catalonia. But don't let that stop you enjoying a quiet moment of national pride, and a cake.

A coffee cake without the cheese is like a kiss without the squeeze!

Bill Granger's Scrambled Eggs on Spelt Toast

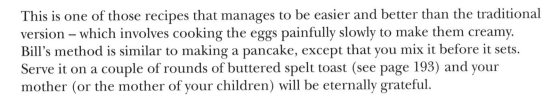

This is one of those recipes that manages to be easier and better than the traditional version – which involves cooking the eggs painfully slowly to make them creamy. Bill's method is similar to making a pancake, except that you mix it before it sets. Serve it on a couple of rounds of buttered spelt toast (see page 193) and your mother (or the mother of your children) will be eternally grateful.

Serves: 1 deserving woman on
Mothers' Day (generously)
Preparation time: 2 minutes
Cooking time: 5 minutes
✓ WF GF

2 really good **free-range eggs**
80ml **double cream**
1 pinch of **salt**
10g **unsalted butter**

1. Place the eggs, cream and salt in a bowl and whisk together.

2. Melt the butter in a non-stick frying pan over a high heat, taking care not to burn it.

3. Pour in the egg mixture and cook for 20 seconds, or until gently set around the edges.

4. Stir the eggs with a wooden spoon, gently bringing the egg mixture on the outside of the pan to the centre.

5. The idea is to fold the eggs rather than scramble them.

6. Leave to cook for 20 seconds longer and repeat the folding process.

7. When the eggs are just set (remembering that they will continue cooking as they rest), turn out on to a plate and serve with hot toast.

TIPS

❖ If you are making more than 2 servings of scrambled eggs, make sure you cook separate batches so as not to crowd the frying pan.

❖ Bill uses milk instead of cream when he cooks them day to day. But that seems a shame.

Bill Granger is a devilishly handsome Australian chef with a smile that would power Cardiff. I was lucky enough to do a food demonstration with him at the Abergavenny food festival, where he taught me how to make these eggs. He discovered this method by chance while trying to make scrambled eggs too fast in his restaurant in Sydney – another great culinary accident.

HENRY

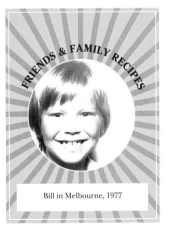

FRIENDS & FAMILY RECIPES

Bill in Melbourne, 1977

Glenys's Desperate Dan Steak Pie

FATHER'S DAY

Henry's next-door neighbour, Glenys, serves this simple old-fashioned pie to Andy (her man) when she wants to treat him right. Horns optional.

Serves: 6
Preparation time: 20 minutes +
cooling time
Cooking time: 2¾ hours

olive oil or vegetable oil

1.3kg **beef steak**, diced

6 **onions**, chopped

8 **bay leaves**

900ml **Newcastle Brown Ale**, or a **similar sweet ale**

sea salt and **freshly ground black pepper**

1 x 375g packet of **ready-rolled puff pastry**
    (or **flaky pastry** from page 38)

1 **free-range egg**, beaten, for glazing

1. Heat the oven to 160°C/325°F/gas mark 3.

2. Heat a dash of oil in a large casserole. Add the beef, brown on all sides and set aside – you might need to do this in batches.

3. Add a dash more oil to the casserole, add the onions and cook until golden.

4. Add the bay leaves and return the meat to the casserole.

5. Add the ale and season well with salt and pepper.

6. Cook in the oven for 2 hours, stirring every 45 minutes or so and checking that it hasn't dried out. You can add more ale if need be.

7. When the meat is tender, take out of the oven, allow to cool and taste for seasoning.

8. When you are ready to assemble the pie, heat the oven to 160°C/325°F/ gas mark 3. Transfer the cooled meat mixture to a pie dish and top with the rolled puff pastry. Press the pastry around the rim to seal. If you are feeling creative, try making a cow's head from the leftover bits of pastry, or some horns. The children can help.

9. Glaze the top of the pastry with the beaten egg, using a pastry brush.

10. Bake for 40 minutes, or until the pastry is golden and you can see the juices bubbling up.

TIPS

✤ You can make the beef and ale filling well in advance of assembling it with the pastry.

✤ Double up on quantities and freeze half. Then you only need to defrost it if you want to make the pie in a hurry.

✤ You can add mushrooms and/or a tin of chopped tomatoes as an alternative.

FRIENDS & FAMILY RECIPES

Glenys in Cynwyd,
North Wales, 1968

DESPERATE DAN PIE

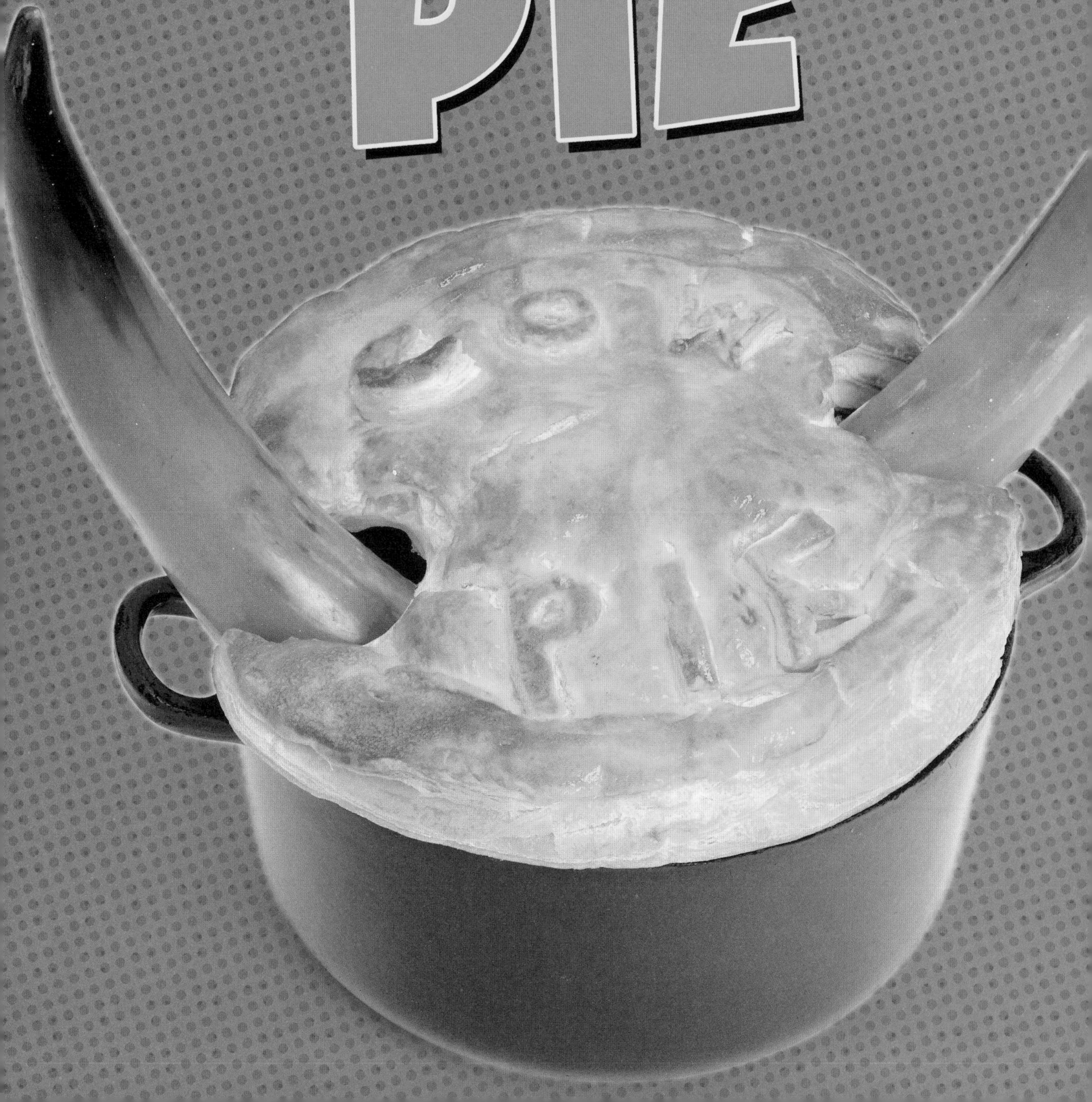

Bruno's Poached Strawberries with Green Peppercorn Ice Cream

People go on about how good strawberries are with pepper – and they are – but without sugar and cream they always seem to be a bit underdressed. This dish, created by chef Bruno Loubet, combines all three. It is sensational. Serve it to friends coming round to watch the Wimbledon final and they will remember it for ever.

Serves: 4
Preparation time: 2 hours
Freezing time: 1–3 hours
WF GF V

For the strawberries:
1 punnet of **strawberries** (about 450g)
250ml **water**
100g **caster sugar**

For the ice cream:
3 **free-range egg yolks**
40g **caster sugar**
125ml **whole milk**
125ml **double cream**
½ **vanilla pod** or 1½ teaspoons **vanilla extract**
2 teaspoons **green peppercorns** in brine, drained and dried
1 teaspoon **golden syrup**

Bruno Loubet was my first boss. At the time he was head chef at the Four Seasons on Hyde Park Corner, the first hotel in the UK to have a Michelin star restaurant. I was a lowly commis chef. Bruno always seemed to stand just the right side of the fine line between pride and arrogance. We were ferociously loyal to him. He is also one of the most creative chefs of his generation. This is just one of his beautiful creations.

HENRY

1. Put 250g of strawberries into a blender or food processor and blend until smooth. Press through a sieve to make a coulis and set aside.

2. Combine the water and sugar in a saucepan and heat, stirring to dissolve the sugar. Bring to the boil and boil for 2 minutes, then pour the syrup into a bowl. Add the remaining strawberries and the strawberry coulis and stir gently to mix.

3. Set a plate on top to be sure the strawberries are completely immersed in the syrup, then leave to cool. When cold, refrigerate.

4. In a large bowl mix together the egg yolks and sugar with a whisk until you obtain a white, creamy consistency.

5. Put the milk, cream and vanilla pod into a heavy-based saucepan (if using vanilla extract, add it at the end). Heat until the milk boils and rises in the pan, then remove from the heat and pour the milk over the egg and sugar mixture, whisking constantly. Return the mixture to the saucepan and cook on moderate heat, stirring constantly with a wooden spoon, until the cream thickens and will coat the back of a wooden spoon. Don't let the cream boil.

FRIENDS & FAMILY RECIPES

Bruno and his dog, 1969

6. Strain quickly through a fine sieve into a cold bowl. If using vanilla extract, add it now. When the custard is cold, cover and refrigerate.

7. Put the chilled custard into a blender and add the green peppercorns and golden syrup. Process until fairly smooth. Alternatively, you can use a hand blender. Pour into an ice cream machine and freeze according to the manufacturer's instructions.

8. With a slotted spoon, remove the strawberries from their syrup to a clean bowl. Strain the syrup through a sieve over the berries.

9. To serve, place scoops of the ice cream into pretty bowls. Divide the strawberries and syrup between the bowls.

 TIPS

❖ This is a good thing to make a day ahead, as the strawberries will benefit from a longer steeping and you will be too excited by the tennis to want to be toiling over the stove.

Halloween Biscuits

Using the recipe for biscuits on page 176, add either half a teaspoon of mixed spice to make some autumnal lightly spiced biscuits or substitute 60g cocoa powder for 60g flour to make them chocolatey.

For each colour icing:
icing sugar
1 tablespoon of **water**
a few drops of **food colouring**, colours of your choice
writing icing tubes, for drawing

1. Make a few coloured icings in different bowls by mixing the icing sugar, water and food colouring together until the icing is thick and smooth (but not too runny).

2. Using the icings as backgrounds and the writing icing tubes for the detail, unleash the creative beast in you.

ANITA (RIGHT) AND BRIDGET, WILLOUGHBY HALL, NOTTINGHAM UNIVERSITY, 1987

MATT (RIGHT) AND NEIL, WALLINGTON, 1981

Anita makes these biscuits with her family every Halloween. She and her husband Matt start off decorating them with the kids, but when they're tucked up in bed, Anita and Matt carry on into the night attempting to make each other laugh with more and more ghoulish and ridiculous efforts. A perfect night of entertainment 'for the kids'.

HENRY

Butterscotch Apples

This is a softer, gooier kind of toffee apple – a little easier on the teeth.

Makes: 6
Preparation time: 5 minutes
Cooking time: 10 minutes +
15 minutes cooling time
WF GF V

6 medium **apples**
90g **unsalted butter**
150g **caster sugar**
2 tablespoons **light brown sugar**
120ml **double cream**
100ml **golden syrup**
a pinch of **salt**
you will also need **wooden dowels**, 1cm thick

1. Wash and dry your apples and push a dowel into the stem (top) end of each one. Line a baking sheet with baking paper.

2. Put the butter, caster sugar, brown sugar, cream and golden syrup into a small heavy-bottomed pan over a medium heat, and stir to dissolve everything together into an emulsified mass.

3. Once the mixture has dissolved, bring it to the boil and cook until it reaches a light golden colour.

4. Remove the toffee from the heat, quickly stir in the salt, then stop the cooking process by plunging the bottom of the pan into a sink full of ice-cold water and place the pan on a trivet to cool. Let the toffee cool for 15 minutes (this helps to stop it sliding down the sides).

5. Dip the apples into the toffee, holding them by their sticks. Place the dipped apples on the prepared baking sheet and allow them to cool and set.

TIPS

✤ If the toffee starts to slip off of the apples, let them cool slightly and dip them again.

Mulled Wine

Spicy and sweet, but with clear flavours that aren't muddy.

Makes: 1.5 litres
Preparation time: 5 minutes
Cooking time: 10 minutes
❤ WF GF DF V

2 bottles of **dry red wine**
200g **caster sugar**
1 stick of **cinnamon**
2 **cloves**
1 **star anise**
1 piece of **lemon peel**
1 piece of **orange peel**, plus extra to serve

1. Pour the wine into a large saucepan. Add the sugar and spices. Heat wine over a medium heat. Do not let it boil but heat it through so that it is steaming and the spices have a chance to infuse. Add the lemon and orange peels, using a vegetable peeler to get nice wide pieces.

2. Simmer the wine for about 10 minutes, stirring occasionally, making sure the sugar has dissolved.

3. Serve with a twist of orange.

TIPS

❖ If you are out of oranges but have clementines, use them.

❖ This is even better with a generous glug of brandy.

❖ This mulled wine is not too sweet (how we like it), but you can add more sugar if you prefer it sweeter.

I came up with this recipe at Henry and Mima's house, when they were hosting a neighbourhood Christmas party. They have a wonderful collection of whole spices in their kitchen, so it was a cinch. The last of the neighbours staggered out at 2 a.m., pretty well spiced themselves.

CLAIRE

Pumpkin Pie

A warm, deeply spicy version of this Thanksgiving classic.

Serves: 8–10
Preparation time: 25 minutes
Cooking time: 35 minutes
♥ V

450g fresh **pumpkin purée** (bought, or see tips)
3 **free-range eggs**
100ml **double cream**
150g **light brown sugar**
1 teaspoon **ground cinnamon**
½ teaspoon **ground ginger**
½ teaspoon **ground star anise**
½ teaspoon **ground allspice**
1 teaspoon **sea salt**
3 tablespoons **maple syrup**
finely grated **fresh ginger** (optional)
black pepper (optional
1 x quantity **Shortcrust Pastry** (see page 38) or
    250g ready-made sweet shortcrust pastry

1. Heat the oven to 180°C/350°F/gas mark 4.

2. Whisk all the ingredients together, except the fresh ginger, in a large bowl. The pie will be silkier if the pumpkin is as smooth as possible, so pour the filling through a fine strainer (even if you have pushed your purée through one initially).

3. Taste the filling. At this point, you can add a little finely grated fresh ginger, along with a good grinding of black pepper to taste.

4. Roll out the pastry as thinly as possible and press into a 23cm fluted flan tin with a loose base, then trim the edges. Pour the filling into the pastry case and bake in the oven for about 35 minutes, or until the custardy filling is just set while retaining a slight wobble.

5. Cool and serve with lots of Chantilly cream (double cream sweetened with caster sugar and a dash of vanilla extract).

(TIPS)

❖ To make your own purée, cut a small cooking pumpkin in half and bake it in a hot oven, cut side down. When it is soft, scrape out the centre and purée.

❖ If the pumpkins are not as sweet as you'd like, some freshly puréed butternut squash will help. If you don't happen to have that, a little extra sugar will do.

Thanksgiving is sacred to Americans because it is a holiday free from the pressures of gift giving, and is all about breaking bread with family and friends and often strangers. This recipe was published on the *Guardian*'s Allotment Blog after I made it for a Thanksgiving dinner celebrated with several other Americans living in the UK.

CLAIRE

Kamal's Meghli

This sweet, scented Lebanese rice pudding is traditionally served at Christmas or to celebrate the birth of a child. We were taught it by our friend Kamal Mouzawak, a celebrated Lebanese cook.

Serves 8
Preparation time: soaking the nuts overnight
Cooking time: 30 minutes
♥ WF GF DF V

50g **whole almonds**, skins on
50g **pistachios**
1.8 litres **water**
150g **rice flour**
300g **sugar**
1 tablespoon **caraway seeds**
1½ teaspoons **ground cinnamon**
1½ teaspoons **ground aniseed**

Kamal at home in Jeita,
Christmas Day, 1975

1. Soak the almonds and the pistachios in water, in separate bowls, overnight. Peel and halve them the next day.

2. Boil 1.6 litres of water in a medium saucepan. Put the rice flour, sugar and spices into a bowl and add the remaining water. Mix well, then add to the boiling water, stirring constantly.

3. Reduce the heat, stir well and then bring to the boil again. Allow the mixture to cook until it thickens. Stir constantly with a wooden spoon so the rice doesn't stick to the bottom of the pan – this will take about 20 minutes.

4. Pour into individual serving bowls and leave to cool. Before serving garnish each bowl with almonds and pistachios.

The centrepieces of my grandparents' Christmases were meghli – to eat – and the Adonis Gardens – for decoration. Meghli is traditionally served to celebrate the birth of a new baby, and prepared by the two grandmas (one more thing for them to compete over). In the mountain regions, it has also become a Christmas treat, in honour of Jesus's birth. It is said that the brown pudding symbolizes a fertile, rich soil, and the nuts on the top are seeds that will sprout and grow.

The Adonis Gardens (see picture opposite) is a traditional homemade nativity scene, decorated with sprouting seeds. On Berbera (our equivalent of Hallowe'en, on 5 December), we would put together the tableau showing the infant Christ in a cave, add layers of wet cotton-wool and plant them with seeds (wheat, lentils, chickpeas). By Christmas, the seeds would have sprouted into tiny fields of green. As the name suggests, it is one of those Christmas traditions that actually has pagan roots: it was originally done by Athenean women to celebrate the life cycle of the god Adonis, who was said to come from Phoenicia (now Lebanon).

KAMAL

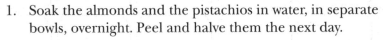

Jossy's Orange Mince Pies

My mum, Josceline Dimbleby, wrote the first supermarket cookery book about Christmas. It sold hundreds of thousands of copies. Wherever I go I meet people who tell me that they still cook her mince pies and Christmas pudding. They are brilliant recipes. HENRY

Makes: 24
Preparation time: 40 minutes
Cooking time: 20 minutes
V

500g **plain flour** or **spelt flour**
125–175g **icing sugar** or **caster sugar**
375g **unsalted butter**, chilled and diced
finely grated zest and juice of
   1 **large orange**
vegetable oil, for greasing
250g **cream cheese**
50g **caster sugar**
500–625g good-quality **mincemeat**
milk, to glaze
caster or **icing sugar**, to decorate

> I devised these pies years ago, and they have proved to be one of my most popular recipes. The addition of cream cheese is optional, but by mixing it with the spicy mincemeat you can give them a really luxurious texture.
>
> JOSSY

1. Sift the flour and sugar into a mixing bowl, then rub in the butter with your fingers until the mixture resembles breadcrumbs.

2. Stir in the orange zest, then the juice using a knife, until the pastry just begins to stick together. Gather up the pastry and pat it into a ball with lightly floured hands. Wrap it in clingfilm and chill it in the fridge for at least 30 minutes.

3. Preheat the oven to 200°C/400°F/gas mark 6. Grease two 12-hole bun tins.

4. Put the cream cheese and caster sugar into a bowl, and beat together until smooth.

5. Remove the pastry from the fridge. Knead it lightly, then divide it in half and roll out one half rather more thickly than usual. Using an 8cm pastry cutter, cut out 24 rounds, re-rolling the pastry as necessary.

6. Line the muffin tins with the pastry rounds. Fill to half their depth with mincemeat, then put a teaspoon of the cream cheese mixture on top and smooth it level.

7. Roll out the remaining pastry, using a 5cm pastry cutter (or star-shaped cutter like we did), and cut another 24 rounds. Moisten the underside of the rounds with milk, water or beaten egg, and place them on top of the filled pies. Press the edges together lightly and make a small slit in the top of each pie.

8. Brush the tops with milk and bake in the oven for 15–20 minutes, until golden.

9. Allow the mince pies to cool slightly before removing them from the tins, then sprinkle with icing or caster sugar. Serve warm or cold.

TIPS

❖ To make the pastry even more crumbly, use two-thirds butter and one-third lard or vegetable fat.

❖ Mincemeat can be hugely improved by adding lemon juice and some finely chopped sharp apple.

Jossy's Favourite Round Christmas Pudding

This is the classic version of Jossy's Christmas pudding. If you want to make it wheat and gluten free, simply substitute the breadcrumbs with cooked basmati rice or gluten-free breadcrumbs.

Serves 8–10
Preparation time: 1 hour
Cooking time: 6 hours
♥ ✓ DF V

350g **pitted prunes**
100g **crystallized ginger**
40g **walnut halves**
225g large **raisins**
grated zest and juice of 2 **oranges**
125g **fresh brown breadcrumbs**
125g **shredded vegetable suet**
¼ teaspoon **ground cloves**
3 large **free-range eggs**
2–3 tablespoons **Cointreau** or **brandy**

1. Generously butter the two halves of a circular mould, 1.7 litre pudding basin or foil-lined rice steamer.

2. Cut the prunes into fairly small pieces and roughly chop the ginger and walnuts. Put the chopped ingredients into a large bowl with the raisins, orange zest, breadcrumbs, suet and ground cloves.

3. In another bowl whisk the eggs until frothy and slightly thickened and stir well into the dry ingredients. Lastly stir in the orange juice and the Cointreau or brandy.

4. Leave for half an hour or more, to allow the ingredients to blend together. If you are using a mould, spoon the mixture into both halves, filling them completely and spreading level. Close the halves to form the circle and wrap thoroughly with more foil. Put a metal biscuit cutter in the bottom of a large saucepan and stand the mould on top. Pour in enough boiling water to come three-quarters of the way up the side of the mould. Then cover the pan and steam gently for about 6 hours, checking now and then and adding more boiling water if it has evaporated at all.

5. If you are using a pudding basin, fill it to the top and smooth it level. Cover the pudding basin with baking paper and then a layer of foil, and tie string tightly just under the lip of the basin. Trim it well so that the foil and paper do not dangle in the water and place the basin in a saucepan. Fill the pan with water to come halfway up the side of the basin, and simmer as instructed above, topping up the water levels every now and then.

6. When the pudding is cold, keep it in a cool place until Christmas Day. Then put it into a saucepan as before and steam for another hour or so before serving. Serve on a warmed plate, stick a sprig of holly on top, pour bubbling Cointreau or brandy round the pudding and set it alight as you approach the festive table.

Over the years I have made countless variations of Christmas pudding and we all think this beats them all. With squidgy prunes, walnuts and a tang of fresh orange, it is dark, full of flavour and gooey, yet crumbly and light because it contains no flour or sugar. People have been known to eat three helpings at one sitting, and even children like it: the fruit makes it quite sweet enough. You can now buy metal moulds to make round puddings, but I still use a large Chinese rice steamer that I line with foil. Of course if you haven't got a mould you can always make this pudding in a 1.7 litre pudding basin. You don't have to make this pudding months in advance.

JOSSY

CHRISTMAS

Champagne Cocktail

The perfect way to toast the New Year – in Scotland or elsewhere.

Serves: 1
Preparation time: 2 minutes
Cooking time: none
♥ ✓ WF GF DF V

Also voluntarily tested by
Anita, Georgia, Issy and Apple

Angostura bitters
1 sugar cube
brandy
Champagne

1. Shake a couple of drops of Angostura on to the sugar cube and pop it into the bottom of a Champagne glass.

2. Pour on a little brandy. It is meant to be just a dash, but they say that fortune favours the bold.

3. Top up the glass with Champagne.

(TIPS)

❖ You can use cava or prosecco or any dry sparkling white wine instead of Champagne (we normally do).

❖ If you don't like brandy, you can leave it out. The original recipe doesn't include it.

Turkish Delight

Eid ul-Fitr
(festivity at the end of the fast)
is the three-day Muslim festival
that ends Ramadan.

These quivering little rosewater jellies are very sweet, but with strong tea or coffee at the end of a feast they will perk you right up. They are eaten to celebrate Eid across the Middle East, as well as by the Turkish community in Dalston, where we both live.

Makes: 30 squares
Preparation time: 10 minutes +
cooling time
Cook time: 40 minutes
❤ ✓ WF GF DF V

450g **caster sugar**
900ml **water**
a pinch of **cream of tartar**
100g **cornflour**
200g **icing sugar**
2 teaspoons **rosewater**
  or 1 teaspoon **lemon oil**
pink food colouring
  (optional)
50g **icing sugar**, for dusting
50g **cornflour**, for dusting

1. Grease a 20–23cm square cake tin or similar, and line with baking paper.

2. In a medium pan, dissolve the sugar, 150ml of the water and the cream of tartar (the acidity of the cream of tartar helps to prevent the sugar crystallizing). Stir to dissolve, then bring to the boil. Boil for 5 minutes and then turn off the heat.

3. In a large bowl, combine the cornflour, icing sugar and 50ml of water to make a paste. Boil the remaining 700ml of water and slowly pour it over the cornflour paste, gradually whisking it in. This is an important step, in order to avoid lumps.

4. Transfer the cornflour mixture to a large pan and place over a moderate heat. Simmer the mixture until thickened and nearly translucent.

5. Take the pan off the heat and gradually pour in the sugar syrup, whisking continuously. Turn the heat down slightly and boil for 30 minutes, until yellowish and thick.

6. Add the rosewater or lemon oil and a few drops of pink colouring (if using) and pour into the tin. Leave to cool completely. This could take overnight.

7. In a bowl, sift together the icing sugar and cornflour. Cut the Turkish delight into cubes and toss in the icing sugar/cornflour mixture.

TIPS

❖ Dip the pieces of Turkish delight in chocolate for an extra special treat (see Tempering, page 34).

❖ Be very careful not to burn yourself, as the boiling mixture is very, very hot. Proceed with caution and use common sense, but by all means, do proceed.

❖ Always use a scrupulously clean and dry pan when doing sugar work.

❖ The Turkish delight will absorb the icing sugar, so if you are making these as gifts, be lavish when dusting on the icing sugar and cornflour mixture, and put extra in the box.

Crème Brûlée

Henry maintains that you can gauge the quality of any restaurant by one mouthful of its crème brûlée. Yet it's not particularly hard to make well, and is terrifically impressive when you do. This – together with its swoonsome creaminess – makes it a perfect Valentine's Day pudding. We recommend the addition of heart-shaped ramekins and Karma Sutra doilies.

Serves: 4
(you can save two for the next day)
Preparation time: 20 minutes
Cooking time: 30 minutes
WF GF V

590ml **double cream**

1 **vanilla pod**

6 free-range **egg yolks**

50g **caster sugar**, plus 4 tablespoons

1. Heat the oven to 150°C/300°F/gas mark 2. Have ready 4 heart-shaped or standard small ramekins.

2. Pour the cream into a pan. Cut the vanilla pod in half lengthwise and scrape the seeds into the cream, also adding the empty pod.

3. Heat to just below boiling point, then remove from the heat and allow the vanilla to infuse for 10 minutes before discarding the empty pod.

4. Meanwhile, whisk the egg yolks together with 50g of sugar until the mixture is pale and thick. Add the infused cream. Stir well before pouring into the 4 ramekins.

5. Place the ramekins in a deep roasting tin. Fill the tin with water to come about halfway up the sides of the ramekins, then cover the tin tightly with foil and bake in the oven for 20 minutes, or until the custard is set but still wobbly. Remove from the oven and allow the custards to cool without the foil covering.

6. To make the brûléed top, sprinkle a tablespoon of sugar over each pudding (do them one at a time) and, using a blowtorch or a very hot grill, heat the sugar until burnt. Let the burnt sugar shell set for 5 minutes before serving.

TIPS

✤ We are opposed to the fashionable habit of adding berries to crème brûlée. It interferes with the pure creaminess of the dish. However, if you must make variations, there are a few interesting flavours that work well:
 • Indian: steep 4 crushed cardamom pods in the custard instead of vanilla.
 • Boozy: add a tot of rum or brandy to the custard.
 • Orange: steep a couple of teaspoons of orange zest in the cream, with, or without, the vanilla pod.
 • Thanksgiving: add a little pumpkin purée and nutmeg. It works. Not on Valentine's Day, please.

✤ These can all be done up until step 6 in advance to save you time. The custard can be made the day before and chilled overnight. You can bake the custard in the morning, then pull the ramekins out of the fridge at the end of supper, brûlée them and send them straight to the table.

VALENTINE'S DAY

Leon's 5th Birthday Cake

This cake looks crazy – like a gigantic, delicious powderpuff, or a Bounty bar turned inside out. It tastes amazing too. The coconut filling has the texture and flavour of very, very fresh coconut flesh.

Serves: 12–15
Preparation time: 40 minutes
Cooking time: 50 minutes

V

For the sponge
125g **unsalted butter**, very soft
200g **caster sugar**
3 free-range **eggs**
½ teaspoon **salt**
300g **self-raising flour**
175ml **coconut milk**

For the syrup
150ml **coconut milk**
100g **sugar**
½ teaspoon **vanilla extract**
a pinch of **salt**

For the filling
100ml **coconut milk**
50g **caster sugar**
40ml **water**
1 tablespoon **cornflour**, mixed with 2 tablespoons **water**
a pinch of **salt**

To decorate
300ml **whipped cream**
100g **coconut shavings**

1. Heat the oven to 160°C/325°F/gas mark 3, with the fan on. Butter a 23cm cake tin and line with baking paper.

2. Cream the butter and sugar until almost white and fluffy. Add the eggs and salt and mix until fully incorporated.

3. Add half the flour until just combined. Add the coconut milk and mix until combined. Then add the remaining flour and mix well.

4. Pour the mixture into the cake tin and smooth the top. Bake in the oven for 40–50 minutes, until a skewer inserted comes out clean and the cake springs back to the touch. Let the cake cool completely in the tin.

5. To make the filling, put the coconut milk, sugar and water into a heavy pan and place over a moderate heat. Stir to dissolve the sugar and then turn up the heat to high. Add the cornflour mixture to the pan with the salt and whisk until thick. Pour the mixture into a bowl and press clingfilm over the surface. Let it cool, then chill in the fridge for at least 2 hours.

6. To make the syrup, heat all the syrup ingredients together in a small saucepan and cook over a medium heat for 5 minutes.

7. Split the cooled cake into 3 layers. Drizzle with the syrup, and sandwich with the coconut filling. Cover the top and sides of the cake with whipped cream and sprinkle with generous amounts of coconut shavings.

BIRTHDAYS

This is a cake that we make at Violet every week. People go wild for the coconut filling, which is adapted from an old Hawaiian pudding recipe. When Henry asked me to create a cake for Leon's 5th birthday this was the first cake I thought of. It just has this outrageous look to it that screams celebration. Plus it was big enough to feed 350. (If you are tempted to make the Leon version from the photo above, simply multiply the quantities by 30. You will need wooden pegs to support the sheer weight of cake on the top.)

CLAIRE

Triple Chocolate Fantasy Cake

Honeycomb, chocolate and a hint of tangy apricot make this a dreamy birthday treat.

Serves: 12–15
Preparation time: 25 minutes
Cooking time: 1 hour

V

Claire developed this recipe for Leon as an extravagant indulgence to add to our cake line-up. During the recipe development we had a meeting with a landlord about a potential site that we wanted dearly. Claire baked a cake for us to take to the meeting (as a bribe). It worked, and in Leon we now talk about our ABC for successful meetings – Always Bring Cake.

HENRY

For the sponge
200g **vegetable oil**
400g **light brown sugar**
1½ teaspoons **vanilla extract**
3 free-range **eggs**
125ml **natural yoghurt**
80g **cocoa powder**
100ml **boiling water**
280g **plain flour**
1½ teaspoons **bicarbonate of soda**
½ teaspoon **salt**

For the icing
200g **unsalted butter**, softened
200g **icing sugar**
4–5 tablespoons boiling **water**
1 teaspoon **vanilla extract**
100g **cocoa powder**

To finish
4 tablespoons **apricot jam**
2 **Crunchie bars**, crumbled
edible glitter

1. Preheat the oven to 160°C/325°F/gas mark 3. Grease two 23cm cake tins and line them with baking paper.

2. Whisk together the oil, sugar and vanilla. Add the eggs one at a time, mixing well after each addition.

3. Add the yoghurt and mix well.

4. In a small bowl, whisk together the cocoa powder and boiling water until smooth

5. Scrape the cocoa paste into the egg mixture and combine into a smooth batter.

6. Sift together the flour, bicarbonate of soda and salt, and beat into the cake mixture just until incorporated.

7. Pour equal amounts into the cake tins and bake in the oven for 55–60 minutes or until a skewer inserted in the centre comes out clean. Leave to cool in the tins.

8. Now to make the icing. Beat the butter until fluffy, then gradually beat in the icing sugar. Add the boiling water and vanilla extract and beat for 3 minutes.

9. Add the cocoa powder and beat until fluffy.

10. To assemble, split the cakes into 2 layers. Place the bottom layer on a serving plate and spread it with some of the apricot jam. Cover with a tablespoon of chocolate icing and follow with another layer of sponge. Repeat with the remaining layers, then ice the top and sides with the remaining icing. Decorate with crumbled Crunchie bars and edible glitter.

TIPS

- For extra decadence, add additional crumbled Crunchie bars between the layers.

- Use the chocolate icing right away for the best results. It will firm up as it sits, making it more difficult to work with.

- Edible glitter can be found online and in many speciality cake decorating shops.

A BAKER WE LOVE

PETRA LEWIS

They say that, before you marry a woman, you should pay close attention to her mother – since that's how she's likely to turn out. I married Mima in the hope that she might, one day, pull something out of the oven to match one of Petra's cakes.

Petra Lewis is one of those unsung 'amateur' cooks who knocks most professionals into a cocked hat. She can make anything, but her particular gift is for the old-fashioned cake or pudding. Her kitchen is always full of nostalgic men of a certain age (her husband among them, it should be said), drooling in anticipation of a gently wobbling junket, a vast suet pudding oozing golden lava, or a tower of warm drop-scones ready to be slathered in golden syrup.

All twinkly eyes and silvery hair – like Mrs Pepperpot but not so shrunken – Petra has the perfect character for cake-making. As well as being generous to the point of lunacy, she has a patient, meticulous brain. She actually seems to enjoy sitting at her kitchen table for hours pulling the tiny stalks off a kilo of currants. Some might call it madness; I call it genius.

HENRY

Petra's Christening Cake

Petra makes a christening cake by icing her Fruit Cake (see page 90) with Royal Icing (see page 179). She is a great cake baker, but a nervous icer. Instead of aiming for smooth perfection, she ices this cake pretty roughly and then covers it with ribbons and a menagerie of little creatures bought from haberdashery shops. The more – and the madder – the merrier.

We always wanted to include a section on wakes because they really can be a celebration of life, and because cooking is one of the ways people instinctively show their love and support in difficult times. On the other hand, we were worried that it might seem a bit gloomy. Then, just as we were about to take these recipes out of the book, someone wrote to Claire asking her what to cook for a wake – so we felt we had to put them back in. Here is how we would like to be remembered – over an Irish coffee and some Guinness cake.

Irish Coffee

Smooth and creamy, a proper Irish coffee is deeply warming and sinfully delicious.

Serves: 4
Preparation time: 15 minutes
Cooking time: none
WF GF V

freshly brewed hot **coffee** (enough for 4)
4 teaspoons **brown sugar**
8 tablespoons **Irish whiskey**
225ml **double cream**, very lightly whipped
4 **Irish coffee glass mugs**

1. Make a fresh pot of coffee.

2. Place a teaspoon of brown sugar in the bottom of each Irish coffee mug and then pour in the hot coffee, leaving about 2–3cm room at the top of the mug. Stir gently.

3. Add 2 tablespoons of Irish whiskey to each mug.

4. Pour the barely whipped cream over the back of a spoon and into the mug.

TIPS

✤ The sugar and alcohol both help to float the cream on top, creating the look of a pint of Guinness, so do not omit them.

✤ The idea is that you sip the Irish coffee slowly through the cream, so it is important that the cream is not too stiff.

Guinness Malt Cake

A very moist and rich cake that marries the flavours of a good stout with malt and dark molasses. The dash of cocoa powder adds to the lovely colour. This cake will keep well for up to a week.

Serves: 8
Preparation time: 15 minutes
Cooking time: approx. 1 hour 30 minutes

V

250ml **Guinness** or other **stout beer**
250g **unsalted butter**
1 tablespoon **molasses** or **black treacle**
200g **dark brown sugar** or **molasses sugar**
70g **cocoa powder**
2 tablespoons **powdered malt** (such as Horlicks or Ovaltine)
2 **free-range eggs**
150g **natural yoghurt**
280g **plain flour**
2 teaspoons **bicarbonate of soda**
200g **caster sugar**
a pinch of **sea salt**

For the stout and cream cheese frosting
100ml **Guinness** or other **stout beer**
60g **unsalted butter**, softened
120g **cream cheese**, softened
½ teaspoon **vanilla extract**
300g **icing sugar**, sifted

1. Preheat the oven to 160°C/325°F/gas mark 3. Butter a 900g/2lb loaf tin and line it with baking paper.

2. Place the Guinness, butter, molasses and brown sugar in a small saucepan and melt over a medium heat.

3. Whisk in the cocoa and malt, then take off the heat.

4. In a large bowl, whisk together the eggs and yoghurt, then add the stout mixture.

5. Sift together the remaining dry ingredients into the bowl and whisk all together to combine. Pour into the prepared tin and bake in the oven for about an hour and 15 minutes, or until a skewer inserted comes out clean. Cool the cake completely in the tin.

6. While the cake is cooling, make the icing: put the Guinness in a small pan and bring to the boil. Boil for about 10–15 minutes, or until the beer has reduced by half its volume. Pour into a container and pop it into the fridge to cool down.

7. In a mixing bowl, beat the soft butter until creamy and light. Add the cream cheese and beat until smooth. Add the vanilla and the sifted icing sugar and beat well. Now add the cooled, reduced Guinness and beat until creamy and light. Turn the cake out of its tin and spread the icing on top.

LEON
LDN.

EXTRA HELPINGS

PICHOT   PARIS   50   DEPOSE

Leon Salted Caramel Banana Split 280

Leon Pie Fest 282

Indexes 294

Bibliography 301

Acknowledgements 302

Leon Salted Caramel Banana Split

We introduced this to the Leon menu after extensive – and very sticky – consultations with the under-tens. Madly theatrical and over-the-top, they have proved a hit with diners of every age.

Serves: 6 (with room to spare)
Preparation time: 10 minutes
Cooking time: 10 minutes
WF GF V

100g organic **flaked almonds**

2 tablespoons organic **icing sugar**

6 Fairtrade **bananas**

500ml organic **double cream**

100g Fairtrade **caster sugar**

sea salt

250ml good quality **strawberry ice cream**

250ml good quality **vanilla ice cream**

25g organic **dark chocolate**

1. Heat the almonds in a non-stick frying pan with the icing sugar until they turn golden and the sugar has caramelized. Put into a bowl and set aside.

2. Slice the bananas in half lengthwise and lay two halves on each plate.

3. Whisk 350ml of the cream until it is thick. Put it into a piping bag (a squirty cream thing from the internet can save time here).

4. Heat the caster sugar in a pan until it has melted and caramelized – not too dark. Add the remaining 150ml of cream and stir well. It will froth right up. Heat through to make sure all the sugar has melted into the cream, stirring occasionally. Add a good pinch of sea salt.

5. Put a scoop of each ice cream on to each split banana.

6. Drizzle the ice cream with the caramel. Pipe on the cream. Sprinkle on the caramelized nuts. Grate over some dark chocolate. Serve.

TIPS

For the truly classic split, top each ball of ice cream with a glacé cherry.

We sometimes use a runny strawberry compote alongside the caramel as a second sauce.

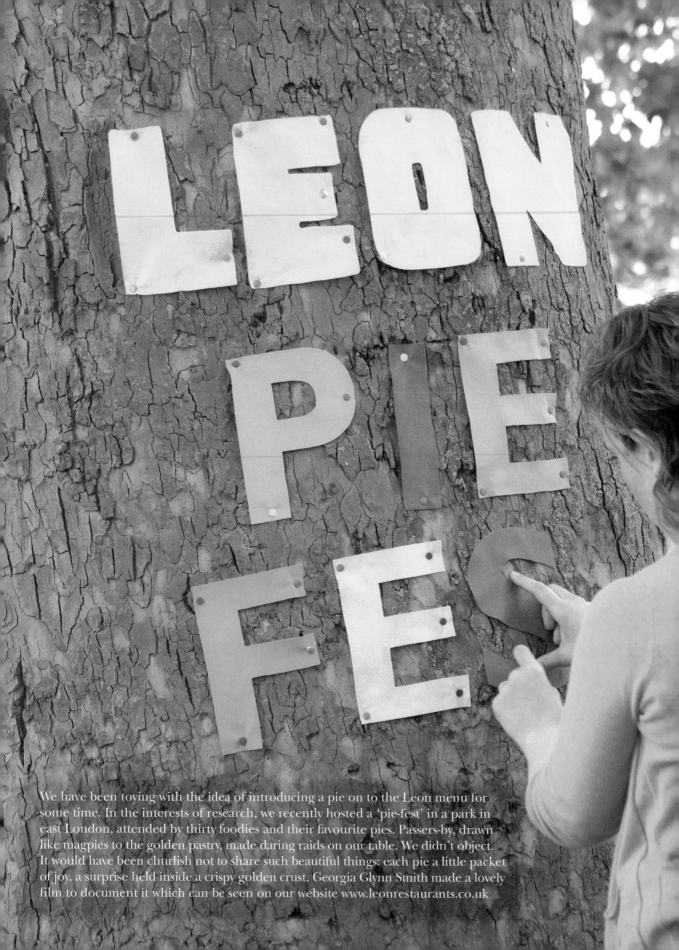

LEON PIE FES

We have been toying with the idea of introducing a pie on to the Leon menu for some time. In the interests of research, we recently hosted a 'pie-fest' in a park in east London, attended by thirty foodies and their favourite pies. Passers-by, drawn like magpies to the golden pastry, made daring raids on our table. We didn't object. It would have been churlish not to share such beautiful things: each pie a little packet of joy, a surprise held inside a crispy golden crust. Georgia Glynn Smith made a lovely film to document it which can be seen on our website www.leonrestaurants.co.uk

Andi's Marshmallow-topped Sweet Potato Pie

Serves: 6–8
Preparation time: 35 minutes
Cooking time: 20 minutes
V

1 x 375g (approx.) pack of **sweet shortcrust pastry**

4 **pink-fleshed sweet potatoes**

6 large spoons of **honey**, or **agave nectar** or any sweetener that you prefer

1 teaspoon **ground nutmeg**

1 teaspoon **ground cinnamon**

1 teaspoon **ground allspice**

1 teaspoon **vanilla extract**

2 tablespoons **desiccated coconut** (optional)

3 **free-range egg whites**

1 packet of **white mini marshmallows**

1. Preheat the oven to 180°C/350°F/gas mark 4.

2. Roll out the pastry with a rolling pin big enough to line a fluted flan tin measuring about 25–28cm. Bake blind for around 25 minutes, until the pastry is golden. Remove from the oven and set aside to cool, leaving the oven on.

3. Peel the sweet potatoes and cut them into cubes. Boil until soft, then mash them well.

4. Put the sweet potatoes into a large bowl with the honey, nutmeg, cinnamon, allspice, vanilla extract and the coconut (if using). Mix thoroughly.

5. Beat the egg whites well in a separate bowl, then add to the sweet potatoes and whip the mixture together for a few minutes. Pour into the pastry case and bake in the already warm oven for around 20 minutes.

6. When the top of the pie has a few browned peaks it is ready to come out of the oven. Gently arrange the marshmallows on top in any design that you like.

7. When you are ready to eat the pie, place it under a hot grill to toast the marshmallows, which will go golden and start to melt very quickly. Keep a close eye on it so that they don't burn.

ANDI AND HER BROTHER SEAN, 1969

Esther's Pork Pie

Makes: 1 large pork pie
Preparation: 2 hours
Cooking time: 1¾ hours

40g **butter**, diced

60g **lard**, diced

100ml **water**

275g **plain flour**

¾ teaspoon **salt**

1 free-range **egg**, beaten, plus extra **beaten egg**
    for brushing

500g **pork shoulder** or **leg**

250g **pork belly**

250g **bacon**

salt, **pepper**, **thyme**, **mace**, **chilli**, or any
    other seasoning you like

30g **powdered beef gelatine** (I use Dr Oetker's)

ESTHER IN OXFORD, 1989

1. Heat the butter, lard and water in a saucepan until it is melted and warm, but don't let it boil. While the fat is melting, put the flour and salt into a mixing bowl and make a well in the centre. Pour the egg into the well and half mix it in with a knife. Once the fat and water have melted together, add to the flour and mix until it forms a dough.

2. The dough will probably be a bit too sticky, so sprinkle on more flour until it takes on the glossy sheen of pastry. Form it into a ball, wrap it in clingfilm and chill in the fridge for an hour.

3. When you take it out of the fridge you can cut off a quarter to put aside for the lid – but I find that if you are using a pie tin (20cm in diameter and 15cm deep) it's easier to roll the whole lot out, lay it over and press it into the tin, then cut off the excess and re-roll that to make the lid.

4. Don't be afraid to make the walls of the pie really quite thick – up to 1cm or more. The crust is just a vessel for the pork inside; it's going to have to be robust enough to contain hot pork fat AND the warm jellied stock you are going to pour in later. If it's a dainty 0.5cm thick, it will tear on cooking.

5. Heat your oven to 180°C/350°F/gas mark 4. Mince up your pork bits quite finely in a food processor. Sort through the meat after it's been processed to pick out any bits of gristle or rind.

6. Add salt, pepper, thyme, mace, chilli or anything else you'd like to the filling. You can test the filling's seasoning by frying a small piece and tasting.

7. Fill your pastry-lined pie dish with the pork filling, really ramming in as much as you can. However much you stuff it, it will all shrink on cooking, so don't be afraid to squash in as much as possible, pummelling it all in, like punching a sleeping bag back into its carry-case.

8. Now roll out your remaining pastry to make the pie lid. You must, *must* brush beaten egg round the top edges of the pie to seal the lid to the sides. Nothing else will do: if you use anything else, the lid will come away from the sides and stuff will fall out and it'll just be a disaster.

9. Lay the lid on top of the pie and press it all around the edges to seal. Trim away the excess pastry round the sides.

10. On the top of the pie, in the centre, make a good, generous hole in the pastry, about the width of your little finger. This is so that juices can escape during cooking and for pouring in the stock at the end.

11. Brush the lid with more beaten egg and shove it in the oven for 30 minutes. Then turn the heat down to 160°C/325°F/gas mark 3 and cook for another 1¼ hours.

12. Leave the pie in the tin to get cool all the way through – this might take 4 or 5 hours. During cooking, the pork will have shrunk away from the sides of the pastry to form a natural cavity to be filled by the jelly.

13. You can make the jelly in two ways: the first of these is to make up a pint of warm stock – any sort will do, from a stock cube or whatever – and set it with powdered gelatine. I find Dr Oetker's powdered beef gelatine to be the most user-friendly. One 30g sachet sets 600ml of stock. The second, if you're feeling very serious, is to ask your butcher for some veal bones or a pig's trotter. Boil it all up for a couple of hours with some carrots and celery and the stock will turn to jelly when it sets, without needing the help of manufactured gelatine.

14. Pour the jelly stock through the hole in the top of the pie while the stock is still lukewarm, and it will set around the pork as it cools. This is quite a tricky process. You can use a turkey baster if you've got one, or a jug and funnel. Don't lose heart if the stock bubbles out of your pie's blowhole and goes everywhere. This kind of pastry is pretty resilient. You may have to repeat the pouring-in of the stock after you've poured in the first lot, as it will slowly disappear into the nooks and crannies of the pie and suddenly there will be a 1cm gap between the lid of the pie and the top of the jelly. Chill the pie in the fridge for at least an hour before eating.

Hattie's Blackcurrant Tart Canelle

Serves: 6–8
Preparation time: 25 minutes
Cooking time: 25 minutes
V

HATTIE IN OXFORD, 1978

170g **plain flour**

85g **unsalted butter**

85g **caster sugar**

2 **free-range egg yolks**

1 tablespoon **water**

1 level tablespoon **ground cinnamon**

225g **blackcurrants**, off the stalk

milk or **beaten egg**, to glaze

extra **caster sugar** to sprinkle over,
   plus more to add to the currants

1. Preheat the oven to 180°C/350°F/gas mark 4.

2. To make the pastry in a food processor, put in the flour, butter, sugar, egg yolks, water and cinnamon and blitz until it comes together into a ball. Remove from the machine, cover with clingfilm and chill well for at least an hour in the fridge.

3. To make the pastry by hand, mix together the flour, butter, sugar and cinnamon with your fingers until you have a breadcrumb-like consistency. Slowly add the egg yolks and water until the mixture comes together into a ball. Cover with clingfilm and chill well.

4. Put the blackcurrants into a pan, cover generously with caster sugar, and put over a low heat. Stir regularly, and when you are sure that all the sugar has melted, turn up the heat until the fruit is bubbling and thick-looking. Remove from the heat.

5. Roll out the pastry 1cm thick and line an 18cm fluted flan tin, gathering up any trimmings. Fill the flan case with the blackberry compote, and roll out the trimmings to make a thin and neat extra strip to go around the edge. There should be enough pastry left to make a lattice pattern over the top of the tart if you wish.

6. Brush the pastry with milk or beaten egg, and bake in the oven for 20–25 minutes, until the pastry is golden. Serve cool, with vanilla ice cream or crème fraîche.

Ana's Cheese Empanadas

Our Ecuadorian cleaner Ana doesn't speak much English, but makes herself understood through the language of laughter, kindness and exceptionally good empanadas. Great party food.

Makes: 20 small empanadas
Preparation time: 30 minutes +
30 minutes resting time
Cooking time: 10–15 minutes

V

ANA, IN EQUADOR, AGED 11

400g **plain flour**
2 teaspoons **baking powder**
1 teaspoon **salt**
115g **butter**
50ml **orange juice**
80ml **sparkling water**
250g **mozzarella cheese**
1 medium **onion** grated or
    finely chopped
1½–2 tablespoons **caster sugar**
1 **free-range egg**, lightly beaten
extra **caster sugar** to sprinkle on
    top (optional)
vegetable oil, for frying (optional)

1. Put the flour, baking powder and salt into a food processor and whiz until well mixed.

2. Add the butter, orange juice and sparkling water and process until a dough forms.

3. Tip the dough on to a surface, bring it together into a ball, wrap it in clingfilm and place in the fridge for 30 minutes to rest.

4. Grate the mozzarella into a bowl and add the onion. Add the sugar and mix well.

5. Preheat the oven to 200°C/400°F/gas mark 6. Line a baking sheet with baking paper, or oil it well.

6. When the dough has rested remove it from the clingfilm and dust your work surface with flour. Cut the ball of dough in half (it's easier to roll out smaller amounts). Roll out the dough so that it's only a couple of millimetres thick.

7. Using a 9–10cm cutter, cut circles out of the dough. Place a teaspoon of the cheese filling in the centre of each circle, fold the dough over to make a half-moon shape, and seal the discs pressing down with a fork. Make sure they are all well sealed, otherwise the filling will ooze out when you cook them.

8. Brush the empanadas with the beaten egg, and sprinkle a little sugar over the top of each one if you want that extra sweetness. Place on the baking tray and cook in the oven for 10–15 minutes, until golden. Cool on a wire rack.

9. If you fancy the fried option, fill a saucepan 3–4cm deep with vegetable oil. When the oil is hot, deep-fry the empanadas until golden, and sprinkle with caster sugar before serving.

Janet's London Fields Apricot & Cherry Galette

Serves 6–8
Preparation time: 30 minutes
Cooking time: 45–50 minutes

V

JANET IN NORTHUMBERLAND, 1978

For the pastry

125g **plain flour**, plus extra for dusting

a pinch of **salt**

a pinch of **sugar**

85g cold **unsalted butter**, cut into 1.5cm pieces

4 tablespoons **ice-cold water**

For the galette

450g fresh **apricots**, washed and halved, stones removed

225g **cherries**, washed and halved, stones removed

2 tablespoons **sugar**

1 tablespoon **plain flour**

1 tablespoon **ground almonds** (optional)

1 **free-range egg**, beaten

1. Combine the flour, salt and sugar in a bowl and either cut in the cold butter with the back of a fork or use two knives.

2. Avoid over-mixing – leaving larger chunks of butter than you would expect will make the pastry more flaky. Drizzle in the water and bring it all together into a ball without working the dough. Wrap in clingfilm, then flatten into a disc and let it rest in the fridge for about 45 minutes.

3. Heat the oven to 200°C/400°F/gas mark 6 and line a baking sheet with baking paper. Allow the pastry to come to room temperature so its easier to work.

4. Dust a work surface with flour and roll out the dough into a circle about the size of a dinner plate. Put it on the baking sheet and return it to the fridge for a few minutes.

5. Remove the pastry circle from the fridge and sprinkle the sugar, flour and ground almonds over, leaving a 5cm border around the outside. Arrange the fruit on top of the almonds – you can put the cherries in the middle and the apricots in circles around them, or make up your own pattern.

6. Fold over the pastry rim to create a crust. Brush the rim with beaten egg, and bake in the bottom half of the oven for 45–50 minutes, until the fruit is squashy.

7. When cooked, transfer the galette on to a wire rack to cool.

8. Serve warm or cold, with vanilla ice cream or whipped cream. Or simply enjoy it on its own with a cup of tea.

TIPS

❖ This is basically a free-form, open-face tart and it can be used for all different kinds of fruit.

London W1F 7JE
LEON.
35-36 Gt. Marlborough St.
Fair Trade & Organic

NOME DEL PASSEGGERO

BAGAGLIAIO

LEON

POWER SMOOTHIE

LEON

LEON
FRESHLY-SQUEEZED
ORANGE JUICE
LEON

FRESH LEON-MADE

LEON

LEMONADE

GRILLED CHICKEN
LEON
SUPERFOOD SALAD
1 2 3 4 5 6 7 8 9 10 11 12 S

LEON · LDN.

LEON

MOROCCAN
MEAT BALLS
MOROCCAN HERBS & SPICES   PLUM TOMATO SAUCE
1 2 3 4 5 6 7 8 9 10 11 12 S

MAGIC MACKEREL
LEON
COUSCOUS

LEON · LDN.

LEON-HOTEL
CASABLANCA

LEON

Maggie's Croatian Pear Pie

This pie can be done in a square, oval or any shape tin you fancy. Also, the pears can be cut into halves, quarters or slices, depending on the look you like.

Serves: 4–6
Preparation time: 50 minutes
Cooking time: approx. 45 minutes

V

Maggie was our son George's nanny for the first three years of his life, and is still a great friend. A former judo champion, she has buns of steel and incredible natural authority. One of the reasons children love her – apart from the fact that she can swing them round her head one-handed without breaking a sweat – is that she's a wonderful cook, thanks in part to the tutelage of her Italian–Croatian parents. This is a typically elegant dish.

HENRY

4–6 ripe **pears**

For the pastry
250g **caster sugar** or **soft brown sugar**
125g **unsalted butter**
375g **plain flour**
1 **free-range egg**
¼ teaspoon **baking powder**
a pinch of **salt**

For the almond filling
200g **unsalted butter**, softened
200g **icing sugar**
2 free-range **eggs**
2 free-range **egg yolks**
a dash of **Calvados** (optional), or other alcohol
200g **ground almonds**
60g **plain flour**

For the glaze
100g **apricot jam**

1. Heat the oven to 220°C/425°F/gas mark 7.

2. To make the pastry, mix together the sugar and butter, until you get a smooth paste. Add the remaining ingredients to the bowl, and mix it together well, adding a little water if you need to. The pastry will be very crumbly, but do not despair, it's supposed to be like that.

3. Roll out the pastry and line a 25cm tart tin, pricking it all over with a fork. If the pastry is too crumbly, press it into the tin by hand a little at a time. It should have a thick crust of pastry, so don't be alarmed by the amount you have. Line it with baking paper and fill with baking beans. Blind bake for 8–10 minutes, depending on your oven, then remove the paper and beans and allow it to cool.

4. Peel the pears, leaving the stalks on. Cut them into slices or halve them, removing the core carefully so they don't break.

5. To make the almond filling, cream together the butter and sugar, then add the eggs and egg yolks one at a time, mixing after each addition. You can do this by hand or using an electric hand mixer. Add the alcohol if you are using it, then the ground almonds and flour, and mix well.

6. Pour the filling into the pastry base, and assemble the pears on top, in any which way you like.

7. Bake the pie in the oven for 30–40 minutes, or until golden brown, but do not let it burn. Allow to cool in the tin.

8. Heat the apricot jam in a samll pan with a teaspoon or two of water until it is runny and spreadable, and whilst still warm, use a pastry brush to glaze your pie.

 TIPS

✤ Eat this pie lukewarm on its own, with cream or a good vanilla ice cream.

✤ To make this in a loaf tin, bake for a further 20 minutes on a low oven shelf.

Croatian Pear Pie by Maggie

Henry's Spiced Chicken Mystery Pie

The mystery is that no one can believe it's made with rhubarb. The pink stems are wonderful in savoury dishes, adding body and a subtle citrus flavour. Worth trying in lamb stews, too.

Serves: 4–6

Preparation time: 10 minutes + cooling time

Cooking time: 2 hours 45 minutes

1 large **chicken**

olive oil

salt and freshly ground **black pepper**

300g **rhubarb**, cut into 2.5cm pieces

2 **bay leaves**

4 **cardamom pods**, crushed with the back of a knife

1 glass of **white wine**

2 **white onions**, peeled and sliced vertically into 8 wedges

1 tablespoon **turmeric**

1 x 300ml tub of **double cream**

1 x 350g packet of ready-made **puff pastry** (or flaky pastry from page 38)

1 **free-range egg**, to glaze

1. Preheat the oven to 180°C/350°F/gas mark 4.

2. Rub the chicken all over with olive oil and plenty of salt and pepper.

3. Put all the ingredients, except the cream, pastry and egg, into a casserole dish. Put the lid on and place in the oven for 1½ –2 hours. The chicken should be falling off the bone. (Check now and then and add a dash of water if it seems dry.)

4. Leave the chicken until cool enough to handle. Pick off the meat and put it into a pie dish with the vegetables and juice from the casserole, discarding only the skin, bones, and bay leaves. Stir in the cream. Season. You can put this into the fridge now until you want to make the pie (several days later, if you fancy).

5. When the filling has cooled completely and you are ready to cook the pie, heat the oven to 160°C/325°F/gas mark 3. Roll out the pastry to make the lid, and use the trimmings to cut out a decoration for the top. I like to write the word 'Pie'. Glaze with the beaten egg.

6. Cook the pie for 40 minutes or until the top is golden.

Claire's Cherry Pie

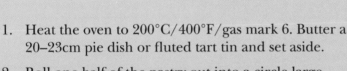

Sour cherries are a favourite pie filling in America. Sour cherries grow in the UK in many back gardens because the bright red fruit is so pretty. They don't survive well going to market, which is why you will not see them in supermarkets. If you can't find them fresh from a friend's tree or from your local farmers' market, frozen ones can be used. A last resort would be jars of preserved ones, but make sure to drain off most of the liquid first.

Serves 8
Preparation time: 40 minutes
Cooking time: 1 hour
V

350g **Shortcrust Pastry** (see recipe on page 38)
500g fresh or frozen pitted **sour cherries**, preferably Morello
200g **caster sugar**
4 tablespoons **cornflour**
a pinch of **salt**
1 **free-range egg**, for brushing
a little **milk**

1. Heat the oven to 200°C/400°F/gas mark 6. Butter a 20–23cm pie dish or fluted tart tin and set aside.

2. Roll one half of the pastry out into a circle large enough to line the pie dish with some excess. Place the rolled-out circle of pastry in the dish, pressing the pastry down well. Roll the other half of the pastry into a rectangle 3mm thick and place it on a baking tray lined with baking parchment. Place both in the fridge while you prepare the filling.

3. Put the cherries, sugar and cornflour into a bowl and add the salt. Toss to coat the fruit evenly.

4. Remove the pie dish from the fridge and fill it with the cherry mixture. Remove the rectangle of pastry from the fridge and use a small knife to slice the pastry into 2cm strips. Arrange the strips of pastry over the cherries in a lattice pattern, saving 3 strips for the edge.

5. Crack the egg into a small bowl and add a few drops of milk. Whisk to combine. Trim the edge of the pastry to the rim of the dish. Using a pastry brush, carefully coat the lattice with egg wash. Use the last 3 strips to cover the rim, then brush this with the egg wash as well.

6. Place the pie in the oven for about an hour, with a piece of kitchen foil underneath to catch any drips. The pie is ready when you see the fruit filling bubbling through.

RECIPE INDEX

LOW SATURATED FAT

a good chocolate cake 183
almond date oat muffins 59
apple sorbet 154
Ballymaloe brown soda bread 204
baked apples 114
bar of good things 80
better carrot cake 98
blood orange & white wine jelly 127
Champagne granita 152
Claire's chocolate hazelnut power
  pills 71
Claire's healthy granola 53
clementine granita 153
dried fruit compote 230
flatbread with zatar 207
Flour Station rye bread 201
french onion tart 208
fresh raspberry jam 226
fresh strawberry jam 226
George's ice cream sandwich 170
gluten-free bread 198
good scones 105
Hannah's banana bread 65
hazelnut milk 56
honeycomb 220
Jossy's favourite round Christmas
  pudding 264
Jossy's jewelled rhubarb & mango
  120
Kamal's meghli 260
luxury granola 55
Maggie's coconut kiss ice cream 170
mulled wine 255
our favourite granola 52
pizza dough 211
poached pears 124
pumpkin pie 258
pumpkin seed milk 56
quince granita 152
Raab the Baker's crusty white rolls
  202
roasted quince compote 229
royal icing 179
simnel cake 238
Soli's floral Persian dates 223
sourdough bread 196
spelt bread 193
spelt hot cross buns 240
spelt pancakes 237
strawberry marshmallows 219
sugar-free vanilla cupcakes 96
sweet popcorn with chocolate
  drizzle 79
vegan vanilla icing 97
Violet's coconut macaroons 101

GOOD CARBS (LOW GI)/ GOOD SUGARS

a good chocolate cake 183
almond date oat muffins 59
baked apples 114
Ballymaloe brown soda bread 204
bar of good things 80
BBQ chocolate bananas 113
better brownie 76
better carrot cake 98
Bill Granger's scrambled eggs 247
Claire's chocolate hazelnut power
  pills 71
Claire's healthy granola 53
courgette bread 99
Flour Station rye bread 201
fresh strawberry jam 226
George's ice cream sandwich 170
Glenys's Desperate Dan steak pie
  248
good scones 105
Hannah's banana bread 65
hazelnut milk 56
Henry's spiced chicken mystery
  pie 292
Jossy's favourite round Christmas
  pudding 264
Leon chocolate mousse 144
Maggie's coconut kiss ice cream 170
oatmeal biscuits 212
pumpkin seed milk 56
simnel cake 238
Soli's floral Persian dates 223
spelt bread 193
spelt hot cross buns 240
spelt pancakes 237
sugar-free vanilla cupcakes 96
sweet popcorn with chocolate
  drizzle 79
Tommi's more-fruit-than-cake cake
  93
vegan vanilla icing 97

WHEAT FREE

apple crisp 132
apple sorbet 154
baked apples 114
bar of good things 80
BBQ chocolate bananas 113
better brownie 76
better carrot cake 98
Bill Granger's scrambled eggs 247
blood orange & white wine jelly 127
Bruno's poached strawberries with
  green peppercorn ice cream 250
butterscotch apples 254
Champagne granita 152
Claire's chocolate hazelnut power
  pills 71
Claire's healthy granola 53
clementine granita 153
clementine polenta cake 89
crème brûlée 268
Dittisham plum crumble 131
dried fruit compote 230
Flour Station rye bread 201
fresh raspberry jam 226
fresh strawberry jam 226
George's ice cream sandwich 170
gluten-free bread 198
gooseberry fool 126
hazelnut milk 56
Henry's chocolate & salted caramel
  ice cream bombe 160
honeycomb 220
ice cream base 158
Irish coffee 276
Jossy's jewelled rhubarb & mango
  120
Kamal's meghli 260
Leon chocolate mousse 144
Leon pecan pie 102
Leon salted caramel banana split
  281
life by chocolate cake 148
luxury granola 55
Maggie's best chocolate chip
  cookies 184
Maggie's coconut kiss ice cream 170
mont blanc 136
mulled wine 255
our favourite granola 52
pavlova 140

plum parfait 157
poached pears 124
pumpkin seed milk 56
quince granita 152
roasted peaches 110
roasted quince compote 229
royal icing 179
Soli's floral Persian dates 223
strawberry & blueberry cobbler 128
strawberry marshmallows 219
sugar-free vanilla cupcakes 96
sweet popcorn with chocolate
   drizzle 79
vegan vanilla icing 97
Violet's coconut macaroons 101
warm gooey chocolate cakes 147

GLUTEN FREE

apple crisp 132
apple sorbet 154
baked apples 114
bar of good things 80
BBQ chocolate bananas 113
better brownie 76
better carrot cake 98
Bill Granger's scrambled eggs 247
blood orange & white wine jelly 127
Bruno's poached strawberries with
   green peppercorn ice cream 250
butterscotch apples 254
Champagne granita 152
Claire's chocolate hazelnut power
   pills 71
Claire's healthy granola 53
clementine granita 153
clementine polenta cake 89
crème brûlée 268
Dittisham plum crumble 131
dried fruit compote 230
fresh raspberry jam 226
fresh strawberry jam 226
George's ice cream sandwich 170
gluten-free bread 198
good scones 105
gooseberry fool 126
hazelnut milk 56
Henry's chocolate & salted caramel
   ice cream bombe 160
honeycomb 220
ice cream base 158
Irish coffee 276

Jossy's jewelled rhubarb & mango
   120
Kamal's meghli 260
Leon chocolate mousse 144
Leon pecan pie 102
Leon salted caramel banana split
   281
life by chocolate cake 148
luxury granola 55
Maggie's best chocolate chip
   cookies 184
Maggie's coconut kiss ice cream 170
mont blanc 136
mulled wine 255
our favourite granola 52
pavlova 140
plum parfait 157
poached pears 124
pumpkin seed milk 56
quince granita 152
roasted peaches 110
roasted quince compote 229
royal icing 179
Soli's floral Persian dates 223
strawberry & blueberry cobbler 128
strawberry marshmallows 219
sugar-free vanilla cupcakes 96
sweet popcorn with chocolate
   drizzle 79
vegan vanilla icing 97
Violet's coconut macaroons 101
warm gooey chocolate cakes 147

DAIRY FREE

a good chocolate cake 183
apple sorbet 154
baked apples 114
bar of good things 80
better carrot cake 98
blood orange & white wine jelly 127
Champagne granita 152
Claire's chocolate hazelnut power
   pills 71
Claire's healthy granola 53
clementine granita 153
dried fruit compote 230
flatbread with zatar 207
Flour Station rye bread 201
fresh raspberry jam 226
fresh strawberry jam 226
George's ice cream sandwich 170

hazelnut milk 56
Jossy's favourite round Christmas
   pudding 264
Jossy's jewelled rhubarb & mango
   120
Kamal's meghli 260
Maggie's coconut kiss ice cream 170
mulled wine 255
our favourite granola 52
Petra's honey bread 104
pizza dough 211
poached pears 124
pumpkin seed milk 56
quince granita 152
roasted quince compote 229
royal icing 179
sourdough bread 196
spelt hot cross buns 240
sugar-free vanilla cupcakes 96
vegan vanilla icing 97
Violet's coconut macaroons 101

INDEX

A

agave nectar 21, 45
Allen, Darina 204, 226
almonds
  almond date oat muffins 59
  better brownies 76
  Claire's healthy granola 53
  clementine polenta cake 89
  Dittisham plum crumble 131
  George's ice cream sandwich 170
  Kamal's Meghli 260
  Leon salted caramel banana split 281
  Lise's cherry almond cookies 73
  Maggie's Croatian pear pie 290–1
  marzipan 238
  our favourite granola 52
  Simnel cake 238–9
  Soli's floral Persian dates, with burnt almond and pistachio 223
Ana's cheese empanadas 287
anchovies: French onion tart 208
Andi's marshmallow-topped sweet potato pie 283
apples
  apple crisp 132
  apple sauce 45
  apple sorbet 154
  baked apples 114
  butterscotch apples 254
  tarte tatin 116
apricots
  bar of good things 80
  dried fruit compote 230
  Janet's London Fields apricot and cherry galette 288
  our favourite granola 52
arrowroot 14

B

bacon: Esther's pork pie 284–5
baked Alaska 139
baking powder 14, 42, 43
baking tins 28
Ballymaloe brown soda bread 204
bananas
  BBQ chocolate bananas 113
  Hannah's banana bread 65
  Leon salted caramel banana split 281

bar of good things 80
Barton, Craig 102
beef: Glenys's Desperate Dan steak pie 248
Ben's classic Victoria sponge 86
bicarbonate of soda 14, 42, 190
Bill Granger's scrambled eggs on spelt toast 247
bird's beak knife 31
birthday baking 270–3
biscuits
  cut-out biscuits 176
  Halloween biscuits 253
  Maggie's best chocolate chip cookies 184
  oatmeal biscuits 212
  storing 40
blackcurrants: Hattie's blackcurrant tart canelle 286
blenders 31
blind baking 42, 43
bloom, on chocolate 35
blueberries
  blueberry cheesecake 123
  luxury granola 55
  strawberry and blueberry cobbler 128
bonfire night treats 254–5
Brazil nuts: Claire's chocolate hazelnut power pills 71
bread 188–207
  Ballymaloe brown soda bread 204
  courgette bread 99
  Flour Station rye bread 201
  gluten-free bread 198
  Hannah's banana bread 65
  Petra's honey bread 104
  Raab the Baker's crusty white rolls 202
  soda bread 190
  sourdough 190, 195, 196–7
  spelt bread 193
  storing 40
  unleavened bread 190
  yeasted bread 189, 190
broccoli and goats' cheese tart 208
brown rice syrup 21
brownies, better 76
Bruno's poached strawberries with green peppercorn ice cream 250

buckwheat flakes: Claire's healthy granola 53
buckwheat flour 13
buttercream icing 39
buttermilk 43, 190
  Ballymaloe brown soda bread 204
butters
  raw nut and seed 57
  salted 17
  unsalted 17
butterscotch apples 254

C

cacao nibs: Claire's chocolate hazelnut power pills 71
cakes 39
  Ben's classic Victoria sponge 86
  better carrot cake 98
  clementine polenta cake 89
  cooling cakes 42
  domed cakes 43
  Eccles cakes 244
  a good chocolate cake 183
  Guinness malt cake 277
  Leon's 5th birthday cake 270
  life by chocolate cake 148
  Petra's christening cake 275
  Petra's fruit cake 90–1
  pineapple upside-down cake 115
  Simnel cake 238–9
  storing cakes 40
  sunken cakes 42
  Technicolor dreamcake 187
  testing doneness 39, 42, 91
  Tommi's more-fruit-than-cake cake 93
  triple chocolate fantasy cake 272–3
  warm gooey chocolate cakes 147
candied peel
  Petra's fruit cake 90–1
  Simnel cake 238–9
cane sugar 20
caramel
  Henry's chocolate and salted caramel ice cream bombe 160–1
  Leon salted caramel banana split 281
cardamom pods
  Henry's spiced chicken mystery pie 292

Maggie's coconut kiss ice cream 170
carrots: better carrot cake 98
cashew nuts
    bar of good things 80
    cashew nut butter 57
    vegan vanilla icing 97
caster sugar 20, 45, 135
Champagne
    Champagne cocktail 265
    Champagne granita 152
cheese
    Ana's cheese empanadas 287
    salmon and dill muffins 58
cheesecake, blueberry 123
cherries
    Claire's cherry pie 293
    Claire's chocolate hazelnut power pills 71
    dried fruit compote 230
    Janet's London Fields apricot and cherry galette 288
    Maggie's coconut kiss ice cream 170
    our favourite granola 52
    Petra's fruit cake 90–1
chestnuts: Mont Blanc 136
chia seeds 45
chicken: Henry's spiced chicken mystery pie 292
chickpeas: gram flour 14
chocolate 35, 142–9
    BBQ chocolate bananas 113
    better brownies 76
    Claire's chocolate hazelnut power pills 71
    Easter eggs 243
    a good chocolate cake 183
    Henry's chocolate and salted caramel ice cream bombe 160–1
    Leon chocolate mousse 144
    Leon salted caramel banana split 281
    life by chocolate cake 148
    Lise's cherry almond cookies 73
    luxury granola 55
    Maggie's best chocolate chip cookies 184
    melting 35
    s'mores 180
    sweet popcorn with chocolate

drizzle 79
    tempering chocolate 44
    triple chocolate fantasy cake 272–3
    warm gooey chocolate cakes 147
Claire's cherry pie 293
Claire's chocolate hazelnut power pills 71
Claire's healthy granola 53
clementines
    clementine granita 153
    clementine polenta cake 89
    St Clement's pudding 166
cobbler, strawberry and blueberry 128
cocktail, Champagne 265
coconut 41
    Claire's healthy granola 53
    luxury granola 55
    Violet's coconut macaroons 101
coconut milk 45
    a good chocolate cake 183
    Leon's 5th birthday cake 270
    Maggie's coconut kiss ice cream 170
coconut oil 17, 45, 98
    coconut oil icing 45
    spelt hot cross buns 240–1
    sugar-free vanilla cupcakes 96
    vegan vanilla icing 97
compotes 225
    dried fruit 230
    roasted quince 229
condensed milk: Key lime pie 119
cookies
    Lise's cherry almond cookies 73
    Maggie's best chocolate chip cookies 184
corn 45
cornmeal 14
cornstarch 14
courgette bread 99
cranberries
    cranberry cheesecake 123
    Nana Goy's cranberry flapjacks 74
cream 36–7
    gooseberry fool 126
cream cheese
    blueberry cheesecake 123
    Jossy's orange mince pies 262
    salmon and dill muffins 58

stout and cream cheese frosting 277
cream of tartar 42, 134
creaming 33
crème brûlée 268
crumble, Dittisham plum 131
cupcakes, sugar-free vanilla 96
curdling 42
currants
    Eccles cakes 244
    Simnel cake 238–9
    spelt hot cross buns 240–1
    spotted dick 162
custard, quick 34
cut-out biscuits 176

D

dairy products 36–7, 45
dates
    almond date oat muffins 59
    George's ice cream sandwich 170
    Soli's floral Persian dates 223
Demerara sugar 20
Dimbleby, Josceline 150, 157, 165, 262, 264
dough
    dough scrapers 31
    kneading 40
drinks
    Champagne cocktail 265
    Irish coffee 276

E

Easter eggs 243
Eccles cakes 244
egg substitute 14
eggs 34–5, 134–5
    alternatives to 14, 45
    Bill Granger's scrambled eggs on spelt toast 247
    crème brûlée 268
    custard 34
    eggy bread 63
    ice cream 150, 157–61, 250
    meringues 134–41
    sabayon 124
Elisabeth's lemon bars 94
empanadas, Ana's cheese 287
Esther's pork pie 284–5

F

fats 16–18
figs
 fig paste 80
 Tommi's more-fruit-than-cake
  cake 93
flaky pastry 37, 38
flapjacks, Nana Goy's cranberry 74
flatbread with zatar 207
flax meal 45
flour 12–14, 43, 45
Flour Station rye bread 201
folding 33
fools 126
French onion tart 208
frosting, stout and cream cheese
 277
fructose 20, 21, 77, 144
fruit
 dried fruit compote 230
 juicing 40
 zesting 40

G

galette, Janet's London Fields
 apricot and cherry 288
George's ice cream sandwich 170
Glenys's Desperate Dan steak pie
 248
gluten-free
 bread 198
 flour 14
goat's cheese: broccoli and goats'
 cheese tart 208
golden syrup 20
gooseberry fool 126
gram flour 14
granitas 150, 152–3
 Champagne 152
 clementine 153
 quince 152–3
granola
 Claire's healthy 53
 luxury 55
 our favourite 52
greaseproof parchment 27
Guinness malt cake 277

H

Halloween biscuits 253

Hannah's banana bread 65
Hattie's blackcurrant tart canelle
 286
hazelnuts
 Claire's chocolate hazelnut power
  pills 71
 hazelnut cracknel 160
 hazelnut milk 56
 luxury granola 55
Henry's chocolate and salted
 caramel ice cream bombe 160–1
Henry's spiced chicken mystery
 pie 292
Herbert, Tom 195
honey 21
 Petra's honey bread 104
honeycomb 220
hot cross buns, spelt 240–1

I

ice cream 150
 baked Alaska 139
 George's ice cream sandwich
  170
 green peppercorn 250
 ice cream base 158–9
 ice cream machines 31
 ice cream scoops 27
 Italian meringue method 150
 Leon salted caramel banana split
  281
 Maggie's coconut kiss ice cream
  170
 plum parfait 157
 raspberry ripple ice cream 159
 traditional custard method 150
icing sugar 20, 33
icings 39
 buttercream 39
 coconut oil 17, 45
 royal icing 39, 179
 vegan vanilla icing 97
ingredients 12–23
Irish coffee 276

J

jams 225–6
 fresh raspberry 226
 fresh strawberry 226
Janet's London Fields apricot and

 cherry galette 288
jars, sterilizing 44
jelly, blood orange and white wine
 127
Jossy's damson ice cream 157
Jossy's favourite round Christmas
 pudding 264
Jossy's jewelled rhubarb and mango
 120
Jossy's lemon pudding delicious 165
Jossy's orange mince pies 262
jugs, measuring 28
juicing fruit 28, 40

K

Kamal's Meghli 260
Key lime pie 119
kneading dough 40
knives 28, 31

L

lard 18
leaveners 14, 42
lemons
 Elisabeth's lemon bars 94
 Jossy's lemon pudding delicious
  165
Leon chocolate mousse 144
Leon pecan pie 102
Leon pie fest 282–93
Leon salted caramel banana split
 281
Leon's 5th birthday cake 270
Levinger, Maggie 56, 71, 80, 170,
 184, 232
Lewis, Petra 90–1, 104, 238–9, 274
life by chocolate cake 148
limes: Key lime pie 119
Lise's cherry almond cookies 73
Loubet, Bruno 250

M

macaroons, Violet's coconut 101
Madsen, Lise 73
Maggie's best chocolate chip
 cookies 184
Maggie's coconut kiss ice cream 170
Maggie's Croatian pear pie 290–1
Maggie's milks 56
mango

Jossy's jewelled rhubarb and
    mango 120
    preparing 41
maple syrup 21
margarine 18
marshmallows
    Andi's marshmallow-topped sweet
        potato pie 283
    s'mores 180
    strawberry 219
marzipan 238
mascarpone cheese: Soli's floral
    Persian dates, with burnt almond
        and pistachio 223
measuring 28, 32
meringues 43, 134–41
    baked Alaska 139
    Mont Blanc 136
    pavlova 140
    Swiss 139
microplane zesters 27
Miers, Tommi 93
milks, Maggie's 56
Miller, Ben 86
mincemeat
    baked apples 114
    Jossy's orange mince pies 262
mixers 31, 134
molasses 20
Mont Blanc 136
mousse, Leon chocolate 144
Mouzawak, Kamal 260
mozzarella cheese: Ana's cheese
    empanadas 287
muffins
    almond date oat muffins 59
    domed muffins 43
    salmon and dill muffins 58
mulled wine 255
muscovado sugar 20

N
Nana Goy's cranberry flapjacks 74
nuts
    nut butters 57
    see also almonds, cashews,
        hazelnuts etc

O
oats 45
    almond date oat muffins 59

Lise's cherry almond cookies 73
luxury granola 55
Nana Goy's cranberry flapjacks 74
oatmeal biscuits 212
our favourite granola 52
oils
    coconut oil 17, 45, 240–1
    olive oil 18
olives: French onion tart 208
onions: French onion tart 208
oranges: blood orange and white
    wine jelly 127
ovens, fan-assisted 43

P
palette knives 31
pancakes
    Saturday 61
    spelt 237
parfait, plum 157
passion fruit: pavlova 140
pastry 37–8
    blind baking 42
    flaky pastry 38
    pressed-crust pastry 37, 38
    rolling 43
    shortcrust pastry 37, 38
    spelt pastry 208
pavlova 140
peaches, roasted 110
pears
    Maggie's Croatian pear pie 290–1
    poached 124
pecan nuts
    Leon pecan pie 102
    luxury granola 55
peelers 28
peppercorns: green peppercorn ice
    cream 250
Petra's fruit cake 90–1, 275
Petra's honey bread 104
pies 282–93
    Andi's marshmallow-topped sweet
        potato pie 283
    Claire's cherry pie 293
    Esther's pork pie 284–5
    Glenys's Desperate Dan steak pie
        248
    Henry's spiced chicken mystery
        pie 292
    Key lime pie 119

pineapple upside-down cake 115
pistachios
    bar of good things 80
    Kamal's Meghli 260
    Soli's floral Persian dates 223
pizzas 211
    dough 211
    potato and rosemary 211
plums
    Dittisham plum crumble 131
    plum parfait 157
polenta 14
    clementine polenta cake 89
pomegranates, preparing 41
popcorn: sweet popcorn with
    chocolate drizzle 79
pork pie, Esther's 284–5
potatoes: Flour Station rye bread
    201
prunes: Jossy's favourite round
    Christmas pudding 264
Ptak, Elisabeth 29
pumpkin pie 258
pumpkin seed milk 56

Q
quinces
    quince granita 152–3
    roasted quince 229

R
Raab the Baker's crusty white rolls
    202
raisins: Jossy's favourite round
    Christmas pudding 264
raspberries
    Ben's classic Victoria sponge 86
    fresh raspberry jam 226
    raspberry ripple ice cream 159
reamers 28
rhubarb
    Henry's spiced chicken mystery
        pie 292
    Jossy's jewelled rhubarb and
        mango 120
rice flour 45
rice milk 45
rolling pins 27
royal icing 39, 179
rye flour 13
    Flour Station rye bread 201

S

sabayon 124
St Clement's pudding 166
salmon and dill muffins 58
Saturday pancakes 61
scales 28
scones 105
seeds
    seed butters 57
    spelt bread 193
    see also chia seeds, pumpkin seeds,
        sesame seeds etc
sesame seeds: bar of good things 80
sieves 27
sifting flour 33
Simnel cake 238–9
s'mores 180
soda bread 190
    Ballymaloe brown soda bread
        204
Soli's floral Persian dates 223
sorbets 150, 154
sourdough 190, 195, 196–7
soya milk 45
spatulas 27
spelt flour 13
    spelt bread 193
    spelt hot cross buns 240–1
    spelt pancakes 237
    spelt pastry 208
spoons, measuring 28
spotted dick 162
steamed puddings 162–9
sterilizing jars 44
stevia 21
strawberries
    Bruno's poached strawberries
        with green peppercorn ice
        cream 250
    fresh strawberry jam 226
    pavlova 140
    strawberry and blueberry cobbler
        128
    strawberry marshmallows 219
suet 18
sugar 19–20, 43
sugar-free vanilla cupcakes 96
sultanas
    Claire's healthy granola 53
    our favourite granola 52
    Petra's fruit cake 90–1
    Simnel cake 238–9
    spelt hot cross buns 240–1
Sussex pond pudding 169

sweet potatoes: Andi's
    marshmallow-topped sweet potato
    pie 283
sweeteners 19, 21, 45
sweets 219–23, 243
Swiss meringues 139
syrups 21

T

tarts
    broccoli and goats' cheese 208
    French onion 208
    Hattie's blackcurrant tart canelle
        286
    Janet's London Fields apricot and
        cherry galette 288
    Leon pecan pie 102
    pumpkin pie 258
    tarte tatin 116
    teatime 84–105
Technicolor dreamcake 187
techniques 32, 44
tempering chocolate 35, 44
thickeners 14
tins, baking 28
Tommi's more-fruit-than-cake cake
    93
tools 26–8, 30–1
treacle 20
Turkish delight 267

U

unleavened bread 190

V

vanilla
    sugar-free vanilla cupcakes 96
    vegan vanilla icing 97
Victoria sponge 86
Violet 101, 270
    Violet's coconut macaroons 101

W

wheat flour 12–13, 45
whisks and whisking 27, 31, 35, 37,
    134
wine
    blood orange and white wine jelly
        127
    mulled 255

X

xanthan gum 14, 98

Y

yacon syrup 21
yeast 14, 190
    yeasted breads 189, 190
yoghurt 43
    Guinness malt cake 277
    Saturday pancakes 61
    triple chocolate fantasy cake 272

Z

zabaglione 124
Zardosht, Soli 223
zatar, flatbread with 207
zesters and zesting 27, 31, 40

a platter of figs and other recipes

THE NATIONAL TRUST

Traditional
Puddings

Sara Paston-Williams

RIVER CAFE COOK BOOK   Rose Gray and Ruth Rogers

DULGE   100 PERFECT DESSERTS   CLAIRE CLARK

LIE LE CLERC   LITTLE CAFE CAKES

The Anatomy of
DESSERT
With a Few Notes on Wine

TART
BRE

EDWARD A. BUNYARD

Introduction by
MICHAEL POLLAN
Preface by
DAVID KARP

MODERN LIBRARY FOOD · RUTH REICHL · SERIES EDITOR

BY CHAD ROBERTSON
PHOTOGRAPHS BY ERIC WOLFINGER

EZ PANISSE FRUIT   ALICE WATER

DAVID   RIPE FOR DESS
LEBOVITZ   100 OUTSTANDING DESSERTS WITH FRUIT INSIDE OUTS

MARTHA STEWART'S PIES & TARTS

PRUEITT/ROBERTSON   TARTINE

«IN THE GREEN KITCHEN»   ALICE

BABYCAKES   Vegan, (Mostly) Gluten-Free, and (Mostly) Sugar-Free
Recipes from New York's Most Talked-About Bakery

elia Smith's   Book of Cakes

Jane Grigson's   Fruit Book

Darina Allen's
BALLYMALOE COOKERY COURSE

The Art of

II   BEYOND NOSE TO TAIL

A year in my kitchen   SKYE GYNGELL

Slater

FERGUS H
JUSTIN PIE

THANK YOU

From Henry:
Claire, who has a rare talent for baking and an even rarer one for having fun.
What a joy to have you as a neighbour • Mum for being the original inspiration and
for continuing to inspire me to cook • My wife, Mima, for proofing, reproofing,
reassurance, rewriting, ideas and even the odd leg rub • Everyone at Conran; in
particular, Jonathan, Sybella and the wise owl Lorraine • John for his continued
support and for providing a little AC current now and then • Dad for getting it
and unflinching support • Liza and Kate, my sisters, for all your useful thoughts
about Leon • Georgia and Anita for putting up with the chaos and producing such
beautiful things out of it • Jeremy, for all those hyphens • All of the Leon
managers for their extraordinary passsion • Simon Drysdale - to mix a metaphor,
a rock in the eye of the storm - without whom everything would grind to a halt
• Tom Ward for your perseverance and moral compass • Justin Ovenden for the
outstanding fridge displays and general hutzpah • Steve and Agnieszka for making
it all add up • James Lee French - what did we do without you • Glenn for an
amazing future. What a difference you have made • Benny O for your love of
narrative • Georgie Sanderson - for caring so much and understanding Leon inside
out • Belinda Giles for the pig days, the board days, and the investment •
Benny and Rich - good luck to you • Bruno Loubet for setting me on my way •
Nick Evans, who had no idea what he was getting himself into • Xander and Hannah
Armstrong for having such faith in the world's worst godfather • Giles, Mark,
Simon and the unflinching workers at the Sustainable Restaurant Association • Petra
for being a baker I love • Roly and Susan Chambers for coming and going but always
being around • Bambi Sloane • Charlie Bigham for the meatballs • All of the people
who have invested in us • Craig from Barton and White • Rick, Sophie and Kate and
the Fusion gang • Jo, Laura and the Saucettes • Greg - we love you really • JD -
for reigniting the fire occasionally • Andy, Glenys and Mel for being so generous
with your children • Pierre and Kathleen Condou - for endless support • Linda Fox
- a truly wonderful person. One day we'll come to the States. • Stan and Tony and
everyone at Reynolds • Adam Longworth for the Ganeshes • Allegra - we'll get there
for you • Tim Smalley for navigational advice in tricky waters • Jacques Fragis
for ferocious focus • Spencer Skinner • Gavyn Davies • James and Hannah Horler -
thanks for Toph • Giles Coren and the way he fights the cynics in the battle for
sustainability • Jason Lowe for the amazing photos on our menu boards • All of
those who gave recipes to the book • All of the recipe testers for making sure the
recipes were easy to understand • All of those who baked wonderful pies at the pie
fest, but which didn't make it into the book •

From Claire:
Henry for creating a fantastic new way to eat good food fast. For being such an
ardent supporter of my business, Violet, and for inviting me to do this terrific
project with him • Hattie Deards for being so jolly in the face of two totally
overcommitted authors • Lorraine for support and confidence • Georgia and Anita for
total dedication and enthusiasm • Kate McCullough and Echo Hopkins for being great
assistants, above and beyond • Special thanks to Dri and the Violet girls for
keeping the shop and stall running so well • Thanks to Sam for the great studio at
The Shop on Haliford Street • Thanks to Sara Tildesley for teaching me so so much
• Finally, thanks to Damian for that ring!

From Anita:
Felicity MacDonald Bing for enthusiasm and support on the shoots • Sam at The Shop
for his patience and cake eating abilities • Matilda Harrison, Sonja Bucherer and
Lucinda Cooper for additional props • Lisa, for help with those kids • Matt,
Maddie and Cy Pie for everything else.

THANK YOU

To all Leon family members, past and present: Ben Peverelli • Marta Klosinska • Peter Kancian • Malgorzata Herda • Ildiko Tanacs • Nicola Bartsch • Agnieszka Chmieliauskas • Justin Ovenden • Navina Senivassen • Ursula Bowerman • Guilherme Turibio Da Silva • Simon Drysdale • Thomas Ward • Remigijus Chmieliauskas • Justyna Konca • Anna Sobczak • Maciej Marek • Piotr Jablonski • Stephen Oakley • Sini Marika Mulari • Kadija Begum • Agata Cyminska • Rodrigo Menezes De Carvalho • Kristal Maley • Thomas Green • Lucy Buckingham • Igor Kurosu • May Kovacova • Rute Christina Coelho da Rocha • Deivid Grigorid • Marta Kowalska • Rachel Little • Bozena Bobowska • Liliya Georgieva • Bruno Lupi • Richard Holmes • Suzanne Carter • Isabela Santos • Ben Iredale • Liang Sun • Jaroslaw Zybowski • Tahsin Kucuk • Orlan Masilu • Jenny Russell • Renan Amorin • Nicolas Bracamonte • Mara Casolari • Roberta Rimkute • Stephen Bage • Lucy Harrison • Holly Clare • Ashleigh Davewport • Jirina Kralova • Christine Noel • Katre Kurosu • Yok Ming Chung • Grace Kyne-lilley • Efemena Okogba • Matthias Abdul-Haiat • Danilo Oliveira • Katrina Hassan • Natalia Koc • Robert Beaney • Gary Marriott • Matthew Ali • Laura Silova • Lara Wrubel • Jenna Brehme • Shipon Miah • Vasilica Cirican • Penny Munn • Ryan Yates • Alexia Farina • Vadims Belovs • Megan Bailey • Monika Jaworska • Pedro Barchin • Thomas Davies • Patricia Ferreira Martins • Saga Levin • Elisabeta Gjovani • Viktor Kanasz • Claire Didier • Ravi Kondru • Oxana Popa • Shaun Ryan • Michaela Boor • Anna Kempi • Christopher Ali • Nuria Olmedo Nieto • Anita Moser • Alessandro Bononi • Karolina Driessen • Joshua Parker • Caio Skua Nagao • Juan Lopez • Pedro Ribeiro • Matthew Alp • James-Lee French • Jean Carlos • Carlos De Oliviera • Shaun Oxenham • Anastasija Nigul • Anderson Gomcalves • Mara Locisano • Joshua Martins • Ilaria Frigerio • Mariana Gontijo Pizeli • Jurgita Lukaseviciute • Bernardo La Porta Da Silva • Maria Laranjeira • Marta Goszczynska • Gentil Silva • Jessica Wratten • Erika Leonaviciute • Rajiv Jaligana • Istvan Szep • Egle Narbutaite • Chanell Scott • Justyna Stanislawa Jesiolowska • Elodie Kouame • Mark Prove • Martyn Trigg • Olga Chwilowicz • Miguel Gonzalez Alonso • Owen Myers • Biodun Adetimehin • Gytis Sirinskas • Jurgita Sirvinskiene • Francisco Luis Gom Silva • Ramos Barbosa • Judith-Ryanatu Gbadamassi • Gustavo Burkle • Naomi Clare Mullins • David Ncube • Denzso Zrinszki • Modesta Peckatyte • Trevor Payne • Vladimirs Gutans • Pedro Simas • Ilona Staniuk • Janis Viksne • Reda El Guebli • Nora Ivette Goboly • Bernando Aragao • Steph Brown • Samuele Raiano • Dan Kenna • Manuela Eller • Didier Bussillet • Giada Zerbo • Alvaro Santamaria • Ineta Bliudziute • Melanie Cunnane • Marcos De Souza • Luca Gennati • Nora Szosznyak • Luis Javier Diaz Moreira • Sandra Navaro • Talita Heshimi • Dominika Staniuk • Matthew Atkinson • Letisha Dyke • Daniele Arcangeli • Toni Kapeli • Silje Graffer • Celine Pelzak • Hector Martin Alonso • Georgina Sanderson • Benjamin Oliver • Monika Mieszczak • Viera Varvaruova • Amita Shrestha • Marisa Batistussi • Janos Szima • Simona Cijunskyte • Henrietta Okai • Elvyra Rekusce • Valentina Manea • Micheline Essomba • Fabio De Micheli • Artur Jakubowski • Anna Marczenko • Yoel Tewolde • Pawel Bojanowski • Amy Browne • Leigha Vigilant-Thomas • Joao Veterano • Egle Ozolaite • Catia Rodrigues • Lacey Lawfon • John Corrigan • Georgina Roper • Remmond Theophilus Johnston • Lukasz Przytarski • Patricia Perez Violan • Susanna Alessandroni • Paloma Solbiati • Kayleigh Goodger • Maxine Haher • Elzbieta Paslawska • Marcelino Vaccaro • Desiree Haley • Sachelle Macgregor • Nicolle Dawkins • Fernando Lopez • Viktoria Marianna Raj • Alejandro Garcia Jinorio • Joseph Balog • Marco Bernardi • Mark Sorsky • Nerijus Latakas • Rodrigo Muniz • Kamila Webb • Eimear White • Donard Marshall • Miriam Poveda Abad • Anna Anuscenko • Vydmante Kalvynaite • Raquel Peralta • Anna Rodero Carro • Thomas Malley • Nicola Kibble • Alessandro Vioto • Ysbrand Iodice • Isis Sitbon • Alan Gullo • Raffaele Coletta • Nina Amaniampong • Jessica Merrett • Julian Gomes • Heider Resende Das Neves • Thomas Malley • Mohamed Ouali • Arnaud Jouin • Kelly Agbo • Guoda Jankunaite • Wilson Inga Orega • Angela Aloy • Antonio Carlos Dos Santos • Lucas Zanca • Matthew Sears • Veronika Prokesova • Nicoline Lyck Bech • Amber Petersen • Janos Francis • Katrina Bulman • Vanessa Mazzi • Anneish Dwyer • Enara Lekanda • Lauren Hounsell • Sebastian Clark • Simone Badiali • Karlie-Sian Meagre • Adriana De Oliveira Viega • Jay Ricketts • Gina Smith • Andew Sabapathy • Franlesco Sponza • Birgit Arumetsa • Dean Leacey • Innocenzo Colacicco • Pablo Sanchez Ruiz • Detroit Williams • Nilton Caboco • Emma Louise Stevens • Rossanna O'Mahoney-Lamb • Nathan Joshua Gordon • Medhi Abdel Haiat

First published in 2011 by Conran Octopus Limited,
a part of Octopus Publishing Group,
Endeavour House, 189 Shaftesbury Avenue, London WC2H 8JY
www.octopusbooks.co.uk

A Hachette UK Company
www.hachette.co.uk

British Library Cataloguing-in-Publication Data.
A catalogue record for this book is available from the British Library.

Publisher: Lorraine Dickey
Managing Editor: Sybella Stephens
Project Manager: Hattie Deards
Design and Art Direction (for Leon): Anita Mangan
Art Director (for Conran Octopus): Jonathan Christie
Illustrations: Anita Mangan (except Victoria Sponge on cover and page 39 by Matilda Harrison
Special Photography: Georgia Glynn Smith
Production Manager: Katherine Hockley

ISBN 978 1 84091 579 2
Printed in China

Jossy, David, Kate, Joseph, Kay,
Ed, Nicholas, Jane & Henry, August 1977

Marion and John, 1973

Jonathan and Johnny, 2011

Claire

Henry's birthday, Putney, 1977

Soli in Dubai, 1989

John and the gang

George, aged 2

Claire, 1978

Anita's birthday, 1974

John at Broadstairs, aged 3

Liza and Henry, 1977